The Films of

FREDRIC MARCH

The Films of

FREDRIC MARCH

by
LAWRENCE J. QUIRK

The Citadel Press
New York

Published by Citadel Press, Inc.
A subsidiary of Lyle Stuart, Inc.
222 Park Avenue South, New York, N.Y. 10003
In Canada: George J. McLeod Limited
73 Bathurst St., Toronto 2B, Ontario
Manufactured in the United States of America
by Halliday Lithograph Corp., West Hanover, Mass.
Designed by William Meinhardt
Library of Congress catalog card number: 71-175831
ISBN 0-8065-0259-2

Acknowledgments

Ernest D. Burns and Cinemabilia, New York; Mark Ricci
and The Memory Shop, New York; Kenneth G. Lawrence
and the Movie Memorabilia Shop of Hollywood; the
Museum of Modern Art Stills Archive, New York; Movie
Star News, New York; Larry Edmunds Bookshop, Hollywood; the staff of the New York Public Library's Theatre
& Film Collection, Library & Museum of the Performing
Arts, Lincoln Center, New York; Pete Sansone and United
Press International, New York; Marty Monroe and Wide
World Photos, New York; Barbara Kaiser and Paul Kahn,
Mass Communications History Center, the State Historical Society of Wisconsin; Warner Bros. Pictures, Inc.,
Wynn Loewenthal; Columbia Pictures, Inc., Hortense
Schorr and John Newfield; Universal, Metro-Goldwyn-Mayer, Paramount, United Artists; James E. Runyan, Alexander Walker, Michael Gordon, Christopher Young, Albert B. Manski, Doug McClelland, Frank Leyendecker,
Ray Gain, Miles Kreuger, Robert Burns Gable, Richard
Rheem, Paul Nemcek, Don Koll, Fred Trebel, Warren
Garland, Robert Sanford, John and Lem Amero, Richard
W. Callahan, Joseph L. Wilkinson, Taysir Badanoro.

And with deep appreciation for the gracious gesture of
Mr. Fredric March, who kindly loaned rare early photographs from his personal files.

To My Mother
MARGARET CONNERY QUIRK
June 2, 1900 — January 12, 1971

Contents

FREDRIC MARCH:

His Life and Career

Fredric March as a baby

Fredric March as a baby

FREDRIC MARCH:
His Life and Career

Fredric March has been an actor for fifty-one years, forty-two of them on the screen. Behind him are seventy movies, a score of Broadway plays, radio and television appearances, narrations of documentaries, dramatic readings, tours for the State Department. He has been married for forty-four years to the talented actress Florence Eldridge, and has two children, now grown, and several grandchildren.

One of America's most respected and admired stars, March's career has brought him two Academy Awards as well as a number of nominations; several Antoinette Perry Awards; numerous citations and degrees; and a variety of plaques sufficient to fill the guest-house walls at his New Milford, Connecticut estate.

The Marches have always cultivated a many-sided life, involving years of busy creative labor (often as co-stars) and much travel all over the world.

In addition to his well-deserved acclaim for solid dramatic triumphs in all media over five decades, March is also a symbol of the romancing, swashbuckling, glamorous Hollywood of the golden days of the thirties and forties, in which he ranked with such male stars as Clark Gable, Gary Cooper, Errol Flynn, Cary Grant, Spencer Tracy, Leslie Howard, and Paul Muni. But though March's screen career was fully as vital and romantic as theirs, his private life was notably more stable than most.

He has appeared opposite a dazzling roster of great feminine stars of screen and stage, including Greta Garbo, Norma Shearer, Joan Crawford, Katharine Hepburn, Claudette Colbert, Olivia de Havilland, Loretta Young, Veronica Lake, Merle Oberon, Carole Lombard, Barbara Stanwyck, Myrna Loy, Ruth Chatterton, Ann Harding, Constance Bennett, Sylvia Sidney, Janet Gaynor, Kay Francis, Miriam Hopkins, Margaret Sullavan, Kim Novak, Sophia Loren, Tallulah Bankhead and Helen Hayes. Though March's references to these ladies are kind, his favorite co-star is Florence Eldridge, with whom he has appeared in all media for forty-five years.

Equally adept in comedy and drama, in costume romance and modern-dress, March as an artist has displayed a thousand faces. He has played Christopher Columbus, Mark Twain, Benvenuto Cellini, pirate Jean Lafitte, Anna Karenina's Vronsky, Mary of Scotland's Earl of Bothwell, the President of the United States, Eugene O'Neill's father, Jean Valjean, Robert Browning, the Angel of the Lord, Death, Arthur Miller's Willy Loman, Joan Crawford's husband in *Susan and God*, Thornton Wilder's Mr. Antrobus; Tolstoy's idealistic Prince Dmitri; George Kaufman's Tony Cavendish; tired businessmen; ambitious corporate executives; returned World War II veterans; Doctor Jekyll *and* Mr. Hyde; intrepid World War I aviators; smug politicians; Philip of Macedonia; inspired clergymen; anti-Nazi refugees; Joseph Conrad heroes; and fading movie star Norman Maine—no variety of characterization has escaped his interpretation.

March's trademarks are a relaxed ease, an effortless delivery, a knack for subtle underplaying, a sharpness in character delineation, a consummate "art that conceals art" that many performers have striven for but few have achieved to so perfect a degree. He is often compared with his contemporary, Spencer Tracy, another master of the natural, underplayed technique. Both careers ran roughly parallel. Both men won two Academy Awards. Both languished under pedestrian studio contracts in a variety of unrewarding parts in the early thirties before finally breaking through to the cinematic major leagues and super-stardom.

March and Tracy, however, are two separate and distinct personalities, and offer highly individual and unique emanations. Of the two, March had the wider range. During all his years in Hollywood, Tracy returned to the stage only once, in 1945. March went back to Broadway eleven times, usually with success.

Many regard March as our greatest American actor. Yet his origins hardly seem conducive to such a destiny.

Born in Racine, Wisconsin, on August 31, 1897, he was christened Ernest Frederick McIntyre Bickel. His father, John F. Bickel, was a prominent Racine manufacturer. His mother was the former Cora Marcher. The youngest of four children, he had one sister, Elizabeth, and two brothers, John and Harold.

March's childhood seems to have been normal, healthy, happy and uncomplicated. He liked, and participated in, all the things "regular kids" of his time and class did: sports, fishing, hunting, water fun. An attractive, outgoing child, he was popular with his schoolmates. As he reached adolescence, his clear, resonant speech attracted the attention of his teachers, and soon he was reciting often and acting in class plays. His family

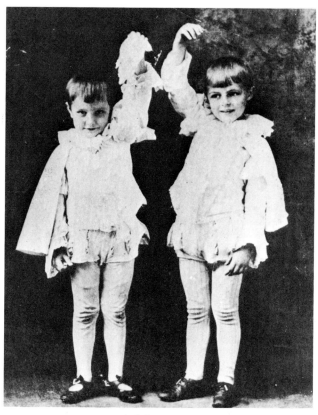

At left, age six, in a school play (1903)

hoped he would become a clergyman, but he became interested, at an early age, in banking and economics.

His father, who ran a loan association as well as his regular business, talked much to him about finance, and he came to think of it as exciting, challenging and glamorous.

With his parents, brothers and sister, about 1904. Mr. March is seated on his father's lap.

14

March graduated from Racine High School in 1915, then went to the University of Wisconsin, where he remained for two years, majoring in finance and economics. He enjoyed at the University the same popularity he had known at Winslow Grammar School and Racine High. When the United States entered World War I in 1917, young Bickel, then twenty, enlisted in the Army, went to Officers Candidate School, and was eventually commissioned a Lieutenant in the Artillery.

After the war ended, he returned to the University of Wisconsin, and managed to pack in a busy academic career before graduating in 1920 with a degree in economics. During this undergraduate period he managed the football team, was a member of the track team, and in his senior year served as class president. The theatrical bug first bit him at this time. He acted in many class plays and was a member of the Harefoot Theatrical Club.

At graduation time he found himself torn between banking and acting. Banking, for a time, won. The summer of 1920 found twenty-two-year-old Fred Bickel working as a teller in the Racine branch of the First National City Bank of New York. Then wanderlust hit him, and he applied for the bank's special training unit aimed at eventual service in foreign branches. He went to New York for the course, but shortly thereafter the bank discontinued it, due to a change of policy, and he found himself in a minor position which he later described as "boring, dry, monotonous, unexciting."

As his twenty-third birthday approached, Bickel found himself weathering a period of depression and ennui. His energetic, imaginative nature, stymied by his dull job, responded to the excitements of New York, which

At age fifteen (about 1913)

in 1920 was a hub of theatrical activity, with hundreds of plays running simultaneously—the golden age of the Broadway theatre. Bickel's brooding was soon cut short by what turned out to be a blessing in disguise: an appendicitis attack. For some weeks after the operation he convalesced, read about the theatre, listened to the theatrical reminiscences of his landlady, a former actress, and, when recovered, went back to catching every show he could.

That fall of 1920 he had photographs made and took them to various agents. He also made the rounds of the casting-offices, patiently and "for what seemed endlessly." One agent took note of his looks, manners and good speech and sent him to one of the movie studios in New York, where he got $7.50 for one day's extra work in a forgettable opus called *Paying the Piper*. This led to some other extra work in films, and a model agency next took note of him.

March reminisced years later about what followed this: "I helped sell cravats, shaving cream, shoes and shirts. Then one day my agent sent me to David Belasco, the producer, who was then casting *Deburau*. I had heard there were several 'bits' in it and hoped to land one of them. I thus barged into my first real break. Rehearsals had already started when I presented myself at the Belasco Theatre and they needed someone right away—for the very small part of Victor Hugo. No experience was necessary and I looked near enough to their idea of Hugo to get by. So I was hired at thirty dollars a week.

With his father, at age twelve

15

At Officers Training School, U.S. Army, 1918

"It was there, in the mechanics of that production, that my nebulous dreams and ideas took on form, were articulated. My silly, adolescent excitements gave way to a more intelligent interest in the theatre. I ceased to dramatize myself and the actors I tried to ape. I began to look upon the theatre objectively—saw it as a vast, endlessly interesting medium. Saw myself no longer as a gift from Heaven, but as a very raw novice with a devil of a lot to learn. And high time too."

Bickel's modelling work for such artists as Neysa McMein, Howard Chandler Christy and Dean Cornwall then gave way to a solid theatrical apprenticeship. In addition to his bit parts as Victor Hugo and The Prompter, Bickel did odd jobs assisting the stage manager. He was well liked in the company.

After out-of-town tryouts, *Deburau* opened on Broad-way on December 23, 1920. Adapted by Granville Barker from the French of Sacha Guitry, the play, which dealt with the life and loves of an 1839-style French panto-mimist, was successful. It starred Lionel Atwill, later a well-known film character actor. Bickel understudied Atwill at a later point, got other roles as vacancies occurred in the cast, and stated years later that his learning-by-doing-style apprenticeship held its own with anything an acting school could offer.

Bickel then went on to do non-Broadway parts, first in a company doing *The County Chairman* and then in a road company production of *Shavings*. Early 1922 found him back on Broadway in *The Lawbreaker*. (He had previously done a brief stint in the Al Jolson musical *Lei Aloha*, but joined the Broadway cast after the opening.)

William A. Brady (father of the famed actress Alice Brady) produced *The Lawbreaker*, which represented Bickel's best break yet. He had been brought to Brady's attention by his friend, the director John Cromwell. Billed as Frederick Bickel, the young man who walked on the stage of the Booth Theatre that February night in 1922 was a polished professional of twenty-four who deserved good reviews and got them—from such eminent critics as Alexander Woollcott and Percy Hammond, both of whom extolled his "genuine promise" (Woollcott) and "remarkably unaffected performance" (Hammond). In his role of Tom Fowler, the guiltless son of a man whose bank was robbed, he found himself working with top professionals, such as the star, William Courtenay, whose techniques Bickel earnestly studied. "While these top-liners polished and sharpened their interpretations from performance to performance, I did the same thing. It was a real acting education," he later said.

After *The Lawbreaker*, March played in a pre-Broadway run of *Zeno*, which dealt with the spirit world (with a touch of homicide thrown in) and at first it looked like promising New York fodder. Somebody changed his mind and it folded in Chicago.

Industrious and determined, March, prior to the *Zeno* episode, had put in some six months of stock company work in Dayton, Ohio "where I played anything and everything." With this toughening and confidence-strengthening background, even the *Zeno* debacle didn't faze him, and back in New York he accepted his friend John Cromwell's offer to star in producer-director Cromwell's touring company of the hit play *Tarnish*. Later Cromwell put Bickel under personal contract and persuaded him that his name wasn't glamorous or theatrical enough for a twenty-six-year-old who was by then giving ample evidence of a starring future. "It reminds me of pickle or bicker or something equally inelegant," Cromwell told him. March said forty years later, "I liked the name Frederick Bickel and I wish now I had left it as was. After all, Theodore Bikel, whose name was similar, though spelled differently, didn't change his, and he did all right."

Because he considered twelve his lucky number, he shortened Frederick to Fredric, shortened his mother's maiden name from Marcher to March, and as of New

Year's Day, 1924, Fredric March was born.

As Fredric March he opened on Broadway in a comedy, *The Melody Man*, which starred Lew Fields. The place: The Ritz Theatre. The night: May 13, 1924. In this bit of nonsense about a classical composer whose sincere musical effusion is jazzed-up into a popular hit, March's role was comparatively negligible. He made his usual good impression. The played closed after forty performances.

About this time March contracted his first, brief marriage, with actress Ellis Baker, niece of the talented character actor Edward Ellis. By 1927 they were divorced.

Puppets, March's next Broadway play, opened at the Selwyn Theatre on March 9, 1925. The stars were Miriam Hopkins, then a popular Broadway leading lady, and C. Henry Gordon, later a well-known film character actor. It ran fifty-four performances, and was frou-frou about a marionette-showowner, a homeless girl, and threatening white-slavers (a popular subject in the twenties). Though it was relatively peripheral to the action, March's role was substantial enough to win him critic Alan Dale's endorsement as having contributed the best work of the evening.

After a European vacation in the summer of 1925, March opened that fall in *Harvest,* by Kate Horton, a play sponsored by the Shuberts in association with John Cromwell. As the city boy who has a brief, doomed romance with country girl Ethel Taylor, March got a pat on the back from critic Burns Mantle for being "a nice juvenile," but the play, which the reviewers castigated as too drab, negative and downbeat, closed after seventeen performances.

On March 29, 1926, March opened at the National Theatre, New York, in Jack McClellan's play, *The Half-Caste,* a "racy" (for that period) melodrama of the kind then fashionable. Though his part was shallow, and indeed stupid, March made the most of it, and again Percy Hammond and other critics remarked on March's good looks, acting authority and charm, and noted that he had done as well as circumstances permitted. To give the reader some idea of what producers thought playgoers wanted to see in the spring of 1926, herewith the plot: Dick Chester, a rich brat who takes to drink,, goes to the South Seas, seduces a native girl who, he later learns, is his father's illegitimate daughter. The father is an old rake who has been thought long dead, but actually he is a beachcomber. March retreats in horror when he learns he has been cohabiting with his half-sister and takes off for home. The girl? She kills herself.

The Half-Caste closed after sixty-four performances, and March went to Denver, where he joined the stock company at the Elitch Gardens Theatre. Here he found himself working with a young actress named Florence Eldridge. She was twenty-four; he was twenty-eight. Within a year, on May 30, 1927, after months of working together in various plays in an association that changed gradually from professional camaraderie to love, Miss Eldridge became Mrs. March.

Florence Eldridge was born Florence MacKechnie in Brooklyn on September 5, 1901. Her parents, Charles James MacKechnie and Clara Eugenie MacKechnie, were non-professionals. The stage urge came to Florence MacKechnie early, and she debuted at seventeen, in 1918, as a chorus girl in Jerome Kern's *Rock-a-bye Baby.*

With his parents, brothers, sister and two nieces, circa 1922

She did not remain long in the chorus. By 1921 she was a hit in the Theatre Guild's *Ambush,* and later scored hits in *The Cat and the Canary, Six Characters in Search of an Author,* and *The Great Gatsby.* At the time March met her, in 1926, Miss Eldridge had been alternating between stock and Broadway appearances for some years and had a reputation as a dependable and gifted young actress of proven expertise and wide range.

There are differing accounts as to just where and when the Marches first met. All concerned agree it was in 1926, but the Marches themselves give different ver-

With wife Florence Eldridge at film opening, about 1933

At a 1932 premiere with Lilyan Tashman and her husband, Edmund Lowe

sions. March claims they first met backstage at the theatre. Miss Eldridge claims it was in a dining car of a train bound for Denver.

In the fall of 1926, March was back on Broadway in Tom Cushing's *The Devil in the Cheese.* It lasted 157 performances, and was a piece of trivia about an archaeologist (Robert McWade) who doesn't want his daughter (Linda Watkins) to marry March, who later saves them all from bandits and wins the father's approval. • The business was banal and silly in the extreme, But March drew excellent personal reviews, with Percy Hammond and Brooks Atkinson terming his performance "earnest, unaffected, heroic, masterful."

The Devil in the Cheese closed early in 1927. March would not be seen on Broadway again until 1938.

Lawrence Langner, founder of the Theatre Guild (who later initiated the American Shakespeare Theatre and Academy at Stratford, Connecticut), next hired the Marches for the Guild's first traveling repertory troupe.

Mr. Langner, in his book of reminiscences, *The Magic Curtain* (1952), has recalled their association thus:

We engaged an excellent acting company headed by Florence Eldridge, George Gaul and Fredric March. Their repertory included *Mr. Pim Passes By* and *Arms and the Man* . . . The scenery could be used in theatres, schoolhouses, auditoriums or what-have-you. This traveling company played in a hundred and thirty-two cities in 1927-28. We visited them on their return . . . to congratulate the actors on their tour, and I have seldom met such a group of indignant, overworked people. What they particularly disliked was that, in the words of Freddy March, "The hotel accommodations in most of the small towns were so bad, that even when we did have an opportunity to sleep, the beds and the inhabitants thereof often made it impossible to do so!" . . . and while the fire has now died out of Freddy's eyes and flames no longer burst out of Florence's nostrils, the verbal chastisement which I have received from time to time at the hands of these two artists has taught me a lesson I will always remember. . . .

For years the Marches ruefully reminisced about the 1927-28 Theatre Guild tour. Friends would say that if anyone mentioned a play like *The Guardsman* or *The Silver Cord,* the Marches would cry out, almost in uni-

Holding his Oscar for Dr. Jekyll and Mr. Hyde, *1932. From left to right, Wallace Beery, who won an Oscar for* The Champ, *Lionel Barrymore and Conrad Nagel*

son, "Oh, we played in that one—on that brutal tour!" Often they didn't even get a theatre to play in; whatever happened to be vacant had to serve; this included barns, gymnasiums, even saloons. When they were lucky they found themselves in a dirty, ill-heated hall that could, with twenty-four hours of applied company ingenuity, be gotten up to resemble a theatre.

"But we *did* enjoy it, for all our complaints," March said years later. "We got to polish our technique in some of the best-written plays ever, it was fun for Florence and me, this working together constantly, and we got to learn a lot about the country and the people in various regions."

The Royal Family had been one of Broadway's biggest hits of the late twenties. Written by George S. Kaufman and Edna Ferber, it was a riotously funny satire of the Barrymores, masquerading as "the Cavendishes." The role of Tony Cavendish was a luscious plum for any good actor, it being a well-written travesty of the speech, manners and mores (or is it morals?) of the irrepressible John Barrymore. With the Theatre Guild tour (and its horrors) completed, the Marches went to Los Angeles, where he had been offered the Tony Cavendish role in the version playing at the El Capitan Theatre.

March played Tony to the hilt and set Los Angeles on its collective ear. John Barrymore, by then a screen star, reportedly appeared at one performance, and after seeing the show went backstage, walked into March's dressing room with a glowering look, then suddenly relaxed, waxed charming and agreeable, and congratulated the jittery actor on a fine performance. (Ethel Barrymore disliked the play intensely and criticized it roundly).

The Royal Family proved the turning point in March's career, for Paramount executives, taking note of his performance, offered him a five-year contract.

March had received other film offers, but until the screen began to talk, he was not too interested. His reviews, and his public, had long since indicated that his voice was not the least of his assets, and he had reasoned: why go into the movies and limit oneself to making faces?

But "talkies" were "in" by late 1928. March realized that Paramount Pictures could get him nationwide exposure in even one film that years of trouping and even Broadway hits could never provide. He was also by this time intent on making the kind of money that would assure his and his wife's future. He was thirty-one years old, which in those days was "getting on" for an actor.

He signed a five-year Paramount contract in late 1928. This time it wouldn't be "extra" parts at $7.50 per day, March had come a long way since 1920.

March, being shrewd and realistic, went into the films with open eyes; he did not delude himself that every picture he made would be of Grade-A quality. Still, he was disappointed with his first release, *The Dummy*, as were a lot of people. *Variety*, after commenting on the primitive sound recording, the lack of a love story, the poor lighting and photography, lamented March's failure to get even one close-up, considering his previous reputation and experience. His part was little more than a bit and had no characterizational depth. The net result was that he failed to register effectively, despite his good looks and fine voice, which even the horrific early sound mechanics couldn't mar. The plot was some nonsense about a young kidnap victim who is rescued by a detective's office boy who pretends to be deaf and dumb to capture the criminals. March played the girl's father whom the mother (Ruth Chatterton) suspected wrongly of kidnapping his child.

Photoplay, then a prestigious and influential film publication owned and edited by James R. Quirk, who was March's earliest and most outspoken booster in films, took what for that then vital publication was a relatively mellow stance. Though commenting pointedly on *The Dummy*'s crude sound, *Photoplay* passed it off as a film "that looks like a convention of new Hollywood faces imported from the speaking stage." Miss Chatterton, whose part was also thankless, was likewise unhappy with the results. John Cromwell, who acted in, but did not direct, this turkey (stage veteran Robert Milton had this dubious honor) once observed: "It made us all miss the theatre."

March made the picture under difficult circumstances. He moonlighted on the stage of the El Capitan Theatre finishing his run in *The Royal Family* while laboring days on *The Dummy* on the Paramount lot. The picture opened in New York in March 1929. Some of the Marches' New York friends went to see it and emerged shaking their heads.

Paramount assured March they had better things in store for him. They purchased the rights to *The Royal Family* with March in mind for a repeat of his Tony Cavendish role. At that point this seemed to March the one light at the end of the tunnel—a five-year one. Miss Eldridge, who had tapered off her own acting career, counseled patience. Determined to make the most of things, and to give his best at all times, March settled down to await Paramount's next choice.

It turned out to be the lead in Clara Bow's first talkie, *The Wild Party*. Dorothy Arzner, soon to be famous as the one successful woman director in films, was assigned to guide Miss Bow through her first vocal travails. The star and March were nervous for different reasons, March because he hoped the recording devices of 1929 would do justice to his hard-earned pear-shaped tones, and Miss Bow because she had no pear-shaped tones and knew it.

The result was not as bad as had been feared, though the plot was negligible pap about a wild college girl (Bow) who falls in love with a professor (March). The critics tactfully issued platitudes to the effect that Miss Bow's voice suited her personality. (Paramount flacks had beclouded the issue with such promotional copy as: "You've had an eyeful; now get an earful!") March garnered fine notices. "Vocally he reigns supreme," one critic wrote.

But ahead loomed a series of one-step-forwards-two-steps-backwards for March, lost as he now was in the wilds of the Paramount studio, circa 1929. He was next shoved into *The Studio Murder Mystery*, playing Richard Hardell, a handsome, vain, woman-chasing actor who gets murdered on a film set. The role was hardly more than a bit, and after the first quarter-hour, no more March. The picture itself was banal, feeble in its attempts at humor, pedestrianly directed by Frank Tuttle—and though only 62 minutes long, it seemed to go on for-ever. Florence Eldridge appeared as the actor's jealous wife who is one of the prime suspects. The film was based on a serial that had appeared in *Photoplay*. That magazine took pains to point out that the plot had been changed in its transference to the screen.

Miss Eldridge made a few more films in the early thirties, but subordinated her career to her husband's continually, and did only one play without him. Domesticity had become the keynote of her life. The Marches had determined from the beginning to make their marriage work, and in mature terms. March told an interviewer about this time: "I do not believe in matrimonial vacations. I am conservative, perhaps old fashioned, domestically speaking. I like being married. I love having a home. All actors appreciate a home. They live in a trunk too much."

At the time he won his second Oscar, for The Best Years of Our Lives *(1947)*

Arthur Hopkins produced, and Edward H. Griffith directed, March's fourth film, *Paris Bound*, which he made on loan-out to Pathé. This time he was paired with the charming stage veteran, Ann Harding, a past mistress at pear-shaped tones, and they played expertly together. The play, a 1927 hit on Broadway, dealt with a couple who adopt a "modern" view toward extramarital affairs, only to find that it boomerangs. Critics noted that the more affectionate scenes between Miss Harding and March went on to excess and there were complaints about the choppy continuity and slow pace. The sound was good, though, considering the period, and both Miss Harding and March fared well with the reviewers, with one calling March's portrayal "sympathetic and human."

Back at his home studio, March did *Jealousy* and counted it a plus that he had as his co-star the noted Jeanne Eagels, of *Rain* fame. Miss Eagels had been dissatisfied with the first version, shot with Anthony Bushell, and demanded that it be redone with March. Because Miss Eagels' earlier film, *The Letter*, had been a success, Paramount honored her request. Miss Eagels was ill

With sculptor Jo Davidson at a "Rally for Roosevelt," Madison Square Garden, New York, 1944

during the shooting, and died later in the year. Based on a Louis Verneuil play, the triangular plot about a young wife, her jealous husband and her ex-"protector" did not register with audiences or critics, and Miss Eagels was criticized for affecting a British accent in a French setting and March for retaining his American accent in his role of a French artist.

Out on loan again, this time to First National for a Colleen Moore feature, *Footlights and Fools,* March found his talents wasted in a second-fiddle role as stage-star Moore's wealthy admirer. Raymond Hackett played the man Moore really loved. The picture was all-Moore, what with her husband, John McCormick, producing,

and elaborate musical numbers written in for Miss Moore to sing (passably) and dance (execrably). March got short shrift in the reviews. When he did get attention, it was favorable.

Again at Paramount for *The Marriage Playground,* March found it his best-received picture to date (December 1929). It had a warm and winning plot based on the Edith Wharton novel, *The Children,* and was ably directed by Lothar Mendes. In this, his seventh film, March's consummate ease before the cameras was noted. He recalled later that Mendes told him: "When they yell 'Camera!' it means *relax*."

The film, about the neglected children of international

At the Stage Door Canteen, 1942

society in Europe, was wistful and affecting in many of its sequences, and contained just enough of its superior literary source to be several cuts above late-1929 fare. It also *moved*—managing to cut free from the fixed-camera, static quality that marred so many primitive talkies. For this March got some of his best reviews to date, and at the end of 1929 found himself a much-sought-after leading man.

For his first 1930 film, March was paired for the second time with Ruth Chatterton. Dorothy Arzner was again on hand to direct. Though Miss Chatterton had the better role as the opera singer who is searching for her long-lost child (with March as the foster parents' lawyer who first opposes, then aids, her) he was praised for his "easygoing and natural" performance.

Then came a slight setback. March was handed a small role as Mary Astor's about-to-be-divorced husband in *Ladies Love Brutes*. March wasn't the "brute"—George Bancroft was, and Bancroft was also the star. Nor did Mary Astor "love" the brute; the title was a mendacity. In fact she wanted to get rid of him. So the Italian building contractor, played with his usual crude gusto by Bancroft, kidnaps Miss Astor's child in order to frame a "rescue," thinking he will thereby win her love. Of course things don't work out that way at all. Reviewers accorded Bancroft sixty percent of the attention, Astor thirty percent—and ten percent to March who, when mentioned, got kind treatment. *The New York Times* said: "[He] tackles a minor role with his unfailing skill."

James R. Quirk of *Photoplay*, who wrote that March was his favorite actor, and also the favorite actor of his beautiful wife, May Allison, the by-then-retired screen star, urged Paramount executives to give March something more worthy of his talents. But since good scripts weren't that frequent in early 1930 and since Paramount wanted to get the most mileage out of its admittedly most able actor (disregarding the dangers of overexposure in the process) March's fortunes did not immediately improve.

After listening to Miss Chatterton sing a torchy lament for a Marine who didn't leave a forwarding address in one of the skits of *Paramount on Parade*, an all-star Paramount extravaganza typical of the period, March found himself reunited with Clara Bow in a trifle called *True to the Navy*. It opened in May 1930 to poor reviews. Paramount was accused of neglecting Miss Bow's interests by surrounding her with careless photography and slapdash production. There was much criticism of the casting of March as a rough-and-ready sailor, the consensus being that he belonged in a drawing room, not on a battleship. His acting was praised but his unsuitability to the role of Gunner McCoy, beloved by his buddies for his expert shooting skills and by Miss Bow for more personal reasons, was universally lamented, except perhaps by March's shopgirl fans, who, Paramount flacks insisted, taped and pasted thousands of pix of March in his sailor suit on their bedroom walls. As for Miss Bow, one critic summed up her performance thus: "She sings . . . and she also weeps."

Finally a combination of Quirk's editorial screams and March's own righteous indignation roused Paramount to a belated and concentrated search for vehicles that were more suitable. *Manslaughter*, which opened in July 1930, cast him to advantage as the district attorney who loves a rich girl (Claudette Colbert) but sends her to prison for killing a motorcycle cop with her car. In prison Colbert learns humility, is later released, at first hates March for convicting her, then winds up in his arms. The picture was praised for its "equal-justice-under-the-law-for-rich-and-poor" angle, and while it stood no particular chance of going down in film history as one of the Ten (or even Twenty) Best Pictures of 1930, it did showcase both March and Miss Colbert to advantage. (It was a considerably updated remake of a Thomas Meighan-Leatrice Joy 1922 silent.)

But *Laughter*, the next film, *could* lay claim to being one of 1930's best films. It had sparkling direction from Harry d'Arrast, a fine script by Donald Ogden Stewart, and excellent performances by March, Nancy Carroll, Frank Morgan and others. A forerunner of the light, gossamer-clever, sophisticated comedies that were to burgeon later in the thirties, *Laughter* was a reworking of the triangle theme (bored wife, ex-lover March, rich-husband Morgan) but done so deftly and humorously that it was five or so years ahead of its time. This is one of March's all-time favorite films and it is one of the few of which he has retained a print.

With his wife, circa 1950

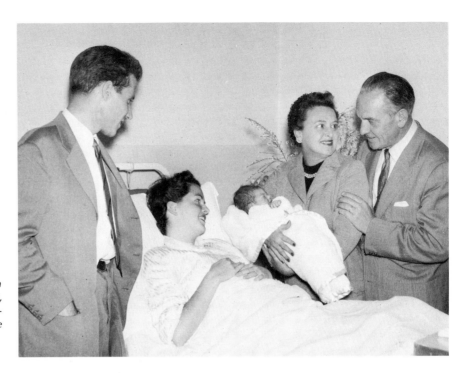

Meeting his one-day-old grandson in Florence, Italy, 1955. Left to right, son-in-law Umberto Fantucci, daughter Penelope March Fantucci, wife Florence Eldridge

Paramount finally got around to producing the screen version of *The Royal Family* that they had bought with March in mind. With its title expanded to *The Royal Family of Broadway*, the film was carefully produced and ably directed by George Cukor and Cyril Gardner. This garnered for March the best reviews for his screen work that he had yet earned. Of course, he knew the role of Tony Cavendish inside and out, after his stage run, and his witty and deft John Barrymore spoof turned out to be as popular with film as with stage fans. Ina Claire was also excellent as the theatre's First Lady who has sacrificed love to career, as were Mary Brian as the sister who deserts marriage for the stage and Henrietta Crosman as the matriarch of the clan, who tours to the glorious end. Typical of March's reviews was that in the *New York World*, which called him "positively brilliant."

March has reportedly said that Tony Cavendish is not one of his favorite roles. Yet for it he received his first Academy Award nomination.

The year 1931 proved to be uneven for March's film work. It came in with the inferior *Honor Among Lovers* but three pictures later went out like a triumphant lion with the superb *Dr. Jekyll and Mr. Hyde*. *Honor Among Lovers* was triangle nonsense about an investment broker (March) and the girl he loves (Claudette Colbert) who marries a weakling (Monroe Owsley.) Though there was some shooting, and some courtroom melodrama, *Honor Among Lovers* was standard fare, got standard reviews, and did nothing for March or Colbert.

Edmund Goulding next guided March and Nancy Carroll through another turkey, *The Night Angel*, written by Goulding and purporting to offer European atmosphere. The arty doings presented March as a Prague district attorney, Carroll as the daughter of a cabaret owner, and Alan Hale as their menace. The critics thought it artificial, a phony travesty of Continental techniques, and

opined that Carroll was no Dietrich (the role had been written with Dietrich in mind) and that March's apple-pie American speech and manner did not correspond to anything in Czechoslovakia.

Nor did he fare any better with *My Sin*. Released in September 1931, this film cast him, under George Abbott's direction, opposite the formidable Tallulah Bankhead, then bidding for major movie fame under Paramount auspices. March played a lawyer who wins acquittal for manslaughter defendant Bankhead, years later urges her to tell the truth about her past to her rich fiance, then gets her for himself. Despite the sincere and expert playing of Miss Bankhead and March, the creaky plot and soapy doings did them in. The reviews were poor.

Then came the picture which metamorphosed March into a major star and won him his first Academy Award. *Dr. Jekyll and Mr. Hyde*, released at the close of 1931, made a sensation with critics and public, and more on account of March's sterling and resourceful performance than the creaky melodrama itself, which had been played on the stage since 1887 and had been done as a silent film by John Barrymore in 1920. Rouben Mamoulian directed imaginatively and March, aided by a graphically hideous, brutishly simian makeup, presented with flair and versatility a meticulously delineated contrast between the dedicated, well-meaning Jekyll and the infinitely evil, lustful, destructive Hyde. Miriam Hopkins was fine as the cabaret girl Hyde seduces and later murders, and Rose Hobart was effectively cast as Jekyll's fiancee. The face of Jekyll changed into that of Hyde via a series of gradual exposures that won much acclaim for the horror they evoked. Though his performance continues after forty years to be widely admired (outranking John Barrymore's sinuous, serpentine portrayal of 1920 and a miscast Spencer Tracy's inade-

With Claire Trevor in NBC-TV's Dodsworth (1956)

quate and inappropriate rendition of 1941) it is not, according to reports, one of March's great favorites. Oscar or not, he is said to feel it was flashy and gimmicky rather than characterizationally deep. Most critics disagree with him. Typical of the praise of the time was that of James R. Quirk, who wrote in *Photoplay:* "No player in pictures or on the stage could surpass his performance in *Dr. Jekyll and Mr. Hyde.* Any man who can handle this heavily dramatic role with such finesse, and also put over an entirely different personality, such as he did as the rollicking brother of *The Royal Family* is a first-class, all around journeyman actor."

Quirk and other film commentators expressed their fervent hopes that, with this sensational hit under his belt, the year 1932 would bring March only first-class roles in prestige pictures. But he had to wait until near the end of the year before he was again handed something decent.

Meanwhile March sweated through a clinker called *Strangers in Love*, in which he essayed the dual role of a twin who is bad and rich and a twin who is poor and good. The good twin, who has been mulcted out of his inheritance via a phony will forged by his bad brother, takes the other twin's place when he dies of a weak heart, eventually winning through to justice and happiness. It was essentially lightweight stuff, with Kay Francis pleasing as a sympathetic secretary.

In *Merrily We Go to Hell*, March, again under Dorothy Arzner's direction, played a reporter-turned-playwright who marries rich girl Sylvia Sidney, disillusions her with his drinking and carousing, then reforms when she undergoes a traumatic pregnancy. Edwin Justis Mayer wrote a screenplay that emphasized wit and smart cracks; Skeets Gallagher and others lent able support, but the result was a forgettable and rarely mentioned March effort. His personal reviews, as usual, were good, though the usual note of regret that he couldn't get better vehicles sounded through.

Next March was one of the guest actors who get a "hi-how-are-you" moment with Stuart Erwin in a remake of the popular play and silent film, *Merton of the Movies* (retitled *Make Me a Star),* in which Erwin played a yokel who wants to be a movie star and wins a reverse kind of stardom with an acting style so lugubrious that it makes him a parody-style comic riot. A number of Paramount luminaries figured, but only momentarily, in the doings.

Then came the first of the two 1932 pictures that gave March a mammoth push up the quality ladder from which he so often had slipped (and through the pictures', not his fault.) Metro-Goldwyn-Mayer borrowed him from Paramount to play Norma Shearer's beloved in *Smilin' Through,* a remake of the play and the silent film starring Norma Talmadge. Again March had a dual role, as the deranged Jeremy Wayne of 1868 who, crazed by jealousy on the day his beloved marries another man, accidentally kills her with a bullet meant for his rival, and fifty years later as the murderer's son who falls in love with the dead bride's niece. A handsome and affecting picture, filled with Thalberg-style production quality and extremely well-mounted, *Smilin' Through* showcased March in important Loews theatres and won him much praise.

Miss Shearer and her husband, Irving Thalberg, had long known the Marches socially, March and his wife having become one of the most popular couples on the Hollywood social scene, and they sympathized with his efforts to get into quality vehicles. The Marches now had a handsome mansion in Beverly Hills, were well liked for their unaffected geniality and quiet dignity, and respected for March's dependability as an actor, his concern for the welfare of his fellow players, and his scandal-free private life.

Though the dearest of their wishes—a child of their own—was to be denied them, the Marches adopted their first child, Penelope, late in 1932. They were reasonably active in fund-raising drives and other philanthropic activities of typical well-heeled Hollywoodians, but they lived quietly, saved their money, and though they maintained a certain standard of living, in keeping with March's Hollywood status, the general conduct of their lives was prudent, and a needed example to less discreet, less disciplined stars.

Thalberg must have given someone at Paramount a quiet nudge, because when he returned to his home studio March found himself in one of their biggest pictures of 1932 or any year, Cecil B. De Mille's spectacular *The Sign of the Cross*. Claudette Colbert was on hand again, giving an excellent performance as the Empress Poppaea, who loves March, who plays Marcus, a Roman

prefect. Charles Laughton practically stole the picture as the perverse Emperor Nero, and Elissa Landi was affecting as a Christian girl loved by March and with whom he chooses to die in the arena.

De Mille ran true to form, lending the picture his usual extravagant touches, though some critics opined that everybody except Laughton tended to get lost in all the epic grandeur, with games, lions, gladiators, soldiers and Roman savagery and excess dwarfing all. But *The Sign of the Cross* was an important, well-promoted film that practically every 1932 movie fan went to see; as such it represented a plus for March.

Paramount execs, feeling possibly that they were furthering March's "quality" ambitions, next put him and Miss Colbert into *Tonight Is Ours,* a film version of Noel Coward's *The Queen Was in the Parlor.* Though sumptuously produced and ably photographed by Karl Struss, the picture, under Stuart Walker's direction, came off as lightweight froth, with Colbert as a queen in love with a commoner (March) and threatened with revolution. Graustarkian themes like this had been often tackled before by Hollywood and would be often tackled again, with varying degrees of success. This particular effort cried out for a Lubitsch touch that was beyond Stuart Walker's range. The play had been one of Coward's weakest, and the film was one of March's. Typical of the reviews were those which thought Miss Colbert "ravishingly photographed" and March "so romantic."

March had something more substantial to work with in *The Eagle and the Hawk,* in which he played an American with the British World War I flying squadron who loses his nerve from watching so many of his buddies die and eventually kills himself. The part was a complex one by 1933 film standards and allowed March

With Nancy Olson, Helen Hayes, Claudette Colbert and Kent Smith, all of whom appeared with him in The Royal Family *on the* Best of Broadway *TV series, 1954*

25

to cover a wide range of emotions. The air action was subordinated to the dramatics, which proved beneficial for the star.

One critic opined that March in this gave "by far his most intelligent and stimulating performance." Seen today, *The Eagle and the Hawk* displays its star most creditably, and underlines another important point about March: that his style has always been a timeless and universal one, since, as previously noted, he is always natural and relaxed and underplays skillfully, as did his contemporary and colleague, Spencer Tracy.

For a time it seemed that Paramount was going to try for all-out quality with each and every March film, for his next was *Design for Living*, one of Noel Coward's great stage hits. Miriam Hopkins and Gary Cooper were the other points of the sophisticated triangular drama, which involved the decision of two men and one woman to pool their emotional investment in one another. This was considered "daring" in 1933, at least in the films; two men sharing one woman was strong stuff then. Accordingly the screenwriter (Ben Hecht informally assisted by director Ernst Lubitsch) took pains to stress the platonic nature of the "arrangement"—which only made it seem absurd.

Moreover, Coward had originally designed the piece for the ultra-sophisticated techniques of Alfred Lunt and Lynn Fontanne plus himself, and it had been played on the stage as a light, fey spoof of sexual mores and manners, with Coward sneaking in much mischievous subtlety.

Some reviewers pointed out that both March and Cooper were too masculine and wholesomely aboveboard for such effete implications, and Miss Hopkins was adjudged to be no Lynn Fontanne.

As the end of the year 1933 approached, March's five-year contract with Paramount drew near its close. After the uncertainties he had known, the disconcerting alternations of quality vehicles with banal trash, and the feeling of artistic freedom truncated, March was reluctant to renew.

A rumor made the rounds that Paramount put him into two of the remaining three pictures due under his contract either to punish him for not signing on again, or to pressure him into signing. Whichever angle was true (if for that matter the rumor itself was true), March drew, in this period, one winner and two turkeys.

The first of the turkeys was a horror called *All of Me*. Miriam Hopkins, George Raft and Helen Mack co-starred, and March drew more attention for his curly hairdo, which for some reason he had adopted, than for his performance. (Some theorized that he had tried the new hairdo in defiant despair after reading the script.)

In this he played a college professor who wants to rough it out West on an engineering project. His snobbish girlfriend, Miss Hopkins, a spoiled rich girl, refuses to go with him until she is softened and humbled by observing the mutual devotion of a criminal couple (Raft and Mack). March was out of the picture for long stretches, there were unbelievable plot developments (Miss Hopkins helps Raft, a thief, to make a jailbreak so

With Christopher Cook ("Tiny Tim") in CBS-TV's Shower of Stars *presentation,* A Christmas Carol, *1954*

he can be reunited with Mack), and the over-all result was highly forgettable.

The picture and March drew weak reviews, for which his role, rather than his performance, was responsible. About this time it became noticeable that when March was dissatisfied with a script he was forced to play, he lapsed into hamming or some other variety of flamboyant performing. He *never* did this with a role worthy of his talents, being a disciplined artist, but his tendency to become what some critics termed "a bouncing boy-o" in certain roles probably dates from the frustrations of the Paramount contract which saw him forced too often to drag too many bad pictures along on the basis of his energies and talents alone.

His next to last Paramount picture, however, was one of his finest. Moreover, *Death Takes a Holiday* proved right as rain for the bravura, flamboyant style March enjoyed adopting on occasion. In this he was Death masquerading as a handsome, sinister, but fascinating Prince at a house party in an Italian castle. The popular play by Alberto Casella was ably directed for the screen by Mitchell Leisen; the production values were first-rate; the dialogue, supplied in part by Maxwell Anderson, was thoughtful and adept, and at times profound, and March gave a strong, haunting performance as Death. Evelyn Venable, as Grazia, the mystically oriented girl who alone does not fear the Prince, and who goes off with him even after he reveals himself to her, was affecting in her role. *Death Takes a Holiday* is one of March's most favorably recalled films, and one of the best he did in his Paramount era.

The Paramount contract finally limped to a close with a film so mediocre that March and everyone connected with it must have despaired. This was *Good Dame*, again with Sylvia Sidney. In this he was a carnival cardsharp redeemed by the love of a sincere and honest girl. That about sums up the plot, and typical of the more charitable reviews was one that read: "It's quite bewildering to see Fredric March, noble brow and all, and who usually plays such grand heroes, portraying a tough guy with an East Side accent."

But all in life ends, and March's travails with Paramount finally ceased with this film. Moving cautiously, he signed on for a two-picture deal with Darryl Zanuck's new company, 20th Century (later 20th Century-Fox). He completed both films but not in sequence, lending himself out for two between the first and the last.

and lavish mounting, however, and was made with care. The bedroom-farce elements and the scene-stealing Frank Morgan notwithstanding, March counted the film as a plus—and certainly a dramatic improvement over *Good Dame* and *All of Me*.

March then lent himself out to Metro-Goldwyn-Mayer, where he was cast in an important "A" production by Irving Thalberg. This was the tasteful and sensitive *The Barretts of Wimpole Street*, in which he again appeared opposite Norma Shearer. While March was praised for his role of Robert Browning, the robust poet who rescues

With Eleanor Roosevelt, Associate Supreme Court Justice William O. Douglas, Florence Eldridge and publisher Gardner Cowles at American Association for the United Nations meeting, 1954. Mr. March served as master of ceremonies.

March's newfound sense of personal freedom and creative liberation is apparent in his work from *The Affairs of Cellini* onward. In this, the first under the two-picture Zanuck deal, March gave a buoyant, sparkling performance as the rakish Florentine artist Benvenuto Cellini. The Renaissance settings were handsome and impressive, the role was a bravura one with a wide range of emotions, plus Douglas Fairbanks-style balcony-climbing, but there were two flies in the ointment: For all director Gregory LaCava's delightful comedy sense and expert timing and the cleverness of the Bess Meredyth screenplay (adapted from Edwin Justus Mayer's play, *The Firebrand*) the movie was basically and irredeemably a romping bedroom farce, and Frank Morgan as the buffoonish Duke of Florence, a role he had played in the stage version, simply walked off with the picture. The plot had to do with the Duke's pursuit of March's beautiful model, Fay Wray, and the Duchess' (Constance Bennett) pursuit of March. The picture reeked of quality

the psychosomatically ill Elizabeth Barrett from the prison her subconsciously incestuous father has built around her, it was Charles Laughton who again stole a March film (the first was *The Sign of the Cross*) with his demoniacally-impassioned performance of the warped, possessive Edward Moulton-Barrett. Miss Shearer too came in for her share of praise. The principal benefit accruing to March was his presence in a Metro-Goldwyn Mayer prestige film of the first rank.

In 1934 the Marches took a boy into their home whom they formally adopted the next year, naming him Anthony March. They continued to live as they always had, entertaining close friends quietly. March kept in good physical trim with tennis, swimming and horseback riding. He was popular with his screen co-workers for his lack of temperament and his professional approach.

Samuel Goldwyn next engaged March for *We Live Again*, a film version of the Tolstoy novel that had been done twice before, as a silent and a talkie. At this point Goldwyn was giving his discovery, the Russian actress Anna Sten, a heavy build-up. An excellent performer, with a natural gift, she somehow failed to catch on with American audiences. Sten and March were very effective together in this handsomely photographed (by Gregg Toland) and richly atmospheric film. It was directed by Rouben Mamoulian, who had guided March through *Dr. Jekyll and Mr. Hyde* three years before. The film dealt with a Russian prince who betrays a peasant girl and later is redeemed from a selfish way of life, rejoining the girl, who has been convicted of manslaughter, as she begins her trek to Siberia. An uneasy attempt by Tolstoy to mix romantic drama with social polemics, and replete with authentic Russian flavor that slowed down the action, the film did not do too well with critics of the day. Seen recently, it is a much better picture than the 1934 reviewers found it, being a careful, disciplined, deliberately paced production, with excellent Maxwell Anderson dialogue touches.

Back at 20th Century, March fulfilled his commitment for the second of his two Zanuck pictures. This was *Les Miserables,* from the Victor Hugo novel, and it is the best of the several that have been made here and abroad based on Hugo's classic. The story is a human and affecting one: a convict, Jean Valjean, is redeemed by a Christ-like cleric (Cedric Hardwicke) from a life of crime and becomes a respected and honored citizen of a French community, circa 1862. But he is dogged by a relentless officer of the law, Javert (superbly played by Charles Laughton), from whom he is in continuous flight. When he eventually surrenders to Javert, whose letter-of-the-law rigidities have finally yielded to compassion, Javert sets him free, but commits suicide, feeling he has affronted his code. This is one of March's all-time best pictures, and for once Laughton didn't steal it from him. Both are equally fine. Richard Boleslawski directed sensitively, the pace was swift, and Zanuck gave it top production values.

When *Les Miserables* was completed, March was invited to sign another contract with Zanuck, but refused. Years later he told an interviewer: "I wanted permanent freedom to pick roles I felt were right for me. At that point (1935) I was moving up toward forty, and I couldn't afford mistakes." Zanuck told him, he said, that he'd never get anywhere in Hollywood without contract protection. March was to prove Zanuck wrong, for in the next three years he climbed, via a succession of pictures that were, by and large, felicitous, to a point where in 1937 he was one of Hollywood's highest-paid actors, listed as earning in that year $484,687. In 1935 he was making $125,000 per picture. "And this," he said years later, "was when you could keep what you earned. Thanks to that period of my life, I will never have money worries."

March then went to Metro-Goldwyn-Mayer for *Anna Karenina* with Greta Garbo. He was a dashing and handsome Vronsky in the Clarence Brown-directed film version of another Tolstoy novel. As the vital and irresistible cavalry officer, he seduces the married Anna. Her husband sends her out in disgrace, she and Vronsky

Delivering Lincoln's Gettysburg Address at joint session of Congress, February 12, 1959

know a brief happiness, then the social structure of the time proves too oppressive for their illicit love. The more shallow Vronsky goes back to his regiment and Anna, deserted and despairing, throws herself beneath the wheels of a train. Tolstoy designed his novel as a commentary on the social evils of the nineteenth century czarist era. The film captured more than a hint of this, thanks to the Clemence Dane-Salka Viertel screenplay. Miss Garbo fared best in the reviews, which was understandable, as the entire picture was built around her. March got off with adjectives like "handsome," "manly," and "stalwart," but as Garbo's co-star he was at the top of the 1935 screen-lover heap.

By that time in great demand as a prestige star of unassailable talent and reliable professionalism, March had his pick of roles, and Samuel Goldwyn got him again for *The Dark Angel,* another remake of a popular silent. March did well as a soldier blinded in the war who wishes to conceal his affliction from the girl he loves, affectingly played by Merle Oberon. He had a tour-de-force scene at the end, in which he memorizes every object in the room to conceal his blindness from his beloved, whom he had avoided since the war. Believing him dead, Miss Oberon is about to marry another childhood friend, Herbert Marshall, but then comes the revelation, and true love conquers all. Sidney Franklin directed with sensitivity, and though the film, as viewed today, seems illogical and unduly sentimental, it was well-mounted and acted, and still has the power to move.

In 1936 March, who had come to enjoy his status as a free agent able to choose or reject his films, did three roles. First there was the Earl of Bothwell in *Mary of Scotland* opposite Katharine Hepburn (he was liked in this RKO film but Hepburn as Mary garnered the most attention, as Garbo's Anna Karenina had). March was a stalwart, impassioned, masterful Earl, though the Dudley Nichols screenplay (which omitted the blank verse of the Maxwell Anderson stage original) made Bothwell out more hero than the knave he actually was.

In the 1935-36 period, March encountered one problem; his pictures tended to be released close together, with three appearing in one month, after which he might not be seen on the screen for nine months or so. His next, *The Road to Glory*, opened in New York one week after *Mary of Scotland* and his third 1936 picture, *Anthony Adverse*, opened three weeks after *that*. Though comparatively minor, this was a penalty of free-lancing. *The Road to Glory* for 20th Century-Fox, was a solid war picture directed by the able Howard Hawks, with Warner Baxter and Lionel Barrymore giving excellent performances, as did March. In this he was a lieutenant who vies with his captain for a nurse's favors. The war scenes were well-handled, with Hawks injecting strong elements of suspense and danger.

Florence Eldridge meanwhile contented herself for the most part with raising their two adopted children. Now and then she appeared in one of her husband's pictures. She was an admirable Fantine in *Les Miserables* (the mother of the child Valjean adopts) and a splendidly serpentine and crafty Queen Elizabeth in *Mary of Scotland*.

March next went over to Warners for the lavishly produced *Anthony Adverse*, which was based on the best-selling 1933 novel by Hervey Allen. The story of an orphan who is raised by a merchant who is actually his grandfather, the period piece tells of the boy named Anthony Adverse, who loves and loses the beautiful Angela, who goes on to become an opera singer and Napoleon's mistress. The movie tends to wander episodically, as did the book, and we find Anthony adventuring in Cuba and Africa, then back in Italy, where he vies for his grandfather's inheritance, then to Paris where he finds that Angela, the girl he had loved and idealized, is now a courtesan—but also the mother of his small son, whom he takes to America to start over, with Angela's blessing. Mervyn LeRoy did a skillful job of blending the disparate story elements, the Sheridan Gibney screenplay captured the picaresque sweep of the novel in capsulized form, and Erich Wolfgang Korngold gave it one of the loveliest scores ever heard from the screen. Seen today, it has a pacing, a bite and an elan that the 1936 critics do not seem to have appreciated, and March underplays his adventurous, action-filled role admirably for first-rate results, which the original reviewers did not sufficiently credit.

One of March's all-time favorite pictures came next. *A Star Is Born* won him a 1937 Oscar nomination, was superbly directed by William A. Wellman, had a trenchant, poignant screenplay by Dorothy Parker, Alan Campbell and Robert Carson and featured Janet Gaynor's finest performance as the girl from the sticks who is helped by Norman Maine (March), a great but slipping star, to win stardom on her own right. Then as he slides into oblivion, finally killing himself to avoid hampering her, she goes on to the heights. The story was not particularly original, but its handling was. The real Hollywood was shown here, in all its bitter reality and its human variety. March's work was universally acclaimed by the critics. Seen today, it is an intuitively shrewd performance, sophisticated yet compassionate.

At this time, he developed an interest in photography, which became his chief hobby. He, Miss Eldridge and the children lived quietly, he invested in trust funds and "sure" stocks, and contributed to causes he and Miss Eldridge adjudged worthy. His kindly philanthropic interest in "worthy" liberal causes was eventually to be betrayed when it was learned that some organizations on which he and other stars had allowed their names to be exploited, were Communist fronts. The Marches forthrightly denied a series of subsequent accusations that they were sympathetic to Communism and in 1938 he made a public statement to the effect that he and his wife were "opposed to dictatorship in any form, be it communism or fascism. We believe wholeheartedly in the principles of American democracy." Summoned to testify before the House Un-American Activities Committee a year after that, he declared later, "I am not a Communist and like all true Americans I am unalterably opposed to such a system . . . I hold no brief for any 'ism' but Americanism." In 1940, when he was accused by one John L. Leech, along with seventeen other Hollywood luminaries, of being pro-Communist, he called Leech "an unmitigated liar." The Marches some years later put a stop once and for all time to the recurring "Communist" rumors by suing *Counter-Attack*, a publication which stated that they were Communists. They won their libel suit and received substantial damages. A number of the Marches' friends in New York and Hollywood rallied to their defense during this difficult period, the consensus of their opinion being: "If Freddie and Florence are Communists, then I'm Stalin's mother."

Late 1937 found March in another hit, *Nothing Sacred*, most amusing of the screwball comedies so popular at that period. William A. Wellman proved as adept at guiding March through high-grade farce as he had been directing him in the tragic *A Star Is Born*. David O. Selznick, who produced, gave the film lavish mounting, and for his co-star March drew Carole Lombard, who had

With Joan Crawford at an MGM luncheon, 1953

forgotten more about screwball screen technique than most actresses were ever to know. The result was highly favorable, with Ben Hecht conjuring up a fast-paced, riotously funny screenplay. The plot dealt with a sensation-chasing reporter who parlays a girl who is allegedly dying of radium poisoning into a sob-brother's journalistic delight. She is wined and dined all over New York. Then comes the revelation: she thought she had it, and didn't. Of course things work out, and she and March fall in love.

The film drew very fine reviews, and then March went back over to his old base, Paramount, where he did Cecil B. De Mille's *The Buccaneer*. The De Mille epic was typically lavish and action-packed, but there was some criticism of March's inadequate French accent and some reviewers thought his performance mannered, artificial and "surface-y." The story dealt with the famed Jean Lafitte, the 1812 privateer who helps Andy Jackson win the Battle of New Orleans, with plenty of romancing on the side.

At this point, March and Miss Eldridge decided to fulfill an ambition they had been seriously contemplating since 1935: a return to the Broadway stage. They opened on January 10, 1938 in *Yr. Obedient Husband*—to poor reviews. The story dealt with the eighteenth century journalist Richard Steele and his domestic life. The Marches' old friend John Cromwell, with whom they had formed Marwell Productions, Inc. to get the play on the boards, also did the staging. Steele likes to drink, and he likes to stay out, and his wife Prue almost loses patience entirely, and threatens to leave him, but she doesn't; so went the plot. Bits and pieces of the Steele journalistic work were thrown in for reference, but the play as a whole didn't jell. The critics complained that March had lost his theatrical technique after years in Hollywood, and moreover played comedy in too heavy-handed and literal a manner.

Accepting their losses with good grace (the comedy had closed after eight performances) the Marches returned to Hollywood. His next film-choice proved almost as unwise as *Yr. Obedient Husband* had been for his stage return. He accepted an offer from Hal Roach to co-star with Virginia Bruce in *There Goes My Heart*. Released in late 1938, the film turned out to be a dull, flat imitation of *It Happened One Night*, with March as the reporter in pursuit of the flighty heiress who in this case works incognito in her grandfather's department store. Most critics felt March was not in his best form. Nancy Carroll, his Paramount co-star of the early thirties, had a small role as a shopgirl.

Next, on a percentage-of-the-profits, reduced-salary basis, March appeared in *Trade Winds*. Tay Garnett based the film on considerable photographic footage he had made while on a world tour; then he had written a story to fit it. Though the result, as in all such cases, had a flimsy look, the whole was redeemed by some witty Dorothy Parker-Alan Campbell-Frank R. Adams dialogue. This was also the picture in which Joan Bennett, as an escaping murderess (who really isn't a murderess) dyed her hair from blond to black, and brought on a hail of "Hedy Lamarr Lookalike" fan-mag gossip.

With Florence Eldridge during visit to Japan, 1960

The plot concerns a special investigator, March, who chases a suspected murderess halfway across the world, finally falling in love with her and uncovering the real murderer. Not without merit, the film as a whole did nothing to enhance March's career. He was not seen on the screen again for over a year.

The *Yr. Obedient Husband* debacle continued to sting, and the game Marches in early 1939 tackled Broadway again, this time far more successfully. Their vehicle this time was *The American Way*, written by George S. Kaufman and Moss Hart, and it traced a family of German immigrants over the forty years from the initial arrival in 1896 to the ripe old age of the protagonists. It had a large cast, and was well-liked by the critics. Typical of March's reviews was one of Burns Mantle, who wrote: "He gave as finely sustained a characterization as the simple hero as any actor has given in any drama this season." The play itself proved refreshing and heartening in grim 1939, extolling as it did the intrinsic virtues in the American style of life.

In 1939 the Marches bought a house in Connecticut, which they used while in the East, along with a New York apartment. They also retained their California home. They had done some radio in 1937 and 1938, and in 1939 March began narrating occasional documentary films, including *China's 400,000,000* (about China's struggle against Japan) and *Lights Out in Europe* (1940).

That same year, 1940, March returned to film-making in Hollywood, co-starring with Joan Crawford in *Susan and God*, the film version of the Rachel Crothers play in which Gertrude Lawrence had made a Broadway success. Miss Crawford and March, ably directed by George Cukor, received fine personal reviews, but the picture as a whole got mixed notices. March played effectively the husband who is neglected by his superficial, shallow wife while she gets caught up in fake religious revivalism. March finally makes her realize that charity begins at home.

Next March did *Victory*, a filmization of the Joseph Conrad novel, at Paramount. His old crony John Cromwell directed, and Betty Field played opposite him ably, but the critics said Conrad's profound ideas had been watered down in favor of the melodramatic elements in this story of a recluse's discovery of his own courage when faced with three evil would-be robbers in the Dutch East Indies.

Then March played in the Loew-Lewin United Artists production, *So Ends Our Night* in which he was affecting as a German refugee from Nazism who meets up with other forlorn types as they wander Europe without passports. Adapted from Erich Maria Remarque's novel, it was well directed by Cromwell and its sincerity was apparent, but critics felt it was slow-paced and episodic. It did help to push forward the burgeoning career of a young Glenn Ford, and Margaret Sullavan was affecting as the girl he loved, as was Frances Dee as March's wife.

Late 1941 saw March in a film hit and a stage miss. The film was *One Foot in Heaven* from journalist Hartzell Spence's novel about life with his Methodist minister father. The reviews for this Warner production directed by Irving Rapper were unanimous raves, with March never in better form as the lovably human William Spence who combines religious fervor with realistic humor and a deep instinctive knowledge of the human heart.

The play was *Hope for a Harvest* and it proved a forlorn hope for all concerned. No *American Way* was this, and it ran for only thirty-eight performances after opening at the Guild Theatre in November 1941. Florence Eldridge appeared with her husband; it concerns a woman (Miss Eldridge) who returns from Europe to a farming community where everything has gone to seed and attempts to redeem March, who had sacrificed the land for a gas station. The Marches' personal reviews were good.

In 1942 March had on his record one hit play and two fairly successful film comedies. Loretta Young co-starred with him for Columbia in *Bedtime Story*, a farce directed by Alexander Hall. In it March is an eccentric playwright who tries to get his "first lady of the theatre" wife, Miss Young, to change her retirement plans. In *I Married a Witch* for Paramount (released by United Artists) March played the descendant of a New England elder who had burned a witch. The witch is reincarnated as Veronica Lake, who sets out to take revenge on her murderer's descendant, then falls in love with him. René Clair's attempts at a light touch were frustrated by American-style censorship. Reviews for both comedies were on the mixed side, but there was no equivocation about the Marches' play. *The Skin of Our Teeth*, which co-starred them with Tallulah Bankhead, kept them busy from November 1942 to June 1943. March himself invested in the play, a fantastic comedy in three acts that covered the adventures of Mr. and Mrs. Antrobus, a couple who lick all the vicissitudes of life over the centuries, and represent the sturdy indestructibility of the human race. The critics were kind to everyone connected with it: the Marches, Miss Bankhead, Elia Kazan who staged it, and Thornton Wilder, who wrote it. The play won the Pulitzer Prize for that year.

During the War years March made tours for the USO, entertaining the troops in farflung parts of the world, and covering nearly 40,000 miles. When he returned he described the troops to a reporter as "gentle, sturdy, reliable, eager to do their job for their country."

The year 1944 brought March a fair success with *The*

Malcolm Cowley presents him with the Medal for Good Speech at the Annual Ceremonial of the American Academy and the National Institute of Arts and Letters

Adventures of Mark Twain for Warners, a film in which his characterization was praised but which was castigated for its episodic, superficial glossing-over of a complex artist's literary and personal life. *A Bell for Adano,* his play, was a long-run hit of the 1944-45 season, and as the understanding Major Joppolo, who takes a kindly, constructive interest in the citizens of a small Italian town where he is stationed, March was much liked. (The play was later made into a somewhat inferior movie with John Hodiak in the March role.) Late 1944 had also seen the release of his film, *Tomorrow the World* in which he again co-starred with Betty Field. Skippy Homeier, who had played the part on the stage (with Ralph Bellamy and Shirley Booth in the March-Field roles), stole the show as the young Nazi who comes to live with his professor uncle, March, after his anti-Nazi parents' deaths and proceeds to disrupt the household. March and Field, while sincere in their playing, had to yield center stage to Homeier at every turn. Some March fans wondered why he had bothered with the role.

March was then absent from the screen for two years. When he returned it was for what many regard as his finest performance, in *The Best Years of Our Lives.* The film won him his second Academy Award, and took nine Oscars in all. William Wyler directed and Samuel Goldwyn produced, from a screenplay by Robert Sherwood, and the result was a picture extolled for its warm human insights and its clear, forceful depiction of the reactions of American servicemen to their homecomings after years away at war. March was unanimously hailed for his depiction of the sergeant reverted to banker who resumes an interrupted life with his family and persuades narrow-minded superiors that ex-GIs are safe loan risks.

The same year, 1946, he made still another stage hit in *Years Ago,* again with Miss Eldridge, and was warm and winning as the father who helps his daughter to achieve her acting ambitions. Ruth Gordon wrote the play, based on her own early experiences in Wollaston, Mass., circa 1913. For his performance in this March won one of the first of the Antoinette Perry Awards given by the American Theatre Wing. (Spencer Tracy did the film version for Metro-Goldwyn-Mayer in 1953.)

After the long run of *Years Ago* ended in 1947, the Marches appeared together in two films under a deal with Universal-International. Both were successful. *Another Part of the Forest,* from the play by Lillian Hellman, displayed them as the progenitors of the vicious Giddenses of Miss Hellman's 1939 stage success, *The Little Foxes,* which had starred Tallulah Bankhead. (Bette Davis made the 1941 movie.) As Marcus Hubbard, a Southern traitor and vicious profiteer who is blackmailed eventually by his own children, March was convincingly malevolent. In the next, *Live Today for Tomorrow,* he projected beneficence with equally favorable impact on the critics. In this he played a letter-of-the-law style judge who finds that his wife is dying of a painful disease and commits a mercy killing. He refuses to avoid responsibility for this, and undergoes trial. Miss Eldridge gave a particularly affecting performance as the dying

wife. The film was later retitled *An Act of Murder.*

The Marches then went to England to do J. Arthur Rank's *Christopher Columbus,* which proved to be long on pageantry and short on drama, with March garnering so-so reviews and critics complaining that the real Columbus didn't show through amidst stilted tableaux and lifeless pageantry.

The year 1950 found the Marches in two stage flops which ran only forty-four and thirty-six performances respectively. *Now I Lay Me Down to Sleep,* a three-act comedy by Elaine Ryan, based on the Ludwig Bemelmans novel, dealt with an Ecuadorean general of eccentric pattern. Miss Eldridge played a spinster governess. March tried hard to limn the general's swaggering self-deceptions and futile eroticisms to good effect, but the critics just didn't like the play.

Late that year the Marches opened on Broadway in an Arthur Miller adaptation of Ibsen's *An Enemy of the People.* Miller gave out interviews stating that he saw in the play an up-to-date protest against "suppression and oppression" but the critics opined that he was better advised to write his own original works and stop tampering with the masters. The Marches again garnered critical kudoes for "earnest" performances.

They fared better on the stage in 1951's *The Autumn Garden,* a fine, witty Lillian Hellman piece about Southerners on a plantation examining their inner problems and attempting to resolve them. March was praised for his depiction of the vain, petty and foolishly self-deceptive painter. Miss Eldridge too fared well.

The year 1951 saw March back on the screen in what many consider one of his all-time best performances, Willy Loman in *Death of a Salesman,* a role Lee J. Cobb had played in Arthur Miller's 1949 play. As the self-deceiving salesman who covers up the shabby and selfish pattern of his life with cheap escapisms, March was never more piercing and true. One critic said he played "a little man's agony with the enormous passion that expands him into a symbol of humanity and therefore a tragic figure." For this role he was nominated for an Academy Award, but he lost to Humphrey Bogart (for *The African Queen*).

At Metro-Goldwyn-Mayer he did the part of an Italian immigrant who thinks it unmanly for his son to wear glasses. It was a segment—the weakest—of an eight-part film that purported to celebrate American life in all its human and geographical variety. Though replete with potent star names and powerhouse directorial talent, the result made it obvious that producer Dore Schary had overreached himself. Some parts were better than others; March's segment—and performance—were soundly criticized when the film opened in January 1952.

In 1953 March was seen on the screen in 20th Century-Fox's *Man on a Tightrope,* directed by Elia Kazan. In this he was a Czech circus owner conspiring to escape from Communist restrictions by brazening his way across the frontier into West Germany. He succeeds, but at the cost of his life. Robert E. Sherwood's literate screenplay complemented March's fine performance and Kazan's taut, suspenseful direction, and the reviews were good.

During the 1950s March was seen less and less on the

With President Kennedy and Mrs. Ernest Hemingway at a White House dinner, 1962

screen—or the stage for that matter. He and his wife began to indulge their taste for travel. He told an interviewer, "Florence and I have always felt that it is narrowing to live only in the world of the theatre, however much we love it. An actor is only as good as the person behind him, only as deep and only as broad-ranging. So we keep busy with a variety of interests, we travel, we study, and I hope, grow as human beings."

In 1954 he gave a creditable account of himself in MGM's *Executive Suite* as a conniving corporation controller who tries to blackmail and pressure his way into the presidency of a furniture company after its head dies suddenly. In a cast that included William Holden, Barbara Stanwyck, Walter Pidgeon and Louis Calhern, most critics adjudged the March performance the best.

The year 1955 saw him acting in sterling fashion in *The Bridges at Toko-Ri* as an admiral who must send pilots to their deaths from an aircraft carrier. And he was most creative in the film version of Joseph Hayes' play *The Desperate Hours,* in which he played the homeowner of conventional background who shows himself a special variety of hero as he confronts three convicts who take over his house and threaten himself and his family while awaiting getaway money. Humphrey Bogart, in one of his final performances, was also excellent.

Occasionally March essayed a television role, but it was far from his chief interest. He was effective opposite Claire Trevor in an NBC-TV "Producers Showcase" version of *Dodsworth* in 1956 and earlier he had been seen in *The Royal Family* (on "The Best of Broadway" TV series) with Helen Hayes and Claudette Colbert. 1958 brought him a good TV role as the father who tries to save his son's reputation in *The Winslow Boy.* He continued also to narrate documentaries. During the war he

had serviced *Black Sea Fighters* as narrator, with his excellent voice drawing favorable notices. He also narrated (in 1949) *The Titan,* the film about Michelangelo. 1957 saw the release of a fine documentary about Albert Schweitzer, with March ably depicting the quiet heroism of the Apostle of Lambarene. His best-known TV appearance (1954) was as Scrooge in a musical version of *A Christmas Carol* on CBS-TV's "Shower of Stars" program.

In 1956 March was seen in two strong film character roles supporting well-known stars of the 1950s. As Philip of Macedonia in *Alexander the Great* he played Richard Burton's father, and gave a vigorous, fierce, deeply human performance in a physically stressful role. He was then 58. (In 1957 he suffered a minor heart upset, and his doctor warned him to slow down.) *The Man in the Gray Flannel Suit* cast him as Gregory Peck's boss in a broadcasting firm, and he and Ann Harding, who had co-starred with him in *Paris Bound* twenty-seven years before, were moving in their scenes, he playing a power-mad executive who has neglected his family with dire results, and she his rueful and resigned wife. Peck carried most of the footage (and there were 152 minutes of it) as a man on the rise who decides that life with his family is worth more than ambition.

In November of 1956 March returned to Broadway after a five-year absence in Eugene O'Neill's monumental *Long Days' Journey Into Night.* Florence Eldridge played opposite him, and Jason Robards, Jr., and Bradford Dillman rounded out the cast. March's role of James Tyrone won him a Tony award. O'Neill's intense and deeply felt autobiographical play was later made into a movie with Sir Ralph Richardson in the March role and Katharine Hepburn as his wife. Many March aficionados regret keenly that March and Miss Eldridge did not repeat their roles in the movie, released in

Giving a dramatic reading for the Kennedys and their guests at the White House, 1962. The affair honored winners of the Nobel Prize

1962. Richard Watts Jr. credited March in this with "the finest and most penetrating performance of his career."

March was not seen on the screen again until 1959, when he co-starred with Kim Novak in Columbia's Middle of the Night, which Edward G. Robinson and Gena Rowlands had done on the stage. Delbert Mann got his usual competent performance from March, with Miss Novak functioning satisfactorily in a relatively undemanding role. Some critics, however, compared March unfavorably with Robinson's stage portrayal of the aging businessman who wants to marry a woman thirty years his junior and has to cope with the opposition of family and friends.

In 1960 March gave a splendid, many-hued interpretation of Matthew Harrison Brady in Stanley Kramer's film version of the hit Broadway play, Inherit the Wind, which Paul Muni (and later Melvyn Douglas) had played on Broadway. Spencer Tracy played the Muni part, based on Clarence Darrow, and March did a fine interpretation of the William Jennings Bryan type Brady represented. The famous "monkey trial" of 1925 Tennessee was recapitulated effectively (allowing for certain dramatic licenses) and March and Tracy both garnered fine reviews. Miss Eldridge, too, came in for her share of praise as March's wife.

The year 1961 brought March two successful appearances, one in the United Artists film, The Young Doctors, with Ben Gazzara and Eddie Albert. One critic said March had stolen the picture with his in-depth portrayal of an old medic who realizes his prime has passed, and joked that it should have been titled The Old Doctors.

On November 9, 1961, March opened in Gideon, his last Broadway performance to date. He played The Angel who argues with Gideon about philosophical and other matters. The Angel is a symbol of, and a representation for, the Deity, and as represented by playwright Paddy Chayefsky, he is a peevish, masterful, contrary Deity indeed—and a prize plum for any actor. Richard Watts, Jr., called March "powerful and enormously impressive as the Lord." March was then sixty-four years old. Shortly after this he was telling friends—and the press—that at that age, he felt he must slacken his pace, that plays were very taxing to the nerves and physique. "My time is limited now," he said, "and I want to enjoy life, travel, rest for what time is left." He has yet to do another play.

From the early 1960s on, March's film appearances have come at ever-widening intervals. The Condemned of Altona, in which he played a German industrialist who cravenly serves whatever government is in power and who has a Nazi son (Maximilian Schell) hidden in the attic of his mansion, was an ambitious attempt directed by Vittorio De Sica and produced in CinemaScope in Germany and Italy. The film was one that March considered "important" when he made it, and for which he had high hopes. The critics disagreed with him, terming it "a ponderous, pretentious, interminable Germanic muddle," and a "pat anti-German tract." March's reviews were not undiluted praise but tended toward the favorable. He was, of course, the star, and not the director or screenwriter, and had only limited responsibility for the dismal result.

In 1964 he was seen in the screen version of the Fletcher Knebel-Charles Bailey novel, Seven Days in May. In this he played a President of the United States menaced by an armed forces coup after signing a nuclear-control treaty with the Soviet Union. Acting in company with such stellar powerhouses as Kirk Douglas and Burt Lancaster, he received the best reviews, with Stanley Kauffmann calling him "easily the best of the three."

Since 1964 Fredric March, obviously in line with his "tapering-off" policy as expressed some years ago, has made only two films. In both he had what amounted to supporting character performances, though he was billed as one of the stars. In Hombre (1967) he was an Indian agent in the West of the 1880s who embezzles from the redmen by passing off dogmeat as beef. Paul Newman played "Hombre," who had been raised from childhood by Indians and who identified with them, and who proves the one passenger in a stage coach ride who has the guts to fight effectively against bandits. March got his usual good reviews.

In his last picture, tick...tick...tick, seen in early 1970, March was the mayor of a Southern town who takes a shrewd, realistic attitude toward a newly-installed black sheriff who must contend with mean white prejudices. The picture tended to be long on action and short on psychological penetration. Jim Brown and George Kennedy shared star billing with March, who was third in the credits. Typical of critical reaction to March was Richard Schickel's Life observation: "The best thing about the film is the presence of Fredric March, too long away and certainly deserving of something more interesting to play than the crusty mayor of a dusty small town."

Always Fredric March has interested himself in causes and political movements that to him enhance the American way of life. The libels of the late thirties that for a time beclouded the thinking of some in relation to his political beliefs has since given way to recognition of him as a truly American, truly Democratic examplar of United States traditions. In the 1960s the State Department honored him and Miss Eldridge by sending them on tours abroad. As far back as 1959 he was accorded the honor of reading Lincoln's Gettysburg address to a joint session of Congress on the 150th anniversary of the Great Emancipator's birth. President and Mrs. Kennedy in 1962 called on him to do a dramatic reading at a White House dinner and "at home" for past Nobel prize winners. Over the past ten years the honors have flooded in: honorary college degrees, a medal for good speech presented by the American Academy of Arts and Letters, continual requests by the State Department and other agencies for play tours. Movie offers keep coming regularly, also scripts from TV. In 1967 he and Miss Eldridge went into CBS Playhouse's Do Not Go Gentle Into That Good Night, but March fell ill and was replaced by Melvyn Douglas.

Son Anthony and daughter Penelope are now grown

With his wife in 1967

and busy with their own lives, but the Marches visit Italy regularly to see their daughter, who is married to Italian-American export-importer Umberto Fantucci, and their several grandchildren.

There have been heart upsets for both the Marches in the past few years, mild ones but, to them, signals that they should slow down and enjoy their vintage years quietly. March was seventy-four on August 31, 1971; Mrs. March was seventy on September 5. "Time," as he told one reporter, "is running out."

Today he spends most of his time on his beautiful estate in New Milford, Connecticut, where he supervises the gardening, reads, and at times meditates about the long, long past of activity and struggle and fulfillment. He dislikes to review his career with the press; "He hates talking about himself; it embarrasses him; he's really a modest guy and he feels his work speaks for itself," his representative has told many members of the press, here and abroad, who wish to interview him.

In December 1970 the distinguished Players Club gave a "pipe night," an honorary dinner and reception for the Marches. He was delighted with the honor, as was Mrs. March, but he came to it, primarily, as one friend put it, "because he enjoys greeting old friends and associates; they give him a warm feeling."

"Keep interested in others; keep interested in the wide and wonderful world," he told a recent interviewer, in line with his often-expressed philosophy. "Then, in a spiritual sense, you will always be young."

The Films of
FREDRIC MARCH

With Ruth Chatterton

The Dummy

Paramount / 1929

THE PLAYERS

Mr. March was *Trumbell Meredith* in a cast that included: Ruth Chatterton *(Agnes Meredith)*; John Cromwell *(Walter Babbing)*; Fred Kohler *(Joe Cooper)*; Mickey Bennett *(Barney Cook)*; Vondell Darr *(Peggy Meredith)*; Jack Oakie *(Dopey Hart)*; ZaSu Pitts *(Rose Gleason)*; Richard Tucker *(Blackie Baker)*; Eugene Pallette *(Madison)*.

THE CREATORS

Robert Milton *(director)*; Herman J. Mankiewicz *(adaptation and screenplay)*; based on the stage comedy by Harvey J. O'Higgins and Harriet Ford; J. Roy Hunt *(photography)*; Hector Turnbull *(supervisor)*; George Nichols *(film editor)*; Morton Whitehill *(assistant director)*.

Opened at the Paramount Theatre, New York, March 3, 1929. Running time when released, 70 minutes.

THE PICTURE

The Dummy was far from an auspicious film debut for March. He was handed a mere bit part as the estranged husband of a woman who suspects him of kidnapping their little girl. Ruth Chatterton, who played his wife, was also given limited footage. The picture, a weak, primitive "talkie," alternated shakily between comedy and melodrama, was sloppily photographed, and the critics of the day complained about the absence of good close-ups and the cavalier treatment of talented stage actors like March and Chatterton in a "weak sister" which was given little more than "quickie" production and compared unfavorably with that other early Paramount talkie, *Interference*, which had been turned out with more care. Paramount scouts had spotted March on the stage in Los Angeles, where he was appearing in *The Royal Family* in a John Barrymore satire role that was discussed in Filmtown with considerable amusement.

Hollywood in late 1928 badly needed goodlooking young actors who were stage-trained and whose voices registered well with the tyrannical and capricious "mike," and March was snapped up by Paramount with a five-year contract. He moonlighted at the theatre doing *The Royal Family*, toiling days at the Paramount studio in his undemanding, indeed thankless and peripheral, role.

Both he and Miss Chatterton played fourth fiddle to a child actor named Mickey Bennett, the "Dummy" of the title because he pretends to be deaf and dumb in order to trap the kidnappers of Miss Chatterton's child. Jack Pickford had played the role in a 1917 silent version, and that was where the whole foolish business belonged—in 1917. The more demanding critics—and audiences—of 1929 were indifferent toward the inane goings-on.

Bennett, the office boy of detective agency head John Cromwell, gets himself kidnapped by the same gang who had taken the girl. They think him a deaf mute, but when he talks in his sleep the jig is up. However, he manages to signal to the pursuing rescuers, who capture the gang, whereupon Chatterton and March, reunited in their mutual concern for their offspring, rush to the cabin to claim her. A happy Mickey Bennett gets a pat on the back and a large reward.

Stage director Robert Milton presided, rather nervously, over this seventy minute pot-pourri of trivia, the badly-synchronized sound track eliciting critical ridicule, and the only genuine novelty offered being ZaSu Pitts, of the fluttery hands—of all people—as a kidnapper! But though his footage was limited shamefully, and his role proved wholly unworthy of his background and expertise, March showed up as a photogenic and well-spoken actor, and the film led immediately to a much better part opposite a major Paramount star.

THE REVIEWERS
Photoplay:
The picture looks like a convention of new Hollywood faces imported from the speaking stage . . . well worth seeing, despite its obvious experimental talkie crudities. It isn't within call of *Interference,* . . . but the fundamental appeal gets it across.

Robert Landry in *Variety:*
Fair program entertainment, including quite a few giggles, but apt to leave audiences cold. No love story, and Ruth Chatterton, number one in the billing, has what amounts simply to a bit. Fredric March is among the three names billed on the main title, although he has even less to do than Miss Chatterton; he doesn't get a single closeup and remains a zero throughout. . . . Talk is good but treatment is leaky at the seams. The failure of the picture to get under the epidermis is in great measure due to the concentration on the vocal phase with the accompanying neglect of good old-fashioned picture technique.

Mordaunt Hall in *The New York Times:*
The antics of the people [in the film] appeared to please [the audience] and even when the voices were as loud as that of a circus announcer, the spectators still remained interested in the story. Perhaps it was because the chief character on the screen was a boy and there were many youngsters in the theatre. The story is a tame, would-be-exciting affair. The persons involved are at various stages of the game so utterly silly that one felt they ought to undergo an examination in a psychopathic ward. On other occasions they appeared to be suddenly endowed with the wisdom of a Solomon. . . .

With Ruth Chatterton and John Cromwell

John Cromwell, a man who knows his footlights and therefore is not intimidated by a mere microphone, is good in his performance but, as in the case of Ruth Chatterton, he can't cope with some of the absurd incidents and violent sound reproduction. . . . One could stand the childish nature of this yarn and take it all in good part if it were not for the bellowing from the screen, which was as if the Paramount management were eager to entertain gratis by sound some of the passengers on incoming steamships in the bay.

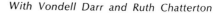

With Vondell Darr and Ruth Chatterton

With Clara Bow

The Wild Party

Paramount / 1929

THE PLAYERS
Mr. March was *Gil Gilmore* in a cast that included: Clara Bow *(Stella Ames)*; Shirley O'Hara *(Helen Owens)*; Marceline Day *(Faith Morgan)*; Joyce Compton *(Eva Tutt)*; Adrienne Dore *(Babs)*; Virginia Thomas *(Tess)*; Jean Lorraine *(Ann)*; Kay Bryant *(Thelma)*; Alice Adair *(Maisie)*; Renee Whitney *(Janice)*; Amo Ingram *(Jean)*; Marguerite Cramer *(Gwen)*; Jack Oakie *(Al)*; Phillips R. Holmes *(Phil)*; Ben Hendricks, Jr. *(Ed)*; Jack Luden *(George)*; Jack Raymond *(Balaam)*.

THE CREATORS
Dorothy Arzner *(director)*; E. Lloyd Sheldon *(screenplay)*; adapted from an original story by Warner Fabian; Victor Milner *(photography)*.

Opened at the Rialto Theatre, New York, March 30, 1929. Running time when released, 77 minutes.

THE PICTURE
Clara Bow, "It" herself, got March as leading man in *The Wild Party*, her first talkie. He played a serious professor and she played a wild student, and a strange combination they made. The 1929 critics were tactful

about the Bow voice, wrote that it suited her personality, and blamed the primitive soundtrack for those occasions when Clara's Brooklynese became downright indistinct. March, of course, contributed all the pear-shaped tones required, and an ingratiating and manly screen personality to boot, but neither the novelty of Clara's speaking voice nor March's evident class and authority could do much for the picture, one of woman director Dorothy Arzner's early efforts, and it did only fair business.

The silly plot had to do with Clara and her equally wild college chums who sign on for Professor March's class because they think he's cute-looking. When they find him serious and scholastically demanding, they indulge in various hi-jinks. Later, Clara is put out of a costume ball because she and her gang sport dresses that are outrageously low-cut. Still later (this girl gets around), Clara is rescued by March from a drunken admirer with rape on his mind. (It is not explained what a college professor would be doing in the roadhouse where this rescue takes place.)

When snoopy schoolmate Joyce Compton sees Clara alighting from March's car, there is gossip; to show that

With Clara Bow and her school pals

he plays no favorites, March bawls Clara out in class; Clara walks out in anger. Then she and pal Shirley O'Hara attend an affair that turns out to be "the wild party" of the title. In this unlikely environment, Miss O'Hara finds romance with Jack Luden.

Then Ben Hendricks, Jr., the drunken admirer who had been put down by March, shoots and wounds him. Clara rushes to March to declare her love, with snoopy Joyce kibitzing. There is some added plot silliness (or have you had enough by now?) about a red-hot letter written by starry-eyed Miss O'Hara to Luden. Chivalrous Clara takes the blame to protect her chum, is disgraced, leaves college and boards a train for home. But lo and behold, her prof joins her on the cho-choo. Seems he has had enough of that wild college atmosphere, too. March comported himself with as much dignity and sense as the silly part and plot permitted; Clara Bow was—well, Clara Bow. The picture, however, did get him some important exposure, and those who came to see Bow did not forget the handsome, mustachioed professor. Though reviewers for the next two years were to continue misspelling his first name "Frederic," his face —and voice—were registering.

THE REVIEWERS
From a Paramount Publix Playbill:
The "it" girl's first all-talking sensation. She listens like she looks in this Paramount all-dialogue hit. You've had an eyeful of "it"—now get an earful!

Bige. in *Variety*:
Boxoffice picture with a b.o. title, a boxoffice star, and more boxoffice than ever, Clara contributes her voice.

Laughing, crying or condemning, that Bow voice won't command as much attention as the Bow this and that, yet it's a voice. Enough of a voice to insure a general belief that Clara can speak as well as look—not as well, but enough. Warner Fabian's story fits the redhead like a red bathing suit. It's impossible, though. So full of all the things everybody knows. But take it or leave it, there's still Clara . . . when Clara flashes a gam, all senses are deadened. . . . E. Lloyd Sheldon's dialogue is as flip and broad as permissible, much of it forced humor, and most of it to be taken seriously by the flaps. . . . Performance of Fredric March as the prof is the picture's best . . . vocally he reigns supreme.

Mordaunt Hall in *The New York Times*:
From Nome to Key West and from John O'Groats to Tahiti be it known that the voice of Clara Bow has been recorded in a motion picture which, provided the theatres are wired for sound, can be heard by all nations. . . . Miss Bow's voice is better than the narrative. It is not over-melodious in delivery but it suits her personality. Sometimes it is distinct and during some passages it isn't. It may fail on account of technical deficiencies of the recording device . . . the story gets sillier and sillier . . . in fact, during the affectionate scenes between [Mr. March and Miss Bow] the audience, instead of being sympathetic, was, despite Miss Bow's good looks, moved to mirth . . . this production is intended for dwarfed intellects, and if they are at all susceptible to the performances that dart hither and thither on the screen, it is perhaps better to deprive them of the questionable enjoyment of gazing upon this picture.

The Studio Murder Mystery

Paramount / 1929

THE PLAYERS
Mr. March was *Richard Hardell* in a cast that included: Neil Hamilton *(Tony White)*; Florence Eldridge *(Blanche Hardell)*; Warner Oland *(Rupert Borka)*; Doris Hill *(Helen MacDonald)*; Eugene Pallette *(Detective Dirk)*; Chester Conklin *(Gateman)*; Lane Chandler *(Martin)*; Gardner James *(Ted MacDonald)*; Guy Oliver *(MacDonald)*; E. H. Calvert *(Grant)*; Donald MacKenzie *(Captain Coffin)*.

THE CREATORS
Frank Tuttle *(director)*; Frank Tuttle *(adaptation and dialogue)*; from the *Photoplay* Magazine serial of the same name, written by The Edingtons. Ethel Doherty *(screenplay)*; Victor Milner *(photography)*.

Opened at the Paramount Theatre, New York, June 9, 1929. Running time when released, 62 minutes.

THE PICTURE
If *The Wild Party* took March two steps forward, this third picture took him one step backward, for once again he found himself in a tiny part, and got killed off before many minutes of the film had elapsed. Perhaps

it was as well he was permitted to make a quick exit, for, as seen today, the picture is a shabby affair indeed— dull, labored, primitive in the worst 1929 manner, with dated jokes and shoddy levity alternating with hunt-the-murderer scramblings and scurryings. For film historians, glimpses of the Paramount studio, where the murder of an actor (March) takes place, may have some interest, and there is more than a little interest in the casting of Florence Eldridge (her first of a number of films with her husband) as the philandering actor's jealous wife who is one of five persons suspected of his murder. Warner Oland plays a film director whose wife spoke the actor's name as she died, so he's on the suspect list, too. And then there's the girl March deceived (Doris Hill), her studio-watchman dad who resented their affair, as did her brother, and some complicated folderol about the murderer substituting the body for a dummy on a set.

The talk (all of it via primitive 1929 microphones) is endless, and makes the 62-minute film seem twice as long as it is. When I viewed the film again a few months ago, I found myself longing for it to end, the tedious

*Doris Hill, Neil Hamilton and
Eugene Pallette*

proceedings being oppressive in the way so many bad 1929 talkies are. Stilted and gauche, the film also features Neil Hamilton as a studio gagman who indulges in endless buffoonery and mutual-insult jokes with Eugene Pallette as the police detective investigating the murder. Miss Hill, convicted by circumstantial evidence, is arraigned for, and finally convicted of, the murder, but is saved by Hamilton, who exposes Oland as the real murderer.

March was as personable and slick in his brief role as circumstances permitted, Oland was a convincing menace, and Miss Eldridge handsome and skillful, but the Hamilton-Pallette juvenilities were given too much footage, and Frank Tuttle's direction was listless and "mikebound" for most of the way. The picture's story had its origin in a serial of the same name commissioned by James R. Quirk, editor-publisher of *Photoplay*, and published in that magazine under the Edingtons' byline. Ethel Doherty, who did the screenplay, and Tuttle, who adapted and did the dialogue, changed quite a bit of the original serial plot (for the worse, it turned out) and Quirk saw to it that the fact was highlighted in *Photoplay's* review, doubtless because he and his magazine wanted to renounce any blame for what resulted on the screen. If that was his intention he was right, for *The Studio Murder Mystery* as a film was nothing of which anyone could be proud. Though *Photoplay* was tactful, charitable, even laudatory in its review, the film, especially as seen in 1971, is one of the worst of 1929 or any year.

THE REVIEWERS
Photoplay:
No doubt you read this thrilling mystery in *Photoplay*.

Perhaps you were among the many thousands who took part in The Studio Murder Mystery Contest. In any event you will still want to see [the film] because it is a corking mystery melodrama, with plenty of dramatic kicks and numerous surprises. . . . Paramount made numerous changes in the story.

Mordaunt Hall in *The New York Times:*
[The picture] is a comedy masquerading as a thriller, for it is far too jocular to be taken with any marked degree of seriousness. There is a murder, to be sure, but the subsequent behavior of a police detective and a gay young spark with a gift for gags affords so much levity that the slaying of an actor seems merely to be an excuse for these two and others to make merry. . . . Florence Eldridge is capital as Mrs. Hardell.

Waly. in *Variety:*
With all the hoke in this story and comedy situations allowed to brew over into things dramatic; with all of the conventional script swerves and a lowly gag writer solving the mystery while conversing to himself over the phone—the thing holds enough interest and suspense . . . to get by as a fair programmer. . . . Major credit for holding the thing together goes to Warner Oland. Continental manner, deep voice, dark appearance and real ability are the Oland assets. . . . A lot of people will like the studio stuff. Camera takes in a couple of sets, some Paramount streets, and something that looks like B. P. Schulberg's sanctum.

With Ann Harding

Paris Bound

Pathé / 1929

THE PLAYERS

Mr. March was *Jim Hutton* in a cast that included: Ann Harding *(Mary Hutton)*; George Irving *(James Hutton, Sr.)*; Leslie Fenton *(Richard Parrish)*; Hallam Cooley *(Peter)*; Juliette Crosby *(Nora Cope)*; Charlotte Walker *(Helen White)*; Carmelita Geraghty *(Noel Farley)*; Ilka Chase *(Fanny Shipmath)*.

THE CREATORS

Arthur Hopkins *(producer)*; Edward H. Griffith *(director)*; Horace Jackson *(adaptation)*; from the play by Philip Barry. Frank Reicher *(dialogue co-director)*. Josiah Zuro *(music score)*.

Opened at the Paramount Theatre, New York, September 20, 1929. Running time when released, 73 minutes.

THE PICTURE

Paramount lent March to Pathé for his fourth picture, *Paris Bound,* and it turned out to be his best chance yet in films. He did full justice to the role of the young husband who agrees with his wife, played charmingly by the fast-rising Ann Harding, that the marital ties need not bind oppressively and that both should feel free to love others while remaining always "spiritually faithful" to each other. The wife is courted by a musician and the husband goes adventuring in Europe, where he indulges in an affair with a girl who had the temerity to declare her continuing love for him on his wedding day.

The 1927 play by prolific Philip Barry had been an enormous hit, titillating would-be sophisticates of the era with its "modern-approach-to-marriage" talk. However, theory and practice, as it turns out, are two different things, and when Miss Harding finds that March had actually been unfaithful, there are hurt feelings. However, she forgives him and takes him back.

This kind of thing was big stuff in 1927—and 1929 for that matter—and the March-Harding combination was chemically right and registered well. Moreover director Edward H. Griffith succeeded in moving the film away from the talky, static deadliness so common to films of the period, and the piece came across on film as bright, smart and well-paced. There was some criticism of the choppy continuity, and it appears also from comments of the day that Mr. March and Miss Harding pitched too much woo too passionately and lengthily for the more delicate mores of the time—they seem to have been the precursors of the Cary Grant-Ingrid Bergman protracted-kissing team of 1946's *Notorious.* But the film did much to showcase March as one of the more accomplished and striking leading men of the

With George Irving, Ann Harding and Ilka Chase

seemingly some extraneous shooting that retards most of its naturally slow action anyway. Yet Pathé has a moderate moneymaker in this talker, mostly because the stage title will get some recognition and again because of this sterling legit actress Ann Harding. Miss Harding is reckoned with as something of a big find out Hollywood way. Unfortunately the screen *Paris Bound* does not do full justice and is only a suggestion of Miss Harding's future possibilities in pictures. No indication anyone in particular erred in picturing the play. Simply a case where necessary appendages and maintenance of continuity slows up the action throughout the film, running into several particularly tedious scenes. . . . Some of the affectionate and vivid embraces executed by Miss

screen. Miss Harding, whose stately blonde beauty, sincere acting style and lovely voice were shortly to make her one of the screen's most important stars, seems to have brought out the best in March, nor was he any mean asset to her own filmic projection. Certainly both lent their portrayals an intelligence and sophistication of a kind that was not on view every week in 1929 films.

THE REVIEWERS
Photoplay:
If you like a problem, see this. None of the intimate marital appeal of the play is lost in the movie version. It is the first film vehicle of Ann Harding (the original "Mary Dugan" of the stage version) . . . sophisticated dialogue . . . smooth acting.

Variety:
Transcribing Philip Barry's medium-weight stage play to the screen left a lot of loopholes to be plugged and

With Ann Harding

With Ann Harding

Harding and Fredric March, that estimable young lead, seem a little too much overdone.

Mordaunt Hall in The New York Times:
Quite a praiseworthy adaptation of Philip Barry's clever play. It is in most respects an effort that bears evidence of a restraining hand and the voices are exceptionally well-registered. E. H. Griffith, the director, often uses his camera to advantage, but there are discursive passages that become somewhat tedious, and so does the constant embracing of the husband and wife. . . . Miss Harding is a most interesting personality on the screen . . . her acting is obviously the result of careful thought . . . Fredric March's interpretation of Jim Hutton is sympathetic and human.

With Jeanne Eagels

Jealousy

Paramount / 1929

THE PLAYERS
Mr. March was *Pierre* in a cast that included: Jeanne Eagels *(Yvonne)*; Halliwell Hobbes *(Rigaud)*; Blanche Le Clair *(Renee)*; Henry Daniell *(Clement)*; Hilda Moore *(Charlotte)*.

THE CREATORS
Jean De Limur *(director)*; Garret Fort *(screen adaptation)*; John D. Williams *(dialogue)*; based on the play by Louis Verneuil and the translation and stage adaptation by Eugene Walter.

Opened at the Paramount Theatre, New York, September 13, 1929. Running time when released, 66 minutes.

THE PICTURE
Proof of March's rising importance as a film leading man came when the famed Jeanne Eagels asked that he play opposite her in the filmization of the Louis Verneuil play, *Jealousy*, which had been done on the stage by John Halliday and Fay Bainter. Anthony Bushell had originally been cast for the role, and indeed he and Miss Eagels had filmed it in its entirety. But then Miss Eagels expressed dissatisfaction, demanded that the footage be scrapped and that March be cast as her husband. Since she was a "prestige" actress, her word was heeded, and March stepped in. Miss Eagels was seriously ill while shooting the film, (she was to die later that year) and she barely managed to complete it.

With Jeanne Eagels

With Jeanne Eagels

woman and Fredric March does what he can with the jealous man. Jean De Limur directed, and badly.

Bige. in *Variety:*
Notable performance by Jeanne Eagels doesn't go far enough to help [the picture] to become better entertainment . . . than its story permits it to. . . . It does little more than sell Miss Eagels as a personality and an actress, although that's doing the same thing over again with Miss Eagels after *The Letter.* All of *Jealousy's* drawing will be done by the star.

Mordaunt Hall in *The New York Times:*
An extraordinarily English Jeanne Eagels is to be heard and seen. . . . Miss Eagels affects a drawl, and during many of her lines it sounds as if she were endeavoring to out-albion the albion. Fredric March, who plays Yvonne's husband Pierre, on the other hand, talks frankly like an American businessman. Halliwell Hobbes, whose work easily excels that of his colleagues . . . quite evidently hails from Britain. . . . Miss Eagels is quite attractive. Mr. March is hardly suited to his part. But Mr. Hobbes is excellent.

The reviews were not good. There was criticism of the British accent that Miss Eagels had affected, and of March's American speech pattern in a piece set in France. Newsboys shouting "Extra!" in some scenes also seemed more reminiscent of Broadway and Times Square than Paris. "Confused," "boring," "devoid of suspense" —the critics damned it in phrases that left no room for doubt that the film was an unfortunate swan-song for Miss Eagels and a cypher in March's career figurings, with *The New York Times'* Mordaunt Hall publicly informing him that he was "hardly suited" to his role. Halliwell Hobbes, the heavy, marched off with whatever praise was left from the debacle.

The plot dealt with a young artist who is jealous of the older man his wife had known before her marriage, and who now poses as her "guardian." When the wife finds herself in dire financial straits, she asks the older man's aid (to the tune of some 500,000 francs) and makes the mistake of going to his apartment after lying to her husband as to her whereabouts. Whereupon the husband, discovering the lie, kills the "guardian." The police at first suspect an innocent man, but finally the husband admits to the crime. Miss Eagels looked extremely wan as photographed, and March, while delivering with his usual efficiency, had certainly found himself more felicitously cast.

THE REVIEWERS
Photoplay:
This one is a bloomer. Originally a brilliant two-character stage play, showing the tragic effects of jealousy on the lives of two temperamental people, it here becomes a confused and boring talkie with more characters and less punch. The late Jeanne Eagels plays the

With Jeanne Eagels

With Colleen Moore

Footlights and Fools

First National / 1929

THE PLAYERS

Mr. March was *Gregory Pyne* in a cast that included: Colleen Moore *(Betty Murphy-Fifi D'Auray)*; Raymond Hackett *(Jimmy Willet)*; Virginia Lee Corbin *(Claire Floyd)*; Mickey Bennett *(call boy)*; Edward Martindell *(Chandler Cunningham)*; Adrienne D'Ambricourt *(Jo)*; Frederick Howard *(treasurer)*; Sidney Jarvis *(stage manager)*; Cleve Moore *(press agent)*; Andy Rice, Jr. *(song plugger)*; Ben Hendricks, Jr. *(stage doorman)*; Larry Banthim *(Bud Burke)*.

THE CREATORS

William A. Seiter *(director)*; John McCormick *(producer)*; Carey Wilson *(screenplay)*; adapted for the screen from a story by Katherine Brush. Stage numbers directed by Max Scheck. Oliver Garretson *(sound recording)*; James Dunne *(assistant director)*. Songs by Alfred Bryan and George W. Meyer: "You Can't Believe My Naughty Eyes," "If I Can't Have You," "Pilly Pom Pom Plee." "If I Can't Have You" rendered by Earl Bartnett's Biltmore Trio. Part Technicolor.

With Colleen Moore

Opened at the Mark Strand Theatre, New York, November 8, 1929. Running time when released, 78 minutes.

THE PICTURE

By this time March found himself in considerable demand among Hollywood's feminine stars, many of whom felt he would enhance their pictures, and Colleen Moore was the next to get him, on loan at First National, where Miss Moore was trying to establish herself in the talkies via a musical in which she emoted (sincerely), sang (passably), and danced (execrably). Miss Moore, who had been a popular silent star, was to find the sound medium rougher going, and perhaps she and her husband, John McCormick, who produced, or one of their advisors, felt that some of March's stage expertise and "mike" aplomb would rub off on her and her picture.

But March found himself saddled with a trivial and limited role, that of the wealthy admirer of one Mlle. Fifi (Miss Moore) a reigning Broadway musical comedy star who is really Betty Murphy from upstate New York. It seems that a backer had sent her to Paris to get some French flavor, then passed her off as the latest Gallic sensation along the Great White Way. If it all sounds familiar, it is—and was even in long-gone 1929. March was not even the authentic leading man, that not-so-enviable spot being held down by Raymond Hackett, who played the racketeering young ne'er-do-well with whom Miss Moore falls in love. She passes up the overtures of young millionaire March, who worships from a distance, and to help her he gets Hackett a job in his firm. Then there is a robbery, the boy claims the millionaire framed him out of jealousy, and Miss Moore believes the lie until March forces Hackett to tell her the truth: that he actually was an accomplice in the robbery. Miss Moore, it seems, had actually married the boy to assure him she truly loved him, but after the revelations, she sadly gives both men their walking papers, and sits alone in her dressing room brooding. Fadeout.

There were songs galore, dancing, elaborate numbers, some of them in a primitive Technicolor process that one critic complained made the performers look "red as Indians." Stage numbers were directed by Max Scheck, who had created the elaborate dance spectaculars for the *Folies-Bergere* of Paris and the *Ziegfeld Follies.* March, philosophically accepting his brief and lustreless role as neither a setback nor an advance, and consoled by the thought that if he hadn't gotten the girl in the picture, neither had the other guy, went back to Paramount to see what else the studio gods had in store.

THE REVIEWERS

Photoplay:

Unquestionably this is Colleen Moore's finest picture since *We Moderns.* Talkies have given her a curious break, which she's taking big. Her voice is pleasant and versatile and the story standards raised by talking films permit her to chuck the synthetic program stuff and turn to something bigger. This is it. The story, by Katherine Brush, is a skillful combination of sophisticated humor and poignant emotional drama.

Variety:

[The film] looks like medium money, and Miss Moore will draw it all on personality and past achievements. . . . Miss Moore's presentation of the one girl with two names and opposite characteristics is a good bit of acting. She is and always was a beautifully sincere performer. Two male leads, Raymond Hackett as the gambling kid and Fredric March as the millionaire, have rather difficult assignments but both pull through neatly. Idea is to keep the customer guessing which is the deserving suitor.

With Virginia Lee Corbin, Larry Banthim and Colleen Moore

With Kay Francis and Mary Brian

The Marriage Playground

Paramount / 1929

THE PLAYERS

Mr. March was *Martin Boyne* in a cast that included: Mary Brian *(Judith Wheater)*; Lilyan Tashman *(Joyce Wheater)*; Huntley Gordon *(Cliff Wheater)*; Kay Francis *(Lady Wrench)*; William Austin *(Lord Wrench)*; Seena Owen *(Rose Sellers)*; Philippe de Lacy *(Terry)*; Anita Louise *(Blanca)*; Little Mitzi *(Zinnie)*; Billy Seay *(Bun)*; Ruby Parsley *(Beatrice)*; Donald Smith *(Chip)*; Jocelyn Lee *(Sybil)*; Maude Turner Gordon *(Aunt Julia Langley)*; David Newell *(Gerald)*; Armand Kaliz *(Prince Matriano)*; Joan Standing *(Miss Scopey)*; Gordon Demain *(Mr. Delafield)*.

THE CREATORS

Lothar Mendes *(director)*; J. Walter Ruben and Doris Anderson *(screenplay)*; based on the novel *The Children* by Edith Wharton; Victor Milner *(photography)*.

Opened at the Paramount Theatre, New York, December 13, 1929. Running time when released, 70 minutes.

THE PICTURE

March then found himself cast in a better-than-average picture, and in a role which highlighted all his most warm and winning qualities. As a young American traveling in Italy in *The Marriage Playground*, he befriends a group of children whose previously-divorced parents have married each other, and who flit about Europe leaving the children more or less on their own in charge of the eldest of the consolidated brood, Mary Brian. At eighteen, Miss Brian is doing her level best to serve as substitute mother to her brood, half of whom are not even related to her, and it taxes her ingenuity and patience, to say nothing of the fact that she is pretty and at an age when a girl seeks romance. Getting scant help from her elders, she does the best she can.

When March comes along, she responds, as do the children, to his kindness and concern, and shortly finds herself in love with him. But the man of her dreams (don't they always?) has a fiancee in Switzerland or someplace, and Miss Brian seems to be in for a bad case of unrequited love until March finally comes around, drops his fiancee (who wasn't much in the first place), and claims the "little mother" for his own, thus sending 1929 audiences home sighing happily.

The film was adapted from an Edith Wharton novel *The Children,* and was several cuts above the usual film fare in its handling of character and atmosphere, in line with the truism that even the sloppiest movie made from a good writer's book will betray its literary origin despite the movie hacks' best efforts.

The critics were, for the most part, kind, and March came in for a goodly share of praise, as did Mary Brian, Lilyan Tashman (who played the bubble-headed mother as only Miss Tashman could) and such child stars of the more precocious type, for instance Philippe de Lacy, whose winsome face popped up in a number of films of the period. Kay Francis was also along for the ride, though this was before her top-liner days, and her role, while displaying her attractively, was essentially peripheral. There were authentic human values in the picture, an appealing March-Brian romance, and workmanlike direction by Lothar Mendes. All in all, March could term his appearance here an advance. This was the last of his 1929 films, and in seven pictures in one year he had become widely and favorably known to the moviegoers.

THE REVIEWERS
Robert Landry in *Variety:*
A peach of a picture, well above the satisfaction-giving average of a program release and the kind that leaves a sense of full-hearted human pleasure behind it. Can be booked in safety and exploited with confidence. It's packed with children, amusingly impudent, touchingly warm youngsters who will carry a tremendous appeal to the great home-keeping, family-loving American public. In the midst of the children, and for this reason, as for others, suggestive of Thomas Meighan, although in no respect similar as to looks, is Fredric March, sharing billing with Mary Brian and getting a great break. A couple of pictures like this one and March will romp upward pronto. Miss Brian is splendid . . . it is a production characterized by quiet, unostentatious elegance.

Mordaunt Hall in *The New York Times:*
Although it has spasmodic lapses and the youngsters are a trifle too precocious even for this generation, it is quite an intelligent production with well-woven strands of humor and sympathy, pathos and an appealing romance. The brunt of the acting falls on Fredric March and Mary Brian, who are thoroughly believable in their roles.

Kay Francis tells off Lilyan Tashman on the left, while March takes on Huntley Gordon at center.

Sarah and Son

Paramount / 1930

THE PLAYERS
Mr. March was *Howard Vanning* in a cast that included: Ruth Chatterton *(Sarah Strong)*; Fuller Mellish, Jr. *(Jim Gray)*; Gilbert Emery *(John Ashmore)*; Doris Lloyd *(Mrs. Ashmore)*; William Stack *(Cyril Belloc)*; Philippe de Lacy *(Bobby)*.

THE CREATORS
Dorothy Arzner *(director)*; Zoë Akins *(adaptation and screenplay)*; based on the novel by Timothy Shea; Charles Lang *(photography)*; Earl Hamen *(sound recording)*.

Opened at the Paramount Theatre, New York, March 14, 1930. Running time, 86 minutes.

THE PICTURE
March was reunited with Ruth Chatterton for Paramount's *Sarah and Son*, in which the old "Madame X" theme was given a fresh whirl, with variations, of course. A lot had happened to both Chatterton and March in one short year. No longer were they playing fourth fiddle to kids and kidnappers, as in *The Dummy*; it was now first-class, center-stage. Miss Chatterton had made a hit in *Madame X* the year before, and by 1930 was climbing to top stardom, her distinctive manner and compelling voice proving big assets.

Adapted by Zoë Akins' from an also-ran novel by Timothy Shea, the film dealt with an Austrian woman who marries a no-good (Fuller Mellish, Jr.). He more or less "sells" their child to a wealthy couple without her knowledge or consent, then disappears. She wanders about looking for her lost family, and as an entertainer, sings for the boys in a World War I army hospital.

There she encounters her dying husband in time for him to whisper the name "Ashmore." Later she locates the family she thinks have her child and claims she can identify him by a birthmark on his neck, but they turn her away and threaten her with incarceration in a mental hospital if she persists in labeling their child her son. Movies being movies, she rises in the world and becomes a grand opera star, no less; meanwhile the lost baby has grown into a boy.

With Ruth Chatterton

The Ashmores' lawyer, March, refuses to believe the boy is Chatterton's when she renews her plea, but when the unhappy mother persists, he arranges finally a meeting in which all is set right. As an added bonus, love blossoms between lawyer and opera singer.

As this outline indicates, *Sarah and Son* was a grand 1930-style weeperoo, albeit well-mounted and skillfully acted. Critical reaction was somewhat divided, but Chatterton and March both won praise for their work. Special

critical attention, and approval, were given Miss Chatterton for essaying, in the film's earlier scenes, a thick Austrian accent which she later subtly modulated throughout the film—no mean trick, given the still-shaky recording devices of 1930. But Chatterton's years on the Broadway stage stood her in good stead, in these and other matters, and she tried an accent again in a later picture.

March registered solidly as the well-meaning but

With Doris Lloyd and Ruth Chatterton

With Ruth Chatterton

stubborn lawyer who finally serves Chatterton's just cause. *Sarah and Son* proved another plus for him. Dorothy Arzner directed in fine style, adding to her growing reputation as Hollywood's only woman director of major status. She had directed March previously in *The Wild Party*. Master Philippe de Lacy of *Marriage Playground* was also on hand with March, this time as Miss Chatterton's long-lost son.

THE REVIEWERS
Variety:
Ruth Chatterton's splendid performance and the occasional fine acting by some of her supporting cast . . . save [the film] from what otherwise would have been a rather doubtful fate. . . . Another *Madame X* with a slightly varied theme. . . . Fredric March is a good type

as the lawyer-lover but occasionally a trifle stiff.

Mordaunt Hall in *The New York Times:*
Ruth Chatterton, who has been highly successful in screen work since the talking pictures came into vogue, gives another splendid performance . . . an intelligently directed narrative . . . in the initial scenes the agony is piled on a little heavily, but the excellent acting of all concerned saves these episodes from being tedious. Later . . . the story is graphic and affecting . . . every performance is restrained. The late Fuller Mellish, Jr., is seen in the role of Jim. It is a good performance. Fredric March is easygoing and natural. . . . A little less attention to pathos and a little more attention to cheer would have made this even a better film than it is.

With Mary Astor

Ladies Love Brutes

Paramount / 1930

THE PLAYERS

Mr. March was *Dwight Howell* in a cast that included: George Bancroft *(Joe Forziati)*; Mary Astor *(Mimi Howell)*; Margaret Quimby *(Lucille Gates)*; Stanley Fields *(Mike Mendino)*; Ben Hendricks, Jr. *(Slattery)*; Lawford Davidson *(George Winham)*; Ferike Boros *(Mrs. Forziati)*; David Durand *(Joey Forziati)*; Freddie Burke Frederick *(Jackie Howell)*; Paul Fox *(Slip)*; Claude Allister *(tailor)*; Crawford Kent, E. H. Calvert *(committeemen)*.

THE CREATORS

Rowland V. Lee *(director)*; Waldemar Young, Herman J. Mankiewicz *(screenplay)*; based on Zoë Akins' play *Pardon My Glove*. Harry Fischbeck *(photography)*.

Opened at the Rivoli Theatre, New York, May 15, 1930. Running time, 80 minutes.

THE PICTURE

For some strange reason known only to the Paramount powers-that-were (perhaps they just had nothing else available) March found himself back in a relatively minor part in *Ladies Love Brutes*, starring George Bancroft. Here he is the husband whom society-wife Mary Astor is in the process of divorcing. Bancroft hogged most of the footage as Forziati, an uncouth but goodnatured building contractor who falls in love with Miss Astor and, to win her, attempts to improve his manners and attire, with sometimes hilarious results.

A comedy-melodrama, the film, based on Zoë Akins' play *Pardon My Glove* and directed by Rowland V. Lee in a manner tailored to the then-popular Bancroft's "crude but well meaning" cinematic image, the story follows Bancroft's persistent attempts to win the elusive Miss Astor, who, as one critic reminded his readers, was a lady who *didn't* love brutes—not really.

When Miss Astor finally tells Bancroft that she can't marry him because she must consider her child's future—meaning "Get lost, you're not good enough for me"—Bancroft is inveigled by one of his shady pals into staging a fake kidnapping of the lady's child, whereupon he will effect a "rescue" and win his lady's gratitude, and, presumably, love. But it doesn't work out as planned; a rival racketeer gets wind of the plot, actually kidnaps Miss Astor's child—and Bancroft's child for good measure—and then our guy is really in a stew. He wins out, of course, in the usual bluff Bancroft fashion, and gets the kids back where they belong.

There are several amusing scenes in which the crude Bancroft tries on a swallowtail coat with the assistance of a supercilious tailor, and another in which he is forced to admit to Miss Astor that he can't tie his own bow after her child has pulled it. Bancroft is crudely amusing all over the place for the eighty minutes the picture runs, and Miss Astor is sleek, knowing and hugely assured. And March? He's just along for the ride—as Kay Francis was in *The Marriage Playground*—and, well, now you see him; now you don't. Doubtless March put the whole thing promptly out of his mind as soon as his scenes were completed.

THE REVIEWERS

Rush. in Variety:

Zoë Akins' play written down to a presumptive neighborhood fan grade of taste, and what it might have held as a class screen production discounted. Result is just pretty good program material. . . . Picture has many slow spots where story progress lags badly; comedy incidents have been inexpertly written in. . . . What the title has to do with the story is another puzzle. This particular lady didn't love this particular brute, anyway, but that's the least of this poorly translated stage play.

The New York Times:

So long as [the film] concerns itself with the comic actions of a rough diamond intent on giving himself a little polish, all is merry and bright, but when this tale turns to implausible melodramatic incidents, it leaves much to be desired. . . . Mary Astor . . . gives an appealing and easy performance. . . . Although the fun in this chronicle is not notable for its novelty or subtlety, it is effective largely because Mr. Bancroft happens to be the target. . . . Mr. Bancroft plays his part well, and toward the close he gives vent to his thunderous laugh. . . . Mr. March tackles a minor role with his unfailing skill.

With Mary Astor

Paramount On Parade

Paramount / 1930

THE PLAYERS

Mr. March was one of the doughboys in a sequence with Ruth Chatterton in a cast that included (alphabetically): Iris Adrian, Richard Arlen, Jean Arthur, Mischa Auer, William Austin, George Bancroft, Clara Bow, Evelyn Brent, Mary Brian, Clive Brook, Virginia Bruce, Nancy Carroll, Maurice Chevalier, Gary Cooper, Cecil Cunningham, Leon Errol, Stuart Erwin (also in the sequence with Mr. March and Miss Chatterton); Henry Fink, Kay Francis, Skeets Gallagher, Harry Green, Mitzi Green, Robert Greig, James Hall, Phillips Holmes, Helen Kane, Dennis King, Jack Luden, Abe Lyman and His Band; Nino Martini, David Newell, Jack Oakie, Warner Oland, Zelma O'Neal, Eugene Pallette, Joan Peers, Jack Pennick, William Powell, Charles "Buddy" Rogers, Jackie Searle, Lillian Roth, Rolfe Sedan, Stanley Smith, Fay Wray.

THE CREATORS

(In alphabetical order): Dorothy Arzner, Otto Brower, Edmund Goulding, Victor Heerman, Edwin H. Knopf, Rowland V. Lee, Ernst Lubitsch, Lothar Mendes, Victor Schertzinger, Edward Sutherland, Frank Tuttle *(directors)*; Albert A. Kaufman *(producer)*; Elsie Janis *(supervisor)*; Harry Fischbeck, Victor Milner *(photography)*;

Merrill White *(film editor)*; John Wenger *(production design)*; David Bennett *(choreography)*. In some sequences, color by Technicolor.

Opened at the Rialto Theatre, New York, April 19, 1930. Running time when released, 101 minutes.

THE PICTURE

Just when it appeared that the revue-extravaganza-all star novelty was on the downswing, Paramount popped up in the spring of 1930 with its own contribution, and it was a lulu. *Paramount on Parade* enlisted the services of the three-dozen stars on the roster, a host of lesser players, musicians, choreographers, dancers, singers—you name it—in a "rise, decline and fall of the Roman Empire"-style jamboree that snapped, crackled and popped its way through two hours of never-ending activity, some of it sparkling, some of it dull.

Seen today, the total effect is wearisome after a while. Let's face it, some of the dramatic stars were not cut out for singing or dancing or light patter; those who were, like Maurice Chevalier, for instance, provided the bright spots. March fared better than some, possibly because Ruth Chatterton carried the burden of his sequence, hogging the spotlight (to fair effect) with a song called "My Marine" (by Richard A. Whiting and Raymond Eagen). Sung in a torchy style by Miss Chatterton in a World War I French bar to a group of doughboys, including a wryly observant March and an admiring Stuart Erwin, the song spelled out the theme, which dealt with Miss Chatterton's loneliness for a Marine who took off without telling her how she could reach him.

While Miss Chatterton looked handsome as usual, and projected well, it was obvious that drama was her chief stock in trade; March, whose contribution consisted mainly of looking and listening and reacting, registered as well as such limitations allowed. No better and no worse than other confections of its kind and period, *Paramount on Parade* offered Technicolor in seven sequences, the over-all supervision of famed World War I entertainer Elsie Janis, who obviously helped with a certain tone and flavor that were not exactly 1930-style, and such items as a Nancy Carroll dance, a Helen Kane song, an *apache* dance between Maurice Chevalier and Evelyn Brent, and a show-stopping Chevalier singing "Sweepin' the Clouds Away."

Elsie Janis and Jack King contributed such songs as "I'm True to the Navy Now," "We're the Show Girls," "Paramount on Parade," "What Did Cleopatra Say?" and "Any Time's the Time to Fall in Love." (Helen Kane, who could sing, and Clara Bow, who couldn't, figured prominently in several). Sam Coslow contributed "Sweepin' the Clouds Away." Richard Whiting and Leo Robin offered "All I Want Is Just One Girl," Abel Baer and L. Wolfe Gilbert offered "Dancing to Save Your Sole," "I'm in Training for You," and "Let's Drink to the Girl of My Dreams." Dave Dreyer and Ballard McDonald offered "We're the Masters of Ceremony," Mana-Zucca came up with "Nichavo," Leo Robin and Ernesto De Curtis got into the act with "Song of the Gondolier"— all in all an impressive display of variegated talent not always wisely deployed and unevenly projected due to the many director-cooks stirring the broth. No doubt the likes of Miss Arzner, Mr. Goulding and Mr. Lee, among others, were glad to be done with this stunt and to get back into the directorial milieus where they shone, or, at least, felt more at ease.

THE REVIEWERS
Variety:
Just when the industry is figuring studio revues are passé, the Zukor organization re-introduces the subject with less gusto but with a picture that is in a class by itself. Real entertainment incorporating everything on the schedule into its twenty numbers, [the film] witnesses the first production of this kind linking together with almost incredible smoothness achievements from the smallest technical detail to the greatest artistic endeavor. It is a prize for all houses and certainly for indefinite runs in the key centers. . . . Technicolor used in seven of the numbers . . . close-ups exceptionally worthwhile . . . excellence of continuity, something virtually impossible in most revues, is responsible for almost a perfect tempo of audience reaction. . . . In the familiar surroundings of a French cafe, Ruth Chatterton sings to a handful of returning doughboys (one of whom is Fredric March) about the lad who forgot to leave a forwarding address. Miss Chatterton does a nice piece of emotionalism, although the song ("My Marine") is insignificant.

Paramount Chorines

True to the Navy

Paramount / 1930

THE PLAYERS
Mr. March was *Gunner McCoy* in a cast that included:
Clara Bow *(Ruby Nolan)*; Harry Green *(Solomon Bimberg)*; Rex Bell *(Eddie)*; Eddie Fetherston *(Michael)*; Eddie
Dunn *(Albert)*; Ray Cooke *(Peewee)*; Harry Sweet *(Artie)*;
Adele Windsor *(Maizie)*; Sam Hardy *(Grogan)*; Jed
Prouty *(dancehall manager)*.

THE CREATORS
Frank Tuttle *(director)*; Keene Thompson, Doris Anderson and Herman Mankiewicz *(screenplay)*; Victor Milner
(photography).

Opened at the Paramount Theatre, New York, May 23,
1930. Running time when released, 70 minutes.

THE PICTURE
Some genius at Paramount decided that March needed
a change of pace, or type, or both, and he found himself cast as a sailor named Gunner McCoy who is the
target-shooting champ of his ship and hangs around a
San Diego drugstore with his cronies, some of whom
make large sums betting on his skill. In this trifle he was
reunited with Clara Bow, with less than felicitous results.
The critics were quick to point out that March was too
intellectual and "drawing-roomish" to play a sailor and
added that it was the most flagrant miscasting of the
year. March's acting was praised, but his bosses took the
strong hint and he never played a sailor again—at least
not that kind of sailor.

Clara Bow was in her cinematic decline by that point,
and her performance was uneven, though her role of a
soda fountain attendant who flirts outrageously with the
gobs and keeps several of them on the string at the
same time, was tailored to her measure. Frank Tuttle

directed the business as if he wanted to get it over and done with at the earliest possible moment.

Of course, Bow falls in love with March, they have their ups and downs, he gets in a bar brawl and she summons his buddies to his aid, they quarrel, make up— and all ends on a cheerful note with Gunner March demonstrating anew his target shooting skills, to his buddies' delight.

Some good character actors were wasted: Jed Prouty as a dancehall manager, Sam Hardy as a slick knock-about, comedian Harry Green as the drugstore pro-prietor. One critic noted the carelessness of the film's production mounting, implying that it constituted sabotage of Clara's star-status. Her husband to be, Rex Bell, was also on hand as a gob.

It's an ill wind that blows nobody good; doubtless some feminine members of the nationwide Paramount audience thought March fetching in a sailor suit— though he was then a ripe thirty-two—but *True to the Navy* will never go down in March's, or anybody else's book as one of his ten best films.

THE REVIEWERS
Robert Landry in *Variety:*
Hardly better than fair. Slow in tempo, sappy in story, and bearing the stamp of perfunctory production, it's the type of picture that's apt to be bigger for the dis-

With Clara Bow (center) and Rex Bell (bottom right)

With Clara Bow

tributor than the exhibitor, and no help to the star. There are laughs, quite a few of them, but it is the laugh that comes from mugging rather than naturally infectious lines or situations. . . . Although Fredric March easily takes the acting honors, he is badly miscast. This sounds paradoxical, but remains the fact. Despite demonstrating some excellent trouping, he is always too much the drawing-room type to look right in those sailor pants. Miss Bow has seldom been so unimportant in a picture. Studio didn't strain themselves looking after her interests. Carelessness is the dominant impression to the trade eye from the entire film. . . . Director Tuttle has all his sailors constantly pulling at the nape of their collars, rather an effeminate manner for able-bodied seamen.

Mordaunt Hall in *The New York Times:*
A moderately diverting summer-weather film, which succeeded in eliciting a good deal of laughter at its showing yesterday. . . . Miss Bow does better work in the lighter scenes than she does in the more serious ones. In fact, the picture would be better if it did not follow the conventional formula, for toward the end it lags and there is a marked absence of both fun and suspense. Fredric March, who is a competent player, is hardly the type for a sailor. . . . Miss Bow sings and she also weeps.

With Clara Bow

With Claudette Colbert

Manslaughter

Paramount / 1930

THE PLAYERS
Mr. March was *Dan O'Bannon* in a cast that included: Claudette Colbert *(Lydia Thorne)*; Emma Dunn *(Miss Bennett)*; Natalie Moorhead *(Eleanor)*; Richard Tucker *(Albee)*; Hilda Vaughn *(Evans)*; G. Pat Collins *(Drummond)*; Gaylord Pendleton *(Bobby)*; Stanley Fields *(Peters)*; Arnold Lucy *(Piers)*; Ivan Simpson *(Morson)*; Irving Mitchell *(Foster)*.

THE CREATORS
George Abbott *(director)*; George Abbott *(screenplay and adaptation)*; based on the *Saturday Evening Post* story of the same name by Alice Duer Miller; A. J. Stout *(photography)*; Otto Lovering *(editor)*.

Opened at the Rivoli Theatre, New York, July 23, 1930. Running time when released, 82 minutes.

THE PICTURE
March was back in his proper element in this film, a remake of the 1922 silent with Leatrice Joy and Thomas Meighan, considerably updated and de-sentimentalized by producer-director-screenwriter George Abbott for 1930 consumption. In this he played a poor but honest young district attorney who sends to prison a rich girl (Claudette Colbert) who had killed a motorcycle cop with her car. Sounding the theme that there is but one law for rich and poor, the adamant March sends this girl

he loves off to the clink for what he righteously presumes will be a decade or so of penance, but politics and "connections" intervene and she gets out in two years. Then she waxes vindictive, but melts into a reasonable facsimile of virtuous breast-beating at the end, of course, and chases her young district attorney down the street for an "I Love You" fadeout.

The prison scenes were sharply delineated and realistically played, with Miss Colbert's acting in these and other scenes getting favorable notice. At first bitter and hostile, she gradually grows accustomed to prison life and when later she discovers her ex-maid is a fellow-inmate, she has unbent to the point where she asks her what her first name is.

Soon the former society girl has become so democratized that she becomes popular with the other inmates, who always want her on their side in spelling-bees. But of course Colbert can't forget that the man she loved and who, she thought, loved her, put her into the clink—and well, it takes time to get all that straightened out after she leaves prison, as before noted—but at the end, all is well.

The screenplay Abbott concocted was based on a *Saturday Evening Post* story by Alice Duer Miller. There was much praise for the courtroom and prison sequences, and both March and Miss Colbert drew good notices. Abbott put care into his direction and the result was a well-tooled product that helped boost both players' careers.

With Claudette Colbert

This was March's first film with Colbert, but it was not to be his last. In films with each other or with someone else, the March and Colbert careers were to accelerate during the early thirties at roughly the same speed, with Oscars for both in the not too distant future.

THE REVIEWERS
Abel Green in *Variety:*
One is always a bit suspicious of those courtroom mellers where the uncompromising D.A. must prosecute his amour and send her to jail, but George Abbott carried it out rather well . . . although never wholly maintaining a consistent pace. No average audience can rationally accept Miss Colbert's carelessness with expensive jewels or her nonchalant distribution of diamond bracelets as bribes to motorcycle cops. The entire structure, so far as Abbott readapted it along these lines, doesn't ring the bell. . . . As a completed product, it will stand up for the average fans because it holds a competent admixture of acting, production and action. It is also susceptible to the usual ballyhoo of "sending his own sweetheart to prison for manslaughter" and that routine.

The New York Times:
A melancholy discussion of the matter of special privilege . . . the courtroom scenes of the picture are well done and so are some of the incidents scattered along the way. It cannot be denied that Claudette Colbert—given an even chance—is capable of excellent acting. She shows some of it in her part of Lydia, although the film is so busy going on its way that there isn't much time. Fredric March also is capable; he does not, however, need to turn so many curiously-built corners.

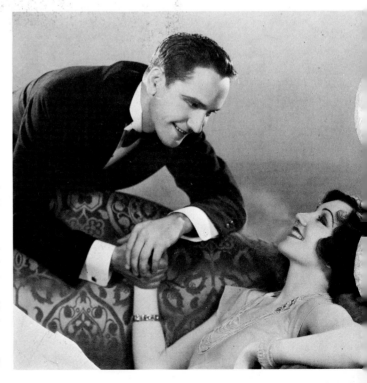

With Nancy Carroll

Laughter

Paramount / 1930

THE PLAYERS

Mr. March was *Paul Lockridge* in a cast that included: Nancy Carroll *(Peggy Gibson)*; Frank Morgan *(C. Mortimer Gibson)*; Glenn Anders *(Ralph Le Saint)*; Diane Ellis *(Marjorie Gibson)*; Leonard Carey *(Benham)*; Ollie Burgoyne *(Pearl)*.

THE CREATORS

Harry D'Abbadie d'Arrast *(director)*; Donald Ogden Stewart *(dialogue)*; based on a story by Harry D'Abbadie d'Arrast and Douglas Doty; George Folsey *(photography)*; Ernest F. Zatorsky *(sound recording)*; Helene Turner *(editor)*; Song, "Little Did I Know" by Irving Kahal, Pierre Norman and Sammy Fain.

Opened at the Paramount and Brooklyn Paramount Theatres, New York, November 14, 1930. Running time when released, 99 minutes.

THE PICTURE

March was then assigned to *Laughter*, a delightful comedy shot in New York. It was smart, witty, sophisticated, with adult and serious aspects underlying the sparkle, and was a forerunner of the clever, shimmering comedies that were to prove highlights of the later

1930s. Donald Ogden Stewart's dialogue was scintillating, and Harry D'Abbadie d'Arrast's direction applied the light, skillful touch required. *Laughter* is one of March's alltime favorite pictures. Reportedly, it is one of the few films of which he retained a print.

Certainly it was five years ahead of its time in execution and atmosphere, and Nancy Carroll, in this her first film with March, was never seen to better advantage. Frank Morgan was excellent as her millionaire husband, too busy with his ticker tapes to give his young wife the excitement she requires, and the other cast members gave fine accounts of themselves.

The film was well-liked by the 1930 critics and when shown in 1970 at the American Film Institute's Eighth New York Film Festival, proved that it had lost none of its charm, though it was then a forty-year-old "antique." Of course, it has to be viewed today in charitable perspective and in proper context; in 1930 it was a trailblazer, clever and original, and in that respect it is a cinema milestone. Other films followed in the thirties that were derivations, and in some cases outright imitators, of *Laughter's* style and general approach. It is important, therefore, to look at it today as it must have appeared when it was fresh and new, forgetful (if one

With Nancy Carroll

goes off to Paris to forget. Money and affluent surroundings soon pall, and when Paul, the composer, returns, they take up with each other again, he insisting that she needs laughter and love in her life.

Paul and Peggy go driving in the country and take refuge in an empty house during a storm. Police arrest them for housebreaking, but her husband gets them released. He then remonstrates with his restless wife, and suggests more discretion for the future. A young Greenwich Village sculptor, Ralph, is also in love with Peggy. When Peggy introduces him to her stepdaughter, Marjorie, he attempts to involve himself with Marjorie on the rebound, but when Peggy tells Marjorie that Ralph really loves her, there is a scene and later Ralph kills himself.

Again Peggy finds herself in an indiscreet situation. Aroused however, at last, to her true inner needs, she returns to her husband and tells him that she cannot go on with the marriage. He reminds her that she needs luxuries and the things money can buy but she replies, "I need love," and goes off with her composer. A mere recital of the plot, which admittedly has its conventional aspects, does not get across the sparkle, wit, fine writing that raise this picture above the ordinary. Certainly it helped to advance both March's and Miss Carroll's careers at a crucial moment.

THE REVIEWERS
Photoplay:
Fredric March as the young composer who loves Nancy and laughter, does his best work. . . . A first-rater. See it.

The New York Times:
It is emphasized in the course of the clever nonsense,

can be) of all the imitations that followed, some of which were quite clever in their own right.

The story deals with an ex-Follies beauty, Peggy, who marries a millionaire because she thinks luxury is the answer to everything. Her young composer boyfriend

With Nancy Carroll

With Nancy Carroll

drama and satire of [the film] that *joie de vivre* is more to be desired than any king's ransom and that dollars are but dross. . . . Endowed with Donald Ogden Stewart's characteristic fun in the dialogue contributed by him . . . Miss Carroll gives a delightful performance. Mr. March is splendid as the impertinent, lighthearted and unruffled Paul. Mr. Morgan's interpretation also is clever, for he shows the worship of Mammon with agreeable restraint.

Herman G. Weinberg in The American Film Institute's 8th New York Film Festival program:
You will look almost in vain for the name of H. D'Abbadie d'Arrast in film histories or encyclopedias. With a few, a very fleeting few, exceptions . . . it is almost as if d'Arrast had never existed. Certainly he occupies no niche at all in the cinema pantheon, where he belongs. [The film] is a wry comedy . . . a typical Hollywood fairy tale, you will say. But all True Love stories are fairy tales. Out of the smallest things d'Arrast made a delight.

With Nancy Carroll

*With Mary Brian, Henrietta Crosman
and Ina Claire*

The Royal Family of Broadway

Paramount / 1930

THE PLAYERS
Mr. March was *Tony Cavendish* in a cast that included: Ina Claire *(Julia Cavendish)*; Mary Brian *(Gwen Cavendish)*; Henrietta Crosman *(Fanny Cavendish)*; Charles Starrett *(Perry Stewart)*; Arnold Korff *(Oscar Wolff)*; Frank Conroy *(Gilbert Marshall)*; Royal G. Stout *(Joe)*; Elsie Edmond *(Della)*; Murray Alper *(McDermott)*; Wesley Stack *(a hall boy)*; Herschel Mayall *(the doctor)*.

THE CREATORS
George Cukor and Cyril Gardner *(directors)*; Herman Mankiewicz and Gertrude Purcell *(screenplay)*; based on the play *The Royal Family* by George S. Kaufman and Edna Ferber; George Folsey *(photography)*.

Opened at the Rivoli Theatre, New York, December 22, 1930. Running time when released, 82 minutes.

THE PICTURE
March then gave his most brilliant performance to date in films, recreating his hit stage role of Tony Cavendish, a thinly-disguised caricature of John Barrymore. Paramount had bought the rights to the play for March, and he came through with a bravura performance that won him his first Academy Award nomination and got the critics to hurling such adjectival garlands as: "preposterous, glamorous, lunatic, tremendously vital, spirited, boisterous." Certainly March had Barrymore down to a T—every lifted eyebrow, every gesture, every fey mannerism—and even though his role was a relatively brief one (he is offscreen for much of the picture) he made his scenes count, and kept the audience thinking of him throughout, and hopeful of his return.

Though he created the role of Tony Cavendish not only on stage and screen, but also on television years later, and though it brought him his greatest acclaim to date as of 1930, it is not among March's favorite roles, reportedly because he regards it, for all its cleverness and virtuosity, as basically a spoofing lampoon of another personality rather than a full-fledged interpretation of a character rooted in his own mystique.

If this be so, March underrates his performance, for it was a wondrous combination of inventive comedy and clever parody, a synthesis which, as any actor will admit, is not easy to get across.

Ina Claire, Henrietta Crosman, Mary Brian, Frank Conroy and other cast members were likewise excellent,

With Ina Claire and Henrietta Crosman

with Miss Claire shining to a greater extent than her film sorties usually permitted—which was the screen's loss, not hers. The story is as zany and wild and spontaneous as the keen wit of George Kaufman and Edna Ferber, as filtered through understanding screen adaptors Herman Mankiewicz and Gertrude Purcell, could make it.

The plot outlined the fortunes of the Cavendishes, Broadway's First Family, Barrymores all, in spirit if not exactly in life. March plays Tony, who whirlwinds into family matriarch Crosman's house with process servers and reporters on his heels; it seems he "broke the faith"

by going Hollywood, where for some time he had been sojourning. A Polish screen star is after him for $200,000 heart balm; "America's Greatest Lover" is also fending off an angry film director he has socked in a moment of temper, and ducking legions of marriage-hungry females. He is in New York en route to Europe. He dazzles the family during his brief stay with his colorful dramatics and unpredictable horseplay, meeting any and all situations with outlandish theatricalism.

Ina Claire, in an Ethel Barrymore-type role, is a theatrical "First Lady" who has long spurned marriage with millionaire Frank Conroy, who waits patiently on the sidelines. Miss Claire's daughter, Mary Brian, rebels against the family stage tradition, and announces she wants to marry society-boy Charles Starrett.

Though old and ill, the outraged matriarch decides to embark on a repertory tour to keep the name alive. March returns from Europe, he and the others learn that his mother has been taken ill on stage, go to her, and she dies surrounded by her family. The thrill of applause had brought on her fatal attack.

Miss Claire decides to continue the tour in her mother's place, once again rejecting Conroy. Miss Brian decides that married life with her society boy is a bore and becomes an actress after all. The dialogue, situations, acting, direction by George Cukor and Cyril Gardner were all first-rate, and the film did much for March's cinematic image and gained him an even wider following.

THE REVIEWERS
William Boehnel in the *New York Telegram*:
A witty and humorous [film] . . . they are a mad, charming, fascinating lot, those Cavendishes, to whom nothing outside of the theatre matters.

With Ina Claire, Mary Brian and Henrietta Crosman

With Mary Brian, Henrietta Crosman and Ina Claire

direction give the comedy a brilliant polish. And the acting is exquisitely finished.

Thornton Delehanty in the *New York Post:*
If [the film] had been shown to an audience in the mountains of Tennessee, they could hardly have failed to recognize any less quickly or forcibly than did last night's audience gathering at the Rivoli just which of Broadway's families was referred to in the title. For, in addition to the many clues offered by the situations and dialogue, it only needed Fredric March's sterling impersonation of America's leading actor, an impersonation that was complete to the last detail of makeup and gesture, to settle the question beyond all doubt . . . not, of course, that any obscurity was intended. In the stage play from which the picture was adapted, the target was plain enough, but in the film version, this target becomes a huge and inescapable closeup; a focal point around which the idiosyncrasies, the temperamental storms, the loyalties and endearments of a celebrated family are deliciously portrayed.

Quinn Martin in the *New York World:*
[Mr. March] gives a performance which is positively brilliant. [His] impersonation is, it seems to me, one of utter perfection, sensitively drawn, true to life, immensely amusing . . . the projection of a personality at once preposterous and glamorous, lunatic and tremendously vital.

Bland Johanson in the *New York Mirror:*
Fredric March gives the performance of the year as the mad matinee idol, Tony, in this hilariously amusing movie about the private life of stage aristocrats. He completely dominates the picture, and five minutes of his comedy are worth the whole price of admission. The hectic homelife of the incurably theatrical family provides riotous fun. Witty dialogue, brisk action, eloquent

Variety:
It is a constant delight when March is on. His conception of the spirited, boisterous, ridiculously dramatic son of a royal theatrical family—a Barrymore takeoff in every gesture—goes beyond just making [the picture]. In a few moments it develops into the frame upon which all further interest is strung.

With Mary Brian, Ina Claire, Arnold Korff and Henrietta Crosman

Honor Among Lovers

Paramount / 1931

THE PLAYERS
Mr. March was *Jerry Stafford* in a cast that included: Claudette Colbert *(Julia Traynor);* Monroe Owsley *(Philip Craig);* Charles Ruggles *(Monty Dunn);* Ginger Rogers *(Doris Blake);* Avonne Taylor *(Maybelle);* Pat O'Brien *(Conroy);* Janet McLeary *(Margaret);* John Kearney *(inspector);* Ralph Morgan *(Riggs);* Jules Epailly *(Louis);* Leonard Carey *(butler).*

THE CREATORS
Dorothy Arzner *(director);* Austin Parker and Gertrude Purcell *(screenplay);* adapted for the screen from a story by Austin Parker; George Folsey *(photography).* Photographed at the Astoria Studios, Long Island, New York.

Opened at the Times Square Paramount and the Brooklyn Paramount Theatres, New York, February 27, 1931. Running time when released, 76 minutes.

THE PICTURE
In line with the two-steps-forward, one-step-backward quality trend of his vehicles in the early thirties, March next found himself in a trivial and highly forgettable potboiler, of the type known in 1931 as "the shopgirl's delight." Again Dorothy Arzner was on hand for directorial chores, and also again on hand was Claudette Colbert. Monroe Owsley was the heavy, and his unique aura of snaky malevolence stole the picture from its nominal stars—that is, whatever was worth stealing, and it wasn't much.

Based on an Austin Parker tale, the business had to do with an investment broker, March, with an attractive secretary, Colbert. At first his intentions are strictly dishonorable, featuring offers of yacht trips and other lures for unwary females, but then his interest begins to

With Claudette Colbert

71

deepen. The sincere bit comes, alas, too late, for Colbert has introduced March to her persistent swain, sharp-but-shifty securities-exec Owsley, and the jealous and insecure Owsley thereupon pressures her into immediate marriage, to which she agrees, for she thinks she's in love with this cad.

When March, who is himself at the point of proposing, finds that the other guy has beaten him to it, he fires her, predicting that the marriage won't last six months. Later he relents and gives Owsley an important account. Owsley begins speculating secretly in wild stocks using some of March's money. When his deals are wiped out, he becomes jittery. Colbert asks March to bail him out and he does so with a check for $100,000. Deranged by financial disaster and the humiliation of his wife's asking March for help, Owsley accuses her of infidelity, whereupon she leaves him.

With Monroe Owsley and Claudette Colbert

With Charles Ruggles (left) and Claudette Colbert (right)

Owsley goes to March and threatens him with a gun; there is an accidental shooting. Owsley is grilled by the police though the wounded March insists it was accidental and self-inflicted. The craven Owsley tries to pin the shooting on Colbert. She is arrested, but the police plant a dictaphone when she is alone with her husband and record his confession. Though disgusted with Owsley, whom she now realizes she no longer loves, Colbert promises to stick with him through the trial. When she visits March in the hospital, he reassures her that he will not push the prosecution. He later saves Owsley from prison by sticking to the accident story. Whereupon Colbert tells a sulking Owsley that he has had it, and goes off with March. As the rat-a-tat-tat plot of this rat-a-tat-tat movie indicates, it was strictly sec-

ness man . . . [he] constantly shows further development, being particularly adept at light comedy. In this feature his handling of various phone conversations can go down as a text.

The New York Times:
[Though it] strikes a popular note, its incidents are frequently far from credible, particularly when the law enters into the story. It has, however, the virtue of being exceptionally well cast, with Claudette Colbert and Fredric March officiating as the principal characters. Mr. March makes his part as believable as it is humanly possible. Mr. Ruggles furnishes some good comedy when he gets the opportunity. Mr. Owsley does good work and Miss Colbert is excellent.

With Monroe Owsley

ond-rate women's magazine stuff, and reflected no particular credit on anyone involved with it, except perhaps Owsley, who as before noted had himself a meaty role and made the most of it. March found himself in a part fatal to any lead: namely one in which he reacted to events rather than implemented them . . . not that he hadn't been in that spot before in other mediocre films.

If ever a Monroe Owsley Film Festival is held (and film buffs are capable of anything) *Honor Among Lovers* should be prominently spotted among the offerings of this relatively obscure but greatly underrated character actor. As for March, Colbert and Dorothy Arzner, if they had skipped it altogether, their careers, and images, would surely have survived the omission.

THE REVIEWERS
Variety:
Miss Colbert, March and Monroe Owsley are collectively and individually a smooth working trio. Miss Colbert flaunts plenty of clothes for the girls to scan. . . . March . . . does a splendid and natural liberally-moraled busi-

With Charles Ruggles (above March)

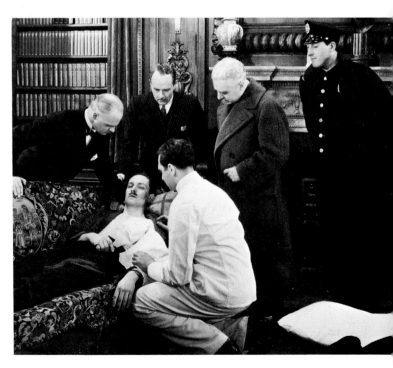

The Night Angel

Paramount / 1931

THE PLAYERS
Mr. March was *Rudek Berkem* in a cast that included: Nancy Carroll *(Yula)*; Alan Hale *(Bical)*; Alison Skipworth *(Countess de Martini)*; Katherine Emmett *(Mrs. Berkem)*; Phoebe Foster *(Theresa)*; Otis Sheridan *(Schmidt)*; Hubert Druce *(Vincent)*; Lewis Waller *(Kafka)*; Clarence Derwent *(Rosenbach)*; Charles Howard *(clown)*; Doris Rankin *(matron)*; Francine Dowd *(Mitzi)*.

THE CREATORS
Edmund Goulding *(director)*; Edmund Goulding *(screenplay)*; from a story by Edmund Goulding; William Steiner *(photography)*.

Opened at the Rivoli Theatre, New York, June 10, 1931. Running time when released, 75 minutes.

THE PICTURE
It was out of the frying pan of *Honor Among Lovers* into the fire of *The Night Angel* next for March. Only it wasn't fire, it was slush, and fake Continental slush at that. In what turned out to be one of the worst films of his career, and Nancy Carroll's, too, for that matter, there was certainly no "laughter"—rather, a plethora of Prague-style heaviness and gloom, with Carroll as the daughter of an infamous cabaret keeper (Alison Skipworth) and March as the district attorney who sends Skipworth to jail for running a place of ill-fame (as Hays office strictures would term it in 1931). There was much presumably-European atmosphere (more Paramount than Prague), arty photography, and self-conscious straining for profundity, but director-writer Edmund Goulding (who when he was good was very very good and when he was bad was horrid) had neglected to provide a plausible or smooth-running story.

The critics called attention to the looseness of the plot construction and the trite unbelievability of the goings-on, and March personally drew the worst reviews he had ever suffered. It was obvious from his performance that he was American, not Czech, both in accent and manner, and that he did not believe his dialogue or identify with his character, nor, all things considered, could he be blamed.

Goulding was obviously trying to out-Von Von Sternberg in this one, handling Nancy Carroll in what he probably thought was the Dietrich manner (the story had originally been designed for Dietrich) but it all came out stilted and muddled and Americanese. Panned unmercifully by the critics, the film was a boxoffice failure.

For anyone who cares by now, the plot rambled on and on to the effect that: March out of pity puts Carroll in a nurses' home instead of a reformatory after he has

With Nancy Carroll

Liberty:
A cinematic disaster ... the usually able Mr. March is as bad as I have ever observed him to be.

Variety:
The story is very loosely knit.... Long gaps in the action. Where it attempts to be unique in motive and situation, each time it reverts to the most conventional plot structure.

The New York Times:
An affected study in direction and acting, which hardly makes for entertainment.... [Mr. Goulding] dawdles when he might hasten matters and he skips over other scenes in a strangely abrupt fashion.... Fredric March endeavors to do what he can with the role of Berkem.

sent her mother to prison; when the mother gets out and returns to her cabaret, Carroll rejoins her. The cabaret bouncer, Alan Hale, is also enamored of Carroll and is jealous of March, and in the inevitable confrontation, March kills Hale accidentally. In an impassioned speech defending him at the trial, Carroll gets March acquitted by a mollified townsfolk, and the leads embrace in the crowded streets of a now-friendly town. Want to know more? We thought not.

THE REVIEWERS
Photoplay:
Fredric March is the hero and struggles pitifully with the stupid story. But it's a hard day's work and no glory.

With Nancy Carroll

With Nancy Carroll

My Sin

Paramount / 1931

THE PLAYERS
Mr. March was *Dick Grady* in a cast that included: Tallulah Bankhead *(Carlotta; Ann Trevor)*; Harry Davenport *(Roger Metcalf)*; Scott Kolk *(Larry Gordon)*; Anne Sutherland *(Mrs. Gordon)*; Margaret Adams *(Paula Marsden)*; Lily Cahill *(Helen Grace)*; Jay Fassett *(James Bradford)*.

THE CREATORS
George Abbott *(director)*; Owen Davis and Adelaide Heilbron *(screenplay)*; George Abbott *(adaptation)*; from the story by Fred Jackson; George Folsey *(photographer)*; photographed at the Astoria Studios, Long Island, New York.

Opened at the Paramount Theatre and the Brooklyn Paramount, New York, September 11, 1931. Running time when released, 77 minutes.

THE PICTURE
Still reeling from the inanities of *The Night Angel*, March next found himself up against the redoubtable Miss Tallulah Bankhead in their first and only film together, and if March's fans considered *The Night Angel* bad, this time around, dah-lings, it was truly Gawd-awful. Not that the March-Bankhead team didn't try; they did, and

their performances were creditable enough (or as creditable as the plot and direction allowed) but even artists cannot make a silk-purse dramatic piece out of a sow's-ear pulp story. *My Sin* was everybody's sin, it seemed, chief sinner being director-adaptor George Abbott. Tallulah was . . . Tallulah, with her deep, throaty, slightly Briticized voice booming out cliches as if they were epigrammatic gems, and March vying with her in what obviously was a conspiracy to make the inane goings-on look reasonably intelligent and mature.

This was Bankhead's second talkie in hers and Paramount's short-lived campaign to metamorphose her from the stage rage of London into a Hollywood superstar. She was attractive, magnetic and forceful in her usual grandiose manner, but that story kept her constantly puffing away like a locomotive hitched to nothing in particular, and the same could be said for March.

The business opens among the dingy dives of Panama. March, a once-respected lawyer who has taken to drink and become a derelict, meets cabaret singer Bankhead, whose blackmailing husband preys on her constantly for money. One night she shoots him in a scuffle and because she has an unsavory name around town, no lawyer will defend her. March is moved to shave and clean himself up and defend the hapless woman, and

With Tallulah Bankhead

his eloquence and legal expertise get her acquitted. The event catapults March into a major reformation and he resumes his legal practice. He loans Bankhead enough to go to New York and make a fresh start.

As 1931 movies liked to have it, a few more years see Bankhead a successful Big Town interior decorator who becomes engaged to a boy of good family. March, who has followed her rise with pride from afar, visits New York and warns Bankhead that she must tell her fiance about her past. She refuses. When an acquaintance who knew both Bankhead and March in Panama thinks he recognizes her at a party, she realizes the past will always dog her and she tells her fiance all. Though he protests that it makes no difference, Bankhead senses

otherwise, and leaves him. Though hurt at first, she is comforted by March, and of course they finally realize that they have loved each other all along.

THE REVIEWERS

The Times: (London)
It says much for the acting of Miss Tallulah Bankhead, first as the disreputable Carlotta and then as the successful Ann Trevor, and Mr. Fredric March as the counsel who is redeemed from drink by the success of his advocacy on Carlotta's behalf, that at times the sequence of events does not seem altogether fantastic. Miss Bankhead looks and speaks as though she is itching to utter the commonsense word that will dissolve the plot's flimsy structure, but even in her restraint it is possible to read, if not sense, at least sensibility, and Mr. March carries a convincing air of fervour into his drinking, chivalry and love-making.

Mordaunt Hall in *The New York Times:*
Considering the talented portrayals contributed by Tallulah Bankhead and Fredric March, it is rather disappointing to find them in such a suspenseless production. In this, her second audible film, Miss Bankhead devotes to her role the same serious and painstaking acting she might give to a really dramatic vehicle. Likewise Mr. March undertakes to make his impersonation as believable as possible. . . . From beginning to end . . . most of the incidents are too readily anticipated and some of the doings are not precisely plausible.

Variety:
It's odd how so many events are crammed into seventy-seven minutes and yet appear to move so slowly. Very few bright moments until the happy ending. Once March livens things up with smart delivery of some well-written dialogue.

With Tallulah Bankhead

With Tallulah Bankhead

Fredric March

Dr. Jekyll and Mr. Hyde

Paramount / 1931

THE PLAYERS

Mr. March was *Dr. Henry Jekyll-Mr. Hyde* in a cast that included: Miriam Hopkins *(Ivy Parsons)*; Rose Hobart *(Muriel Carew)*; Holmes Herbert *(Dr. Lanyan)*; Halliwell Hobbes *(Big. Gen. Carew)*; Edgar Norton *(Poole)*; Arnold Lucy *(Utterson)*; Colonel MacDonnell *(Hobson)*; Tempe Pigott *(Mrs. Hawkins)*.

THE CREATORS

Rouben Mamoulian *(director)*; Samuel Hoffenstein and Percy Heath *(screenplay)*; adapted from the novel by Robert Louis Stevenson; Karl Struss *(photography)*.

Opened at the Rivoli Theatre, New York, December 31, 1931. Running time when released, 98 minutes.

THE PICTURE

It is often darkest just before the dawn, for cinema actors as for other mortals, and after three bad films in a row, it dawned on Paramount executives that they were short-changing their most talented performer. They decided to give him his head in something worthwhile, and March found himself handed a plum role in an expensive production, and a role, moreover, of the bravura kind calculated to propel the right actor to international fame. That is exactly what *Dr. Jekyll and Mr. Hyde* did for March, and it won him his first Academy Award. Due in part to the startling and sensational (for 1931) nature of its theme, the tasteful and perceptive direction of Rouben Mamoulian, and a screenplay that, while labored and slow in spots, did sufficient justice to the story, March's perfect characterization was given a proper showcase, and he delivered in superior style.

The Robert Louis Stevenson classic had first appeared in 1885 in England, becoming a best-seller after publication. By 1887 Richard Mansfield was touring America in the dramatic version, which he revived for the following ten years. Other famed actors who essayed the role were Daniel Bardmann, the German-American thespian (1888), and Henry Irving (London, 1899).

The first film version was made in 1920, with John

Barrymore displaying his virtuosity in a sinuous and serpentine performance that was much praised. The third and last cinema transcription of the theme came in 1941 when Spencer Tracy offered a characterization that eschewed horrific makeup and relied rather on character changes facially delineated. While Barrymore's was commendable if Barrymoresque, and Tracy's a failure (Tracy just wasn't the type), March's interpretation, easily the best of the three, is the most favorably recalled. Though he acted as Hyde under heavy and elaborate makeup of a particularly grotesque and simian kind that would have won Lon Chaney's approval, March nonetheless succeeded in delineating Jekyll-to-Hyde personality changes in a forceful yet subtle depiction.

As the more balanced and amiable Jekyll, he got across the inquiring, dedicated scientific nature and the despair that accompanied Jekyll's realization that the powers-of-evil had overtaken him after the potion he laboriously concocted take him into another personality and another sphere of being. As the despicable, sensual Hyde, March limned graphically the ever-alert concupiscence and the infinite capacity for evil that were Jekyll's "other self."

Cameraman Karl Struss depicted the horrifying facial transmogrifications in brilliant successive exposures. Miriam Hopkins was splendid as the cabaret singer who falls victim first to Hyde's lust and then to his murderous instincts, and Rose Hobart was dignified and tragic as the girl who might have married Dr. Jekyll had that hapless scientist been content to let the unknown remain unknown.

At the close, after embarking on an orgy of unmitigated evil, Hyde is tracked down and shot by the police, and as he lies dying, the unspeakably malignant and simian face returns, again via gradual exposures, to the serene, affirmative, almost boyish features of Jekyll. After

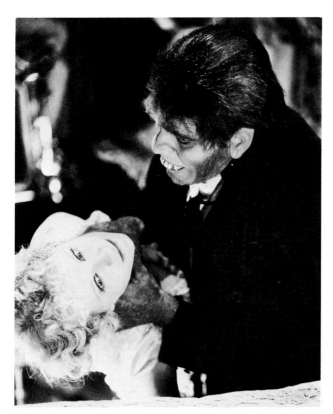

With Miriam Hopkins

this picture, there was no longer any doubt that March was a major star of infinite creative resource, but he still was under contract to Paramount, forced to do whatever commercially-oriented potboilers "the factory" saw fit to assign, and two more years were to elapse before his five-year contract was up and he was free to pick and choose roles he deemed right for him.

THE REVIEWERS

Photoplay:
Here is a picture that partakes of the dual nature of its principal role. The first part is a "Dr. Jekyll" of beauty and drama. But when *Dr. Jekyll* becomes *Mr. Hyde,* the picture follows suit. Fredric March's work is splendid and Miriam Hopkins shares the honors. Too bad this filming of the Stevenson classic is not good fare for children or even for adults who are easily unnerved.

Rush. in Variety:
Labored adornment of the original simplicity weakens the production for mob appeal. High pitch of emotional horror is difficult to maintain beyond some certain degree of elapsed time and the ninety-eight minutes this picture runs carries it past that human limit. . . . The more resourceful camera must improve on the simple form [of the stage play] by expounding principles and motives, weaving in a thread of modern psychology that interprets the adequate original, and telling it all with a wealth of distracting symbolism. The picture is infinitely better art than the old stage play—indeed, in many passages it is an astonishingly fine bit of interpreting a classic, but as popular fare it loses in vital reaction. . . . The picture doesn't build to an effective climax and it seems that the reason is the too slow and essentially too labored approach to the climaxes. . . . March does an outstanding bit of theatrical acting. His Hyde make-up is a triumph of realized nightmare.

Mordaunt Hall in The New York Times:
What with the audibility of the screen and the masterful

With Rose Hobart

Fredric March

photography, the new pictorial transcription of Stevenson's spine-chilling work . . . emerges as a far more tense and shuddering affair than it was as John Barrymore's silent picture. . . . [March's] makeup as Hyde is not done by halves, for virtually every imaginable possibility is taken advantage of to make this creature "reflecting the lower elements of Dr. Jekyll's soul" thoroughly hideous. . . . Rouben Mamoulian, the director of this film, has gone about his task with considerable enthusiasm, and the ways in which Jekyll changes into Hyde are pictured with an expert cunning, for it is a series of gradual exposures during which the changing face does not leave the screen. The first time the transition takes place it is effective, but it is still more so in subsequent sequences. . . . Mr. March's portrayal is something to arouse admiration, even taking into consideration the camera wizardry. As Dr. Jekyll he is a charming man and as the fiend he is alert and sensual. . . . Miriam Hopkins does splendidly as the unfortunate Ivy. . . . The atmosphere, that of London in Stevenson's day, is quite pleasing. There are the gas lamps, old-fashioned feminine costumes and other details. Likewise the settings enhance the scenes, particularly of the interesting twisted little byways.

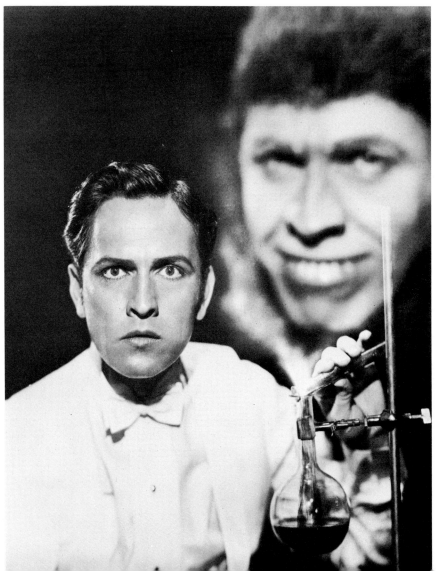

Fredric March

With Lucien Littlefield

Strangers In Love

Paramount / 1932

THE PLAYERS

Mr. March was *Buddy Drake-Arthur Drake* in a cast that inclued: Kay Francis *(Diana Merrow)*; Stuart Erwin *(Stan Keeney)*; Juliette Compton *(Muriel Preston)*; George Barbier *(Mr. Merrow)*; Sidney Toler *(McPhail)*; Earle Foxe *(J. C. Clarke)*; Lucien Littlefield *(Professor Clark)*; Leslie Palmer *(Bronson)*; Gertrude Howard *(Snowball)*; Ben Taggart *(Crenshaw)*; John M. Sullivan *(Dr. Selous)*.

THE CREATORS

Lothar Mendes *(director)*; William Slavens McNutt and Grover Jones *(adaptation and screenplay)*; based on the novel *The Shorn Lamb* by William J. Locke; Henry Sharp *(photography)*.

Opened at the Paramount and the Brooklyn Paramount Theaters, New York, March 5, 1932. Running time when released, 68 minutes.

THE PICTURE

Though impressed with March's tour-de-force in *Dr. Jekyll and Mr. Hyde*, and though quite aware that in simple justice he should be given better-mounted pictures henceforth, Paramount executives found themselves forced to remain boxoffice-minded as the Depression sank to new depths in 1932. They continued to cast about nervously for what they considered safe "compromise" fare, and since March had done so well in a dual role (of sorts) in his Oscar-winning picture, some bright boy at the studio decided that their new golden boy would appear to equal advantage in another type of dual portrayal, this time as twin brothers—a good one and a bad one, of course. This already-hackneyed good twin-bad twin gambit was to get quite a whirl over the next two decades, being especially popular among the actresses (Bette Davis in *A Stolen Life* and *Dead Ringer* and Olivia de Havilland in *The Dark Mirror*, etc.)

March's work in *Strangers in Love* was praised, as was Kay Francis's, and it was noted that he did succeed in portraying two disparate personalities rather convincingly. But there was a taste of soap, pot-boiled soap, to the proceedings nonetheless, and it must be ranked with March's also-ran fare.

As Arthur, the bad twin, March forges his father's will to disinherit his more easygoing brother, Buddy, who becomes a derelict. Meanwhile Arthur, an amateur anthropologist with a weak heart, is writing a book on anthropology with the help of his secretary, Kay Francis. Buddy comes to ask Arthur's help, and in the course of an argument, Arthur drops dead of his ailment, for which he had been taking constant medication. Sensing

With Kay Francis and George Barbier

him who are not in on the imposture begin to think that "Arthur's" mind is unhinged. Meanwhile he gets around the unfinished book by telling an astonished Diana that he has lost interest in it. Lothar Mendes, the director, kept all this deceptive stuff rotating nicely, and of course all comes out right in the end, with Buddy managing to expose his twin's forgery of their father's will and achieving a romantic understanding with Miss Francis. Though it was pretentious and essentially light-weight fare, the picture did give March a chance to get in some clever characterizational nuances.

THE REVIEWERS
Mordaunt Hall in *The New York Times:*
In this story of a young vagabond who masquerades as his well-to-do but conscienceless twin brother, Fredric March assumes both roles. Through clever photography Mr. March is thus beheld and heard talking to himself, and this actor gives his usual excellent performance. . . . Lothar Mendes, the director, has incorporated into the picture several so-called "process shots" which are very poor. Some of the direction in other respects is fair. Kay Francis is charming and alert as Diana. Mr. Erwin is good in his rough-and-ready fashion.

Char. in *Variety:*
A romance with numerous laughs, ably done by its cast, adaptor and director. . . . March turns in one of his best performances to date. . . . It has a flavor of sophistication, yet is played and written down to the masses.

Photoplay:
In the capable hands of Fredric March and Kay Francis an old bewhiskered theme becomes an entertaining and amusing movie. You could write the plot blindfolded—twin brothers, one a crook with heart trouble, the other a supposed prodigal but actually a sterling character. But how that boy March shades the characters of the two *Drake* brothers! Stuart Erwin gets over some grand laughs. Good stuff.

a chance at a better life, Buddy quickly changes apparel with the corpse and then brazenly proceeds to pose as Arthur. But it is not to prove the lark he supposed, for there are bothersome details like correct recognition of strangers and correctly penned signatures and the matter of finishing that book, which Miss Francis keeps urging on him.

Complications abound as the plot thickens. He learns that his twin was being blackmailed, for one thing; he inherits his girlfriend, for another; though physically identical, he tends to be easygoing where the dead twin was stern, affable where Arthur was frosty.

He is forced by circumstances to confide his true identity to a Negro servant, from whom he elicits enlightening facts on Arthur's habits and associations that enable him to keep up a passable bluff. Those around

With Juliette Compton, George Barbier

With Sylvia Sidney

Merrily We Go to Hell

Paramount / 1932

THE PLAYERS
Mr. March was *Jerry Corbett* in a cast that included: Sylvia Sidney *(Joan Prentice)*; Adrianne Allen *(Claire Hempstead)*; Richard "Skeets" Gallagher *(Buck)*; Florence Britton *(Charicle)*; Esther Howard *(Vi)*; George Irving *(Mr. Prentice)*; Kent Taylor *(Dick Taylor)*; Charles Coleman *(Damery)*; Leonard Carey *(butler)*; Milla Davenport *(housekeeper)*; Robert Greig *(baritone)*; Rev. Neal Dodd *(minister)*; Mildred Boyd *(June)*; Cary Grant *(stage leading man)*.

THE CREATORS
Dorothy Arzner *(director)*; Edwin Justus Mayer *(screenplay)*; based on the novel *I Jerry, Take Thee, Joan* by Cleo Lucas; David Abel *(photography)*.

THE PICTURE
Opened at the Paramount Theatre, New York, June 10, 1932. Running time when released, 82 minutes.

THE REVIEWERS
The studio next bought Cleo Lucas' novel, *I Jerry, Take Thee Joan,* and retitled it *Merrily We Go To Hell.* (Boxoffice worries in the Depression era and all that, you know. The studio was even running scared with its titles.) The title also indicates the toast the hero likes to give when drinking with his buddies. March, as a

journalist-turned-playwright, does a great deal of drinking and carousing in this film, and to a repetitious extent. There is a lot of joking and assorted bar buffoonery, to which Skeets Gallagher, as March's pal, contributes his share. There are also attempts to contrast "old-fashioned" with "modern" (meaning 1932) views on life and love.

The plot meanders, and rather sparsely at that. Certainly the eighty-two minutes' running time gives March a great deal of exposure in various moods, so he must have reckoned that a plus for him. He needed whatever plusses presented themselves, for the film itself is no great shakes in any department, and today seems quite dated in its dialogue and ideas. Moreover, the temperamental writer that March plays seems a very self-centered and prickly and unreliable fellow for any girl to romance—let alone marry. Yet that is exactly what heiress Sylvia Sidney does, after meeting him at a party.

Of course, being the person he is, March doesn't cotton well to responsibilities, schedules or anything else he finds tiresome, and when he adds to his alcoholic and other rogueries a dalliance with the leading actress in his play, Miss Sidney decides enough is enough and goes home to her millionaire papa.

Of course, this being 1932, a year of determinedly happy endings, nobody really goes to hell at all, and

With Sylvia Sidney

when March learns that his wife is critically ill in a maternity hospital he rushes to her despite papa's opposition and there is the requisite stuff about repentance, forgiveness and a fresh marital start. Though considering the character's record up to that point, any wife would be a fool to bet on it. Oh well, it was only a movie. Miss Sidney was appealing in her long-suffering-wife role, and the supporting cast was competent. Dorothy Arzner was on hand as director (her fifth time around with March) and did what she could with material that might have looked bright and lively enough in 1932 but comes off mighty stale today. Or maybe it was then, too, for people of any discernment. Critical opinion at the time was divided.

THE REVIEWERS

The London Times:
[The film] is cut to a stupid and conventional pattern, and there is nothing in the cutting, no attractive flourish, no decorative border, to make up for the dullness of the main design. . . . The director, Miss Dorothy Arzner, is handicapped throughout by the lack of pliability in her material. It is so obvious what is going to happen. . . . Since the film is not concerned with character, [Miss Sidney] has nothing to fall back on while the mechanism of the plot runs its appointed course.

Mordaunt Hall in *The New York Times:*
There have been many strange changes in story titles

With George Irving

With Edwin Maxwell, Adrienne Allen and Sylvia Sidney

but few of them as strange as that of the picture at this theatre. Imagine Cleo Lucas's novel, *I Jerry, Take Thee, Joan* being known in shadow form as *Merrily We Go To Hell*. This production is another with excellent acting, especially by Sylvia Sidney and Fredric March, but the many scenes showing the constant intoxication of a newspaperman who writes a successful play are not particularly interesting or edifying.... This picture was directed by Dorothy Arzner, who has done some good work, although the church marriage scene is a Hollywood notion of what such a ceremony looks like. Miss Arzner, however, has evidently been handicapped by the script. In the course of the hectic proceedings, there is a fling at modern ideas, which are contrasted with those of years gone by. The theme, so far as this is concerned, is however, quite a little vague in its real meaning.

Rush. in *Variety*:
Immaculately played by Fredric March in a light and graceful way...the playing of the two leads by March and Miss Sidney is the substance of the entertainment. What happens isn't of great moment, except as it affects two engaging characters...story opens in a cheerful spirit of comedy, moves along to a romantic measure and comes to a strong finish in a burst of sentimental seriousness that rounds out a fairly absorbing, if slightly commonplace, history...fine direction accounts for much of the picture's effect...dialogue often extremely "literary" and must have been a sore trial to director and players both.

With Richard "Skeets" Gallagher (left)

Stuart Erwin visits a March set

Make Me a Star

Paramount / 1932

THE PLAYERS
Mr. March was a guest star, playing himself. The other guest stars included: Tallulah Bankhead, Clive Brook, Maurice Chevalier, Claudette Colbert, Gary Cooper, Phillips Holmes, Jack Oakie, Charlie Ruggles, Sylvia Sidney. All played themselves. The regular cast included: Stuart Erwin *(Merton Gill)*; Joan Blondell *("Flips" Montague)*; ZaSu Pitts *(Mrs. Scudder)*; Ben Turpin *(Ben)*; Charles Sellon *(Mr. Gashweiler)*; Florence Roberts *(Mrs. Gashweiler)*; Helen Jerome Eddy *(Tessie Kearns)*; Dink Templeton *(Buck Benson)*; Arthur Hoyt *(Hardy Powell)*; Ruth Donnelly *(the Countess)*; Sam Hardy *(Jeff Baird)*; Oscar Apfel *(Henshaw)*; Frank Mills *(Chuck Collins)*; Polly Walters *(Doris Randall)*; Victor Potel, Bobby Vernon, Snub Pollard, Billy Bletcher, Bud Jamison, Nick Thompson *(actors)*.

THE CREATORS
William Beaudine *(director)*; Sam Wintz, Walter De Leon, Arthur Kober *(adaptation)*; Allen Siegler *(photography)*; based on the book *Merton of the Movies* by Harry Leon Wilson and the play by George S. Kaufman and Moss Hart; Leroy Stone *(editor)*; Earle S. Hayman *(sound recording)*.

Opened at the Paramount Theatre, New York, July 1, 1932. Running time when released, 83 minutes.

THE PICTURE
In this remake of Glenn Hunter's 1924 silent, *Merton of the Movies*, starring Stuart Erwin and Joan Blondell, March was seen fleetingly as one of the Paramount stars Erwin encounters in his peregrinations about the studio. The plot is a revamped version of the 1922 novel, the 1923 stage play, and the 1924 silent. (Some revamping was certainly warranted, considering that sound-era, "modern" 1932 had arrived when Erwin was handed the role.) Director William Beaudine tried for gentle irony, fey lightness and lively pacing, and generally succeeded. He moved his hero through all areas of the Paramount studio and got him on a number of sets of pictures either completed or shooting. The rather simplistic and elementary, but human and likeable, plot deals with a yokel grocery clerk, Erwin, who hungers for Hollywood acting fame. He eventually winds up in the Mecca of his dreams and wangles his way into the studio via a ruse. There he meets Blondell (charming and vital in the role of a movie extra) and she maneuvers him into a

Stuart Erwin before guest-star photos (Erwin's head conceals March's photo)

picture that burlesques westerns. Since he plays his role in all seriousness, he unconsciously lends to the film the comic touch desired. At the preview he realizes he has been "taken" (Merton is a sort of ancestor of Mr. Deeds) and prepares to return home. But Blondell waylays him and persuades him that he has a great future as a comedian; hence a long Hollywood sojourn for Merton seems assured after all.

THE REVIEWERS
Photoplay:
What a title for this gale of mirth! For Stuart Erwin, a perfect knockout as the movie-struck boy from the crossroads, will be a star after this picture has roared and howled its way across America! The talkie version of Harry Leon Wilson's great *Merton of the Movies* is swell entertainment. Erwin's performance is rib-rattling, button-busting. And right beside him charges Joan Blondell, as the hard-boiled little fairy-godmother of the lots. A magnificent blending of laughs and tears, with the

chuckles winning. Moreover, it's another fascinating expose of picture-making, with Hollywood secrets paraded. Whip-like dialogue, smart direction, stunning performances. Laurels to director William Beaudine and to Sam Hardy, who *plays* a director. Certainly one of the year's best.

Abel Green in *Variety:*
It's the forerunner of the latest Hollywood production cycle dealing with insights on filmland . . . it conveys to the muggs the general futility of busting into the movies and at the same time holds the dramatic interest, nicely mixing up the pathos and buffoonery. The laugh punctuations are at times robustly hilarious, although the general background of pathos is sustained throughout. . . . Chevalier, Colbert, Brook, Sidney, March and Bankhead (among others) of the Paramount player roster are introduced in brief shots on the lot or at the preview. . . . Beaudine's direction and general Paramount production are altogether workmanlike and professional.

Smilin' Through

Metro-Goldwyn-Mayer / 1932

THE PLAYERS

Mr. March was *Jeremy Wayne-Kenneth Wayne* in a cast that included: Norma Shearer (*Moonyean Clare; Kathleen Clare*); Leslie Howard (*John Carteret*); O. P. Heggie (*Doctor Owen*); Ralph Forbes (*Willie Ainley*); Beryl Mercer (*Mrs. Crouch*); David Torrence (*gardener*); Margaret Seddon (*Ellen*); Forrester Harvey (*orderly*); Cora Sue Collins (*young Kathleen*).

THE CREATORS

Sidney Franklin (*director*); Ernest Vajda and James Bernard Fagan (*adaptation and screenplay*); based on the play by Jane Cowl and Jane Murfin; Lee Garmes (*photography*); Margaret Booth (*film editor*).

Opened at the Capitol Theatre, New York, October 14, 1932. Running time when released, 96 minutes.

THE PICTURE

March was then loaned to Metro-Goldwyn-Mayer, where again he played a dual role, Jeremy Wayne and Kenneth Wayne, his son, in the handsome and affecting Norma Shearer version of the much-loved sentimental romance, *Smilin' Through*. This had originated as a stage play authored by Jane Cowl and Jane Murfin and had been produced in 1922 as a Norma Talmadge silent. This role represented a definite plus for March, as he was given a

With Norma Shearer

With Norma Shearer and Ralph Forbes

chance to delineate two very different personalities, got to co-star with the prestigious Miss Shearer, then at the apex of her stardom, and moreover was accorded the benefit of exposure in Loew's as well as Paramount theatres, and in a Grade-A picture opposite one of the top feminine stars of Hollywood's golden era.

Miss Shearer and her husband, the famed producer Irving Thalberg, had long admired March's artistry, considered his presence in the picture an asset, and he was to figure within two years in another of their important MGM films. Certainly March and Miss Shearer complemented each others' personalities and acting styles exceptionally well, and their scenes together were delicate and affecting, constituting as they did the essence of glamorous star-teaming, 1932-style.

Leslie Howard was also excellent, as were O. P. Heggie and a fine supporting cast, and Sidney Franklin, whose depthful and discerning directorial style always showcased the sensitively gifted and shimmeringly radiant Miss Shearer at her best, gave the picture, along with talented photographer Lee Garmes, all the romantic power called for by the script.

Miss Shearer, who was a far better actress than some of her latter-day detractors are willing to admit, and who had won an Academy Award, the year before March got his, for her scintillating performance in *The Divorcee*, was lovely and affecting as the tragic Moonyean Clare, who in the year 1868 married her beloved, Howard, but was shot and killed at the church by

With Norma Shearer

With Norma Shearer

her tormentedly jealous and rejected suitor, March, with a bullet he had meant for Howard. Before she dies, Moonyean promises Howard she will always be with him in spirit and that one day they will be happily together again in eternal union.

As the decades go on, she comes to him on occasion as a supernatural vision, consoling his more dejected and lonely moments. (Garmes' delicately expressive photography is particularly effective in the scenes where the wraith of Moonyean appears.) After the passage of many years, Moonyean's niece, also played by Miss Shearer, comes to live with Howard after her parents' death. The young girl and the old man become deeply attached to each other, and establish a close father-daughter relationship.

She grows to womanhood. Fifty years have now passed since Moonyean's tragic death on her wedding day, and to the little English community comes Kenneth Wayne, the murderer Jeremy's son. Kathleen (Miss Shearer), out for a jaunt with a friend (Ralph Forbes), takes shelter from a storm in the old Wayne mansion, where the drawing room, though dusty and cobwebbed, remains exactly as it was on the fatal day, complete with 1868 newspaper and overturned chair. Kathleen succumbs to the strangeness of the room. Kenneth enters and they meet. An attachment soon grows between them but when John Carteret (Howard) discovers that Kenneth is the son of the man who destroyed his happiness, he bitterly refuses sanction of their union.

Later, Kenneth returns wounded from the war, and the now-aged Howard is visited again by the tender wraith of Moonyean, who counsels him to forgive and forget and leave the young people to their happiness. Kenneth and Kathleen are seen in the final sequence walking together back to the house while near them the wraiths of Moonyean and Carteret, who has joined her in death, look on fondly.

The theme song, "Smilin' Through," a haunting and expressive melody, has remained a perennial favorite through the years. If I may add a personal note, I recall being powerfully affected by this film as a boy of nine in the Paramount Theatre in Lynn, Massachusetts in 1932, and it has lingered long in my memory and feelings. Certainly its like is not to be encountered today, for it belongs to an era when sincere emotions were expressed by cinema artists with true feeling and consummate creativity, and the supernatural was held in fond reverence and respect, as it deserves to be in any era.

Jeanette MacDonald made a version for MGM in 1941 that closely followed the Shearer original. Miss MacDonald was charming and sincere, and was ably supported by Brian Aherne and Gene Raymond in the Howard and March roles respectively, but it somehow lacked the freshness, spontaneity and charm of the 1932 picture, though enough lingered of its source to make it reasonably affecting.

THE REVIEWERS
Rose Pelswick in the *New York Journal-American:*
A tender romance to which the star brings a genuine

With Norma Shearer

sweetness and sympathy. Made with taste and skill, the picture is at all times delightful, for its sentimentality is moving, its emotions are sincere and it is beautifully mounted . . . one of the very few old stage plays that stand up in their talking picture revival, and credit for this goes not only to the three principals, but also to Sidney Franklin for his smooth and understanding direction.

Bland Johaneson in the *New York Mirror:*
The production is a sensitive and beautiful one, distinguished by exquisite settings and rich photography. The acting is perfectly finished. The March and Shearer love scenes are tender and charming.

Mordaunt Hall in *The New York Times:*
Distinguished by the able direction of Sidney Franklin . . . it is a beautiful production, too immaculate, if anything, in its scenes of the past. It is rich in sentiment, but Mr. Franklin has permitted sufficient gentle comedy to relieve the romance and the tragedy of bygone years. It is another venture that benefits by expert photography, particularly in those scenes in which a wraith-like figure appears and talks. . . . Mr. March is very good. . . . He is far better than the ordinary choice for such a role. He does make the character determined and sympathetic.

With Elissa Landi

The Sign of the Cross

Paramount / 1932

THE PLAYERS

Mr. March was *Marcus Superbus* in a cast that included: Claudette Colbert *(Poppaea)*; Elissa Landi *(Mercia)*; Charles Laughton *(Nero)*; Ian Keith *(Tigellinus)*; Harry Beresford *(Favius)*; Arthur Hohl *(Titus)*; Tommy Conlon *(Stephanus)*; Vivian Tobin *(Dacia)*; Ferdinand Gottschalk *(Giabrio)*; Joyzelle Joyner *(Ancaria)*; Nat Pendleton *(Strabo)*; William V. Mong *(Licinius)*; Harold Healy *(Tyros)*; Robert Alexander *(Viturius)*; Robert Manning *(Philodemus)*; Joe Bonomo *(The Mule Giant.)* Also included in the cast were: Otto Lederer, Lillian Leighton, Lane Chandler, Wilfred Lucas, Jerome Storm, Gertrude Norman, Florence Turner, Horace B. Carpenter, Ynez Seabury, Carol Holloway.

THE CREATORS

Cecil B. De Mille *(producer and director)*; Waldemar Young and Sidney Buchman *(adaptation and screenplay)*; from the play by Wilson Barrett; Karl Struss *(photography)*; Anne Bauchens *(film editor)*; Rudolph Kopp *(music)*.

Opened at the Rialto Theatre, New York, November 30, 1932. Running time when released, 124 minutes.

THE PICTURE

Back at Paramount for his final 1932 film, March found himself cast in a Grade-A Cecil B. De Mille super-spectacular, *The Sign of the Cross*. This film version of the famous old play by Wilson Barrett, expertly photographed by Karl Struss, was the most expensively mounted and produced film under Paramount auspices that March had ever found himself in. He responded well to De Mille's seasoned direction, turning in a glamorously forthright and manly performance as Marcus Superbus, Prefect of Rome, who desires a Christian maid, Elissa Landi, but discovers eventually that he must accept her on her own sublime spiritual terms.

Some critics opined that March, Landi, Claudette Colbert and Charles Laughton tended to get lost under all the spectacle and gargantuan goings-on, but recent viewings of the film reveal this is far from the case. Laughton was brilliant as the Emperor Nero, the essence of pagan cruelty and rigidity, though not devoid of a human side, and Claudette Colbert as Empress Poppaea, was serpentine, coolly authoritative, and frankly amorous in her overtures toward an unresponsive Marcus. She was handsomely photographed, as was Elissa Landi, who as the Christian Mercia, turned in a performance that reflected with clarity the purity and integrity of soul that the character was designed to encompass.

DeMille's direction was never more expert, well-paced, relentless in its search for all possible cinematic values, and the production itself reflected meticulous care in all departments. March's clear, resonant speech

With Charles Laughton and
Claudette Colbert

and graceful, heroic stances were well suited to the role of Marcus. Colbert took spectacular baths in asses' milk, in typical DeMille style; Ian Keith swaggered expertly as the heavy; Nero did his dirty work in epic style, and March tried valiantly to rescue Christian Landi from her inevitable doom, contending meanwhile with the jealous Poppaea and the hostile Keith.

Eventually Landi and her cohorts are doomed to face the lions in the arena, despite Marcus' plea for her life before Nero, and which Poppaea subtly frustrates by appealing to Nero's self-protectiveness. Landi is offered her life and freedom if she renounces her faith, but she refuses. Marcus goes to the dungeon where the Christians wait to ascend to the arena where the lions await them. As he observes Mercia's radiant faith and indomitable courage, he realizes that his love for her is true and eternal, joins her faith in spirit, and ascends with her the staircase that leads to death and eternal spiritual togetherness.

This 1932 DeMille effort can hold its own with many more ambitious Roman spectaculars of a later era of color and CinemaScope, for even in conventional black-and-white and a 1932-size screen, nobody knew his "spectacle business" better than the Master. The film manages to remain engrossing in its action and crowd sequences and affecting in its emotional passages. Certainly this film contained a worthy role for March (he and DeMille were to work together again), in a 1932 that had seen him rise to the top of the Hollywood heap.

THE REVIEWERS
Mordaunt Hall in *The New York Times:*
The principal roles are all well played, even though they are more or less in the modern manner . . . no DeMille picture would be complete without some suggestion of a bathtub and here this director goes himself one better by having a small swimming pool filled with the milk from asses. . . . The picture is staged impressively and finely photographed. There is an abundance of imagination throughout its scenes and the story is well told. One feels, however, that the players must have been relieved when the production was finished, for all work

With Ian Keith and Elissa Landi

hard and thoroughly, even to those who merely figure for an instant or so in a death scene in the arena, or the more fortunate who are spatting about their seats.

Bige. in *Variety:*
Religion triumphant over paganism, and the soul is stronger than the flesh. Religion gets the breaks, even though its followers all get killed in this picture. It's altogether a moral victory. Neat, deft and probably beyond reproach is the manner in which the scarlet punches are inserted. Every sequence in which religion wins out is built upon lurid details. The censors may object to the method, but they can't oppose the motive, and in the way "Cross" was produced, one can't be in without the other. Cast is uniformly good, but only one exceptional performance is registered. That's Laughton's. . . . Misses Colbert and Landi and Messrs. March and Keith are called upon chiefly to look their parts, and they manage. Frequently some badly written and often silly dialogue holds them down.

With Claudette Colbert

Tonight Is Ours

Paramount / 1933

THE PLAYERS
Mr. March was *Sabien Pastal* in a cast that included: Claudette Colbert *(Nadya)*; Alison Skipworth *(Grand Duchess Emilie)*; Paul Cavanaugh *(Prince Keri)*; Arthur Byron *(General Krish)*; Ethel Griffies *(Zana)*; Clay Clement *(Seminoff)*; Warburton Gamble *(Alex)* and Edwin Maxwell *(leader of the mob)*.

THE CREATORS
Stuart Walker *(director)*; Mitchell Leisen *(associate director)*; Edwin Justus Mayer *(screenplay)*; adapted from the play *The Queen Was in the Parlor* by Noel Coward; Karl Struss *(photography)*.

Opened at the Paramount Theatre, New York, January 21, 1933. Running time when released, 75 minutes.

THE PICTURE
The March-Colbert team had proven a popular one in *The Sign of the Cross* and they were seen for the fourth time together in a Graustarkian trifle called *Tonight Is Ours*, released early in 1933 to only fairish critical notices. Revamped by screenwriter Edwin Justus Mayer from a second-rate Noel Coward play called *The Queen*

Was in the Parlor, it won such reviewer designations as "trite, labored, monotonous, nice, delightful, slow, talky, heavy"—which is really running through all colors of the critical rainbow but in the final analysis spells: mixed reaction, veering toward thumbs-down.

There was some speculation as to what Ernst Lubitsch or René Clair could or would have accomplished with this Coward frou-frou about a Princess who falls in love with a commoner while visiting Paris, has a brief romance with him, then is suddenly recalled to take over the throne of her eastern European country when her father and brother are killed by revolutionists. Of course they try to marry her off to a Prince (delightfully played by an intelligently-wry Paul Cavanaugh) whom she doesn't love and who doesn't particularly love her either, and of course the amorous March shows up, circles for the kill, saves the Queen from an assassin's bullet and prior to the inevitable wedding with the Prince offers her that "tonight that is ours" as consolation.

But then comes the revolution (with convenient timing) and the revolutionists take pity on the lovers, and Queen Claudette finds herself ensconced as a constitu-

*Claudette Colbert and
Alison Skipworth*

tional monarch, with March winning the revolutionists' enthusiastic approval as her future consort. And what could be a nicer ending than that? Richard Watts, Jr., of the *New York Herald Tribune* sounded a typical critical note when he commented on the heaviness of Stuart Walker's direction and the lack of a "thistledown" quality that the aforementioned Herr Lubitsch or Monsieur

Clair might have lent to it. Colbert seemed to garner more plaudits for her clothes and her expertly photographed (by Karl Struss) beauty than for her acting, and the *New York American* seemed to capsulize the general reaction to March with the words "Isn't he romantic!" His profile, especially in the more horizontal love scenes, also won favorable notice. A film, it would appear, that

With Claudette Colbert

With Claudette Colbert

both Miss Colbert and Mr. March have long contrived to forget. The public certainly has. Even the film buffs rarely mention it, which is the ultimate in damnation.

THE REVIEWERS
Philip K. Scheuer in the *Los Angeles Times:*
Miss Colbert has gained in prettiness, at the expense, possibly, of her individuality. . . . March is, as always, heroic with the saving grace of a sense of humor.

The *New York Daily News:*
Some of Miss Colbert's closeups are ravishing. And more than a few damsels in the audience sighed over Fredric March's handsome profile during the hottest of the love scenes . . . we think the picture will give you a nice sort of feeling and that you'll leave the theatre liking it, in spite of its little shortcomings.

William Boehnel in the *New York World-Telegram:*
At no time in its monotonous progress is there any evidence of the intelligence, showmanship and wit that have established Mr. Coward as one of the most brilliant playwrights of the day. . . . Some of it might be entertaining if it were done with Mr. Coward's customary magic. But it is all pretty drab and uninteresting.

Abel Green in *Variety:*
Too slow and talky, steeped in legity motivation, to be popular cinema. . . . It requires an hour to attain the situation which the title explains . . . there is much horizontal posturing by the pair [March and Colbert] . . . in line with the boxiffice intent of the motivation . . . not undeftly recounted in some bright dialogue that is as much Edwin Justus Mayer as Noel Coward. But it's not good film fan fare.

The Eagle and the Hawk

Paramount / 1933

THE PLAYERS
Mr. March was *Jerry Young* in a cast that included: Cary Grant *(Henry Crocker)*; Jack Oakie *(Mike Richards)*; Carole Lombard *(the beautiful lady)*; Sir Guy Standing *(Major Dunham)*; Forrester Harvey *(Hogan)*; Kenneth Howell *(John Stevens)*; Leyland Hodgson *(Kingsford)*; Virginia Hammond *(Lady Erskine)*; Crauford Kent *(general)*; Douglas Scott *(Tommy)*; Robert Manning *(Major Kruppman)*; Russell Scott *(flight sergeant)*.

THE CREATORS
Stuart Walker *(director)*; Screenplay by Bogart Rogers and Seton I. Miller; based on a story by John Monk Saunders; Harry Fischbeck *(photographer)*; Mitchell Leisen *(associate director)*.

Opened at the Paramount Theatre, New York, May 12, 1933. Running time when released, 86 minutes.

THE PICTURE
The Eagle and the Hawk originated in a story by John Monk Saunders, of *Wings* fame, and it proved neither better nor worse than many World War I aviation films that had preceded it. Reportedly the film was designed to give March a change of pace, as he had never been a flier in any of his previous films. He was his usual assured and expert self, and his role gave him an opportunity for some solid characterization; in fact the per-

With Sir Guy Standing

99

sonal drama took distinct precedence over the action stuff, which, in a March film, was all for the best.

In this effort he was an ace American member of the Royal Flying Squadron who has lost too many observers and other comrades in the flaming skies for his own peace of mind. Fed up with the meaningless slaughter of war, March becomes gradually demoralized. Jack Oakie is on hand for some lighter moments, and Cary Grant plays a dour observer with a chip on his shoulder because he has been unable to get his wings. He has it in for March because the latter had advised against giving him the wings.

March's deteriorating emotional state is recognized by his flight commander, Sir Guy Standing, who sends him to London for what he hopes will be a restful leave. Here he encounters (for two scenes) Carole Lombard, with whom he has a brief romantic interlude. (There was some criticism of the gimmick of dragging in a feminine star for such a short running time just to bolster the sex-lure on the marquee.) What little she was given to do, Lombard did well.

In London, his hostess' child has told him that he too wants to be a flier when he grows up, which saddens him. When he returns he finds that Oakie is the next to die. Though in his next engagement he kills a German ace, he loses his new young observer, who, green in combat, falls from the plane during a loop. After drunkenly haranguing his comrades at another fete to celebrate his latest "accomplishment," March goes to his room and kills himself, his overwrought, sensitive nature having finally broken. Grant, who though his rival, understands March's sincere and dedicated nature, spirits

With Carole Lombard

the body aboard a combat plane, then takes it up, riddles it with bullets, then crashes them both deliberately to save his dead comrade from the disgrace of a suicide report and get him remembered as a hero to the end.

The bulk of the reviewers thought March effective in his role. Certainly it gave him a change of pace, and did him no harm, without particularly enhancing his image at the time. Seen today, the film reveals dated ele-

With Jack Oakie

With Cary Grant

ments in its plot and general handling, though March's performance is as fresh and sincere as when he made it.

THE REVIEWERS
John S. Cohen, Jr. in the *New York Sun*:
Extremely exciting aerially, although what stands out is its intimate drama.... Fredric March gives by far his most intelligent and stimulating performance as the noble pilot who killed himself before he would kill another German.... Carole Lombard plays well in a brief role.

Mordaunt Hall in *The New York Times*:
An impressive account of the effect of battles in the clouds upon an American ace ... fortunately devoid of the stereotyped ideas which have weakened most of such narratives. Here is a drama told with a praise-worthy sense of realism and the leading role is por-trayed very efficiently by Fredric March.

Variety:
Strictly a formula story of the Royal Flying Corps by the man who wrote "Wings" with a laboriously dragged in romantic bit to get a feminine star's (Lombard's) name on the program. But it takes more than fifty or sixty feet of sex stuff to make love interest. It might better have been left out. Nothing much new in the matter of plot, the same old yarn of the man who gets fed up on the uselessness of war. Story owes much to the deftness with which it has been developed than to any basic interest.... Carole Lombard contributes little in spite of sincere playing. March offers a finely sensitive study, acting with force but entirely without bombast. Cary Grant is more along usual lines, but he supplies the complementary action effectively.

With Jack Oakie and Cary Grant

Design for Living

Paramount / 1933

With Miriam Hopkins

THE PLAYERS

Mr. March was *Tom Chambers* in a cast that included: Gary Cooper *(George Curtis)*; Miriam Hopkins *(Gilda Farrell)*; Edward Everett Horton *(Max Plunkett)*; Franklin Pangborn *(Douglas)*; Isabel Jewell *(stenographer)*; Harry Dunkinson *(Egelbauer)*; Helena Phillips *(Mrs. Egelbauer)*; James Donlin *(fat man)*; Vernon Steele *(first manager)*; Thomas Braidon *(second manager)*; Jane Darwell *(house-keeper)*; Armand Kaliz *(Burton)*; Adrienne D'Ambricourt *(cafe proprietress)*; Nora Cecil *(Tom Chambers' secretary)*; Wyndham Standing *(Max Plunkett's butler)*; Grace Hayle *(woman on staircase)*; Olaf Hytten *(Englishman at train)*; Mary Gordon *(theatre attendant)*; Lionel Belmore, Charles K. French *(patron of theatre)*; Rolfe Sedan *(salesman)*.

THE CREATORS

Ernst Lubitsch *(producer and director)*; Ben Hecht *(screenplay)*; Victor Milner *(photography)*; Hans Dreier *(art direction)*; Travis Banton *(costumes)*; based on the play by Noel Coward; M. M. Paggie *(sound recording)*; Francis Marsh *(editor)*.

Opened at the Criterion Theatre, New York, November 22, 1933. Running time when released, 90 minutes.

With Miriam Hopkins

THE PICTURE

When Ernst Lubitsch got around to directing, and Ben Hecht to writing, a film version of Noel Coward's ultra-sophisticated, witty and ironic play about the *ménage à trois* consisting of two men and a woman, their Hollywood overlords apparently developed a bad case of boxoffice nerves and urged the two artists (who reportedly collaborated on the screenplay) to tone down the far-out implications of Coward's brazen jape. As a result,

the play was entirely rewritten, the sharp, biting, character-elucidating observations on art and life in which the threesome of the play had indulged were eliminated, and the emphasis was put on action and farcical convolutions.

Coward, Alfred Lunt and Lynn Fontanne had played it on the stage for sophisticated laughter, with cerebral overtones. The screen version, designed for a larger, less subtle-minded, less discriminating audience, accordingly diluted all the irony, shrewd observations and recondite philosophizing that had made the play such a hit with its more aware audiences. Moreover Fredric March, Gary Cooper and Miriam Hopkins were so directed that a heavy-handed, serious patina of poignancy was laid on the romantic scenes when they should have been played, as on the stage, with ebullience and a light touch.

March and Cooper, moreover, talented as they were in their proper cinematic métiers were simply too All-American-Boy in aura rather than the decadent hedonists and social icon-smashers that Coward had visualized, and, with the Lunts, had projected with outrageous cunning. As a result the film barely made sense in its basic situation. Though Ben Hecht, who had smashed a few icons of quite another stripe in his time, gave it a good try, both he and Lubitsch were obviously stymied by the necessity of pleasing Hays Office bluenoses and conventional 1933 audience standards, in adapting the play of a man who was the most brilliantly subtle nose-thumber around.

The plot, as cinematized? Hopkins, a commercial artist, meets March, a budding playwright, and Cooper, a

With Miriam Hopkins and Gary Cooper

With Miriam Hopkins

burgeoning painter, on a Paris-bound train. Both fall in love with her, and since she cannot make up her mind which one she wants, all three set up a "design for living," a platonic (to please Hays) set-up in which all share and share alike. Hopkins inspires the boys to push their careers, but of course they are constantly jealous of each other's place in Hopkins' scheme of things, and finally she throws up her hands in despair and settles for a peace-and-quiet marriage with her rich, stuffy boss, Edward Everett Horton.

She goes off to New York with Horton, but after a year of this existence, during which she is bored to distraction, she wants out, and is enormously relieved when the boys show up in New York at her husband's party and break it up with their assorted buffooneries. Realiz-

ing that she prefers their "gentleman's agreement" to life with Horton (who is relieved to be rid of her anyway), Hopkins goes happily back with the boys to Paris.

THE REVIEWERS
Richard Watts, Jr. in the *New York Herald Tribune:*
The picture, played without the charm that Miss Fontanne, Mr. Lunt and Mr. Coward brought to it, is, despite Mr. Lubitsch's expert job, lacking in the proper air of high comic deftness. The actors seemed to me lacking in the necessary quality of brilliance. Miss Hopkins is realistic and invariably believable in the Lynn Fontanne role but she fails to bring to the part the air of sparkling grandeur that Miss Fontanne introduced to the part. You could hardly expect Mr. Cooper to be properly at

With Edward Everett Horton

104

home as a witty sophisticate, and I fear that he isn't. Mr. March, as the playwright, is well cast, but this is not one of his best performances.

William Boehnel in the *New York World-Telegram:*
No end of praise is due to Ben Hecht for his admirable work rewriting the Coward play, and to its four principal players, each of whom does truly fine work.

Regina Crewe in the *New York American:*
A delightfully smart, crisp piece of entertainment, cleverly conceived, delightfully executed. . . . Fredric March as the suaver, more "civilized," city slickerish of the two lovers, portrays him with deft understanding.

The Literary Digest:
It is not being especially critical to say that the film players are very far from as expert as their predecessors. . . . Despite its great faults, [it] was on the stage a witty, brilliantly acted comedy, while the screen version is lacking in both wit and wisdom, and is not excitingly performed. Lubitsch's direction is smart, but it is hardly first-rate Lubitsch.

Campbell Dixon in the *London Daily Telegraph:*
Fredric March and Gary Cooper as the rivals, Miriam Hopkins as the girl, and Edward Everett Horton as the temporary husband, all give perfect performances. Hecht's dialogue sparkles continuously and Lubitsch has never directed better.

The Times: (London)
The relation between this film and Mr. Noel Coward's play is a rather distant one, so distant, indeed, that nothing of the stage dialogue remains, and the point of the play's argument is passed off as a farcical extravagance. But that is not to say the film lacks justification. Herr Lubitsch, who presumably considers it a waste of time to photograph what is intended for the theatre, has insisted on having the subject matter of *Design for Living* thought out in terms of the screen; and the result is a farce with a sparkle all its own. The characters parade no theories about themselves. They are too actively engaged with their farcical predicament to find time for those slick generalizations upon art and life that gave their prototypes of the stage an intelligent background of sorts. . . . Mr. Gary Cooper and Mr. Fredric March depict with humour and precision the rivalry, the friendship and the embarrassment of the men between whom the butterfly lady flits with such disconcerting impartiality.

With Miriam Hopkins

All of Me

Paramount / 1934

THE PLAYERS
Mr. March was *Don Ellis* in a cast that included: Miriam Hopkins *(Lyda Darrow)*; George Raft *(Honey Rogers)*; Helen Mack *(Eve Haron)*; Nella Walker *(Mrs. Darrow)*; William Collier, Jr. *(Jerry Halman)*; Gilbert Emery *(the Dean)*; Blanche Frederici *(Miss Haskell)*; Kitty Kelly *(Lorraine)*; Guy Usher *(district attorney)*; John Marston *(Nat Davis)*; Edgar Kennedy *(guard)*.

THE CREATORS
James Flood *(director)*; Louis Lighton *(producer)*; Sidney Buchman and Thomas Mitchell *(screenplay)*; Thomas Mitchell *(dialogue direction)*; adapted from Rose Porter's play *Chrysalis*; Ralph Rainger and Leo Robin *(music and lyrics)*; Victor Milner *(photography)*.

Opened at the Paramount Theatre, New York, February 4, 1934. Running time when released, 70 minutes.

THE PICTURE
Typical of several poor films in which Paramount put March as he neared the end of his five-year contract was *All of Me*, a confused and murky melodrama in

With Miriam Hopkins

With George Raft and Helen Mack

With Helen Mack

which March played a professor who wants to go to Boulder Dam and work on an engineering project. His pampered, rich-girl student girlfriend, Miriam Hopkins, doesn't relish "roughing it" and living in surroundings that do not appeal to her.

One of those pictures that feature two distinct stories running concurrently—in this case in opposite directions—the picture was adapted from the Rose Porter play *Chrysalis*—and the whole idea might well have been left alone. March and Hopkins encounter a thief, George Raft, and his girlfriend, Helen Mack. For reasons that psychologically and dramaturgically make no sense, the two sets of lovers socialize briefly, then Raft lands in jail for theft and Mack in a girls' reformatory. March tells Hopkins he is disillusioned with her selfishness and they part. Then for no reason that remotely makes sense, Hopkins finds herself drawn into helping a reunion of Raft and Mack by aiding and abetting Raft's jailbreak, during which he kills a cop.

The melodramatic windup finds Hopkins on hand as a witness when Raft and Mack, who are deeply in love with one another and never again want to be separated, jump out a window together while the cops are closing in. This—so the plot would have us believe—arouses Hopkins to the essence of true loyalty and devotion between a man and a woman, and she goes back to March, humbler and wiser. Many critics thought the picture absurd, melodramatic, stupidly motivated and unworthy of March's and Hopkins' talents. There was also a measure of criticism of the "unhealthy" and "socially deleterious" glorification of criminality and the romanticizing of the essentially sordid Raft-Mack relationship. Among other uneven elements, the picture talked itself to death in a static Part One, then went hogwild with busy melodrama in a busy Part Two, with March himself disappearing for long stretches of the action, being dragged back for an unlikely clinch with Hopkins toward the end. It is, understandably, another of those pictures that March and his admirers prefer to forget.

With Miriam Hopkins

THE REVIEWERS

New York Sun:
One of those pictures filled with a false Hollywood sentimentalism, with the most startling glorification of criminals that even the movies have ever dared, its whole essence more subversive than the most radical of propaganda pictures.

The New York Times:
An unhealthy piece of work and it gives persons who assert that there are few films to take their children to a strong opportunity to complain . . . yet in this fatuous drama one finds cast such players as Fredric March and Miriam Hopkins. . . . It is a waste of rich talent.

The London Times:
The film is not free from sentiment and it's too facile in its generalizations but Mr. Flood keeps the suspense taut and makes the most of the dramatic opportunities his material gives him. The acting is consistently good.

Robert J. Landry in Variety:
It may be set down as a reasonable truism of dramaturgy that any story which ultimately converts its principal actors into spectators for things happening to secondary characters is going to end up by getting lost in a cul-de-sac. For considerable footage March drops out altogether and when reappearing is definitely subordinate. . . . March unveils a new coiffure in this picture. It's a hair dressing that may be authentic for a college professor but it's a strain on his boxoffice rank. With the hair in one scene goes a collar and tie worthy of a Charles Dawes. All in all, while March hands in an in-

With Miriam Hopkins

telligent performance, it's scarcely the kind of thing his fans will fancy. . . . Direction of James Flood is finely shaded. In spite of the basic story mistakes the picture does keep going.

Death Takes a Holiday

Paramount / 1934

THE PLAYERS

Mr. March was *Prince Sirki* in a cast that included: Evelyn Venable *(Grazia)*; Sir Guy Standing *(Duke Lambert)*; Katherine Alexander *(Alda)*; Gail Patrick *(Rhoda)*; Helen Westley *(Stephanie)*; Kathleen Howard *(Princess Maria)*; Kent Taylor *(Corrado)*; Henry Travers *(Baron Cesarea)*; G. P. Huntley Jr. *(Eric)*; Otto Hoffman *(Fedele)*; Edward Van Sloan *(Doctor Valle)*; Hector Sarno *(Pietro)*; Frank Yaconelli *(vendor)*; Anna De Linsky *(maid)*.

THE CREATORS

Mitchell Leisen *(director)*; Maxwell Anderson and Gladys Lehman *(screenplay)*; based on a play by Alberto Casella; Charles Lang *(photography)*; Hans Dreier and Ernst Figte *(art direction)*.

Opened at the Paramount Theatre, New York, February 23, 1934. Running time when released, 79 minutes.

THE PICTURE

Death Takes a Holiday was the next-to-last picture on March's original five-year Paramount deal, and he was, for once, confronted with a role to which he could conscientiously lend his best efforts. The role of Prince Sirki is one of his best-liked characterizations and one of his most glamorous. The film was sumptuously produced in tasteful settings and sensitively directed by Mitchell Leisen.

Based on the famed play by Alberto Casella, it relates how Death, bored with his usual pursuits, decided to assume human guise and find out for himself why people feared him so. He masquerades as a handsome young prince and becomes for three days the houseguest of an Italian nobleman, Sir Guy Standing, who is in on his secret and cooperates reluctantly.

There he encounters a variety of people, including several aristocratic women who are at first attracted to the prince's enigmatic, mysterious charm, then recoil in terror as he makes himself better known to them. The Duke is rendered constantly uneasy by the Prince's ironic offhand remarks. For instance, to one famous guest who is getting on in years, the Prince remarks that he is surprised that Fate had not yet brought them to-gether. Meanwhile in the world outside the castle, no accident fatalities are reported, no plants die, no casualties are reported in current wars. Death is truly on a furlough.

The only one of the guests who is not afraid of the Prince, and who indeed, is drawn to him wholeheartedly, is Grazia, a young girl of lyrically mystical leanings. The Prince in turn is drawn to her, despite the annoyance of her fiance, and soon they are in love with each other. In fairness to her, the Prince decides to tell her who he really is and give her an opportunity to withdraw, but when he appears to her as the ominous shade in which he had first made himself and his wishes known to Duke Lambert, the girl still responds to him as the lover of her dreams.

So, despite the shocked grief of her family, her friends and the young man who loves her, to all of whom the Duke has finally confided Prince Sirki's true identity, the shade wraps his cloak around the girl and they depart together. At the time there was considerable debate over the mystical and philosophical implications of Casella's theme, which a number of critics labeled obscure. This seems surprising, as the implicit message has cropped up in the literature of Man countless times through the ages, though in various forms, this being that the deepest and most perfect love is eternal and not subject to the tyrannies of time or the vagaries of human frailty, and so-called death is but the harbinger of it, the messenger, the intimator.

Death has down through the centuries come legendarily in the form and guise of a handsome young man. Prince Sirki represents this image to the romantic and idealistic Grazia, and so she welcomes him, Death, in her mystically-oriented view, being not an affliction but a gift. March gave one of his finest performances in this

With Evelyn Venable

film, complete with monocle, makeup and clothes that gave him a mysteriously handsome aura. He also managed a foreign accent very well. Evelyn Venable struck just the right note as the sensitive Grazia, and Sir Guy Standing was particularly fine among the distinguished supporting cast as Death's half-terrified, half-intrigued nobleman host.

THE REVIEWERS
Time:
The impossibility of assaying the philosophical content, if any, of the play by Alberto Casella from which this picture was adapted does not diminish the charm.... It remains a serious poetic riddle ... thoughtful, delicately morbid.

Richard Watts, Jr. in the *New York Herald Tribune:*
An interesting, frequently striking and occasionally beautiful dramatic fantasy that somehow ends by being unsatisfying. Its chief virtues in the current version are the rather sensitive dialogue ... the intelligent direction ... the settings, the photography, and the playing of Fredric March. Mr. March is at his best in this florid sort of part and, although he doesn't seem cast as accurately to type in the title role as was Philip Merivale in the theatre, his performance is admirably managed ... an imaginative fantasy based on a good poetic idea.

Variety:
Though highly fantastic, the plot provides many interesting situations.... The tendency to sermonize, at times, by long stretches of dialog that will go over the

With Kathleen Howard

heads of many filmgoers, is evident throughout. . . . March again turns in a skillful performance, here playing a foreigner in an accent from which there is never a break or slip.

Mordaunt Hall in *The New York Times:*
It is an impressive picture, each scene of which calls for close attention. Undoubtedly Maxwell Anderson's share in the adaptation had a great deal to do with the effectiveness of this screen contribution . . . so long as one does not give it too much deep thought, it is joyous indeed when Death takes a holiday, for wilted flowers regain life, a man leaps from the Eiffel Tower and gets up and walks away, no one is even injured in a school fire and no casualties are reported in fighting between rival nations. . . . In portraying his role, Mr. March affects a monocle and speaks with a foreign accent. His performance is pleasing.

With Evelyn Venable

With Evelyn Venable

With Sylvia Sidney

Good Dame

Paramount / 1934

THE PLAYERS

Mr. March was *Mace Townsley* in a cast which included: Sylvia Sidney *(Lillie Taylor);* Jack La Rue *(Bluch Brown);* Noel Francis *(Puff Warner);* Russell Hopton *("Spots" Edwards);* Bradley Page *(Regan);* Guy Usher *(Fallon);* Kathleen Burke *(Zandra);* Joseph J. Frazer *(Scanlon);* Miami Alvarez *(Cara);* Walter Brennan *(Elmer Spicer).*

THE CREATORS

Marion Gering *(director);* William R. Lipman, Vincent Lawrence, Frank Partos, Sam Hellman *(screenplay);* from a story by William R. Lipman. Leon Shamroy *(photography).*

Opened at the Paramount Theatre, New York, March 16, 1934. Running time, 72 minutes.

THE PICTURE

In his final picture under his Paramount contract, March was handed one of his most mediocre vehicles, possibly

With Sylvia Sidney

With Sylvia Sidney

the worst film of his career. This was *Good Dame*, a confused and meandering trifle in which he was grossly and inappropriately miscast as a tough-talking, cheap-minded carnival card-sharp who is eventually redeemed by his love for a forlorn girl, Sylvia Sidney.

After getting fired from the carnival, they go off together. Though ensconced in adjoining hotel rooms their relationship is platonic, though not through any choice of the card-sharp, and the "good dame" refuses to give in to his importunities. Though frustrated and annoyed, he finds he respects the girl all the more for it, and though he is a wise-cracking hard-guy on the surface, a genuine feeling for her grows in him. All this is played out against a would-be impressionistic back-

ground of cheap and sordid surroundings and people. Sidney is maneuvering toward a genuine love relationship leading to marriage, but it takes time for March to react affirmatively to the idea. He tries various jobs, is eventually arrested for burglary. Sidney is also hauled in on a suspended-sentence hangover from a past misfortune. March's chivalrous instincts are aroused, and when he makes a sincere plea to the judge on the girl's behalf, the judge (being one of those sentimental old dears one always finds in such situations—in 1934 movies anyway) marries them instead of sentencing them. So all ends happily.

It would, we suppose, be reasonably accurate to style this seventy-two-minute screenplay a "mood-piece," though of a rather gross, low-life kind, with March punching assorted characters at every opportunity and swaggering around in a style that some critics thought distinctly overdone. The screenwriters in adapting William R. Lipman's story, doubtless imagined they had a nice little human-interest-type thing about two forlorn, essentially lost people, outside the pale of "respectable" society, who find a harbor in each other. The lowlife March played, with latently decent instincts aroused by his "good dame," *could* have been an appealing figure, and the situations confronting him and Sidney *might* have possessed a wistful charm and a basic common-denominator human warmth, but the confused writing, the meandering plot, the disconcerting reversals of character in midstream, plus indifferent direction and slapdash production all kept this film solidly plunked on Mother Earth, from which it at no point rose. One would be inclined to suspect that Paramount was trying to "punish" March for not signing another five-year contract and signaling his desire to go his own way in self-chosen vehicles. If true, it was a mean way to do it.

THE REVIEWERS
New York World-Telegram:
A couple of good actors wasting their talents in a des-

With Sylvia Sidney (right)

113

With Noel Francis

perate effort to sustain a story that is only half-way worthy of them. Miss Sidney and Mr. March do what they can to make their roles seem less trite than they are but they are so handicapped by poorly written and characterized parts that their efforts are of no avail.

Grace Kingsley in the *Los Angeles Times:*
It's quite bewildering to see Fredric March, noble brow and all, and who usually plays such grand heroes, portraying a tough guy with an East Side accent.

New York Sun:
A plot too involved in its action to be a highly effective film. Its psychology gets decidedly off center at times, both tough guy and good dame at times suddenly reversing the entire characterizations so carefully built up for them. . . . Not one of Fredric March's better pictures. It's rather a pity to have it follow so closely upon *Death Takes a Holiday.*

Variety:
March suggests the tough showman most of the time, but occasionally bears down too hard. Miss Sidney delivers a more even performance as the girl who's wise but decent. She holds straight to the character.

With Joseph J. Frazer

114

The Affairs of Cellini

20th Century   United Artists Release / 1934

THE PLAYERS
Mr. March was *Benvenuto Cellini* in a cast that included: Constance Bennett *(Duchess of Florence)*; Frank Morgan *(Alessandro, Duke of Florence)*; Fay Wray *(Angela)*; Vince Barnett *(Ascanio)*; Jessie Ralph *(Beatrice)*; Louis Calhern *(Ottaviano)*; Jay Eaton *(Polverino)*; Paul Harvey *(emissary)*; John Rutherford *(captain of guards)*.

THE CREATORS
Gregory La Cava *(director)*; Bess Meredyth *(screenplay)*; adapted from Edwin Justus Mayer's play *The Firebrand*, Charles Rosher *(photography)*.

Opened at the Rivoli Theatre, New York, September 5, 1934. Running time when released, 90 minutes.

THE PICTURE
March, once-burned and twice-warned, had signed with Darryl F. Zanuck's 20th Century pictures, but had refused a long-term contract, his deal calling for several

With Constance Bennett

115

pictures only. His first film under that deal was *The Affairs of Cellini*, an adaptation of the Edwin Justus Mayer play, *The Firebrand*, which had starred Joseph Schildkraut on Broadway.

It dealt with the amours of that Florentine hedonist, rascal and rake, Benvenuto Cellini, a talented artist who dabbled in all manner of colorful vice and had a fantastic record as a womanizer. He is having an affair with his lovely model, Fay Wray, but catches the attention of the Duchess of Florence (Constance Bennett) whose husband, the Duke (Frank Morgan), in turn takes a fancy to the model. Frank Morgan repeated the role he had played in the stage version and walked away with the picture, delivering one of those delightfully zany prize-bumbler interpretations that had become one of his trademarks (Morgan could also be a dignified, serious

actor of great depth and skill, as in 1933's *The Kiss Before the Mirror*, an aspect of his talent that is too often overlooked).

Attired fetchingly in close-fitting tights and glamorous Renaissance silks, and sporting goatee and curled hair, March was called upon in this to engage in Douglas Fairbanks-style feats of derring-do, climbing balconies and fending off assorted villains with colorful sword play. While the role suited him temperamentally, critics continuing to insist that he was tapping one of his most rewarding fortes in such floridly romantic parts, some reviewers liked him and some didn't.

The piece was basically a bedroom farce dressed up in sixteenth-century Florentine settings and costumes. The Duchess pushes her romantic intrigue with Cellini, the bumbling old Duke pursues the model; Cellini wangles and flatters and double-talks his way out of torture chambers and other punishments devised for him by his enemies; there is much scurrying in and out of bedchambers and clashes with such heavies as Louis Calhern.

The production mounting provided was first-rate and director Gregory La Cava (an expert with farce, be it high or low-level) gave the whole waggish affair the deftly tongue-in-cheek approach that such nonsense deserved. It was all light, diverting and often amusing, but Frank Morgan, playing a buffoonish role that he was born for, got the most out of the proceedings, as well he deserved to. Granted its fragilities, *The Affairs of Cellini* must have represented a welcome relief for March from the kind of films he had been doing. His aficionados still recall the film with pleasure, but it is distinctly lightweight material.

THE REVIEWERS
Richard Watts, Jr. in the *New York Herald Tribune*:
Benvenuto Cellini, braggart, wastrel and artist, is just the romantic hero of a well costumed musical without the music (here).... Even on the stage...this farcical account of Florentine life in the days of the Medici was little more than a conventional sex comedy of the bedroom, doorslamming and deceived-husband school, pleasantly decorated by its Renaissance settings and graceful verbiage. In the screen version, carefully acted by such popular performers as Fredric March and Miss Constance Bennett, it seems to lose some of its grace and dash, if none of its usual visual attractiveness, and emerges as something less than a masterpiece of gaiety and wit. As upon the occasion of its stage premiere, it

With Fay Wray

is Frank Morgan, in his original role of the amiably imbecilic Duke of Florence, who walks off with all the acting honors involved in the proceedings.... Mr. March seems...less comfortable than usual in this part. An admirable actor who is at his best in florid romantic

With Louis Calhern

117

roles, with a suggestion of comedy, [Mr. March] should have been not far from perfect as the great Cellini, but for some reason he seems curiously restrained and retiring, and although he is pleasant and engaging in the part, he is far from the brilliant success that I, for one, had anticipated.

Mordaunt Hall in *The New York Times:*
Although Miss Bennett and Mr. March are able performers, the brunt of the comedy is shouldered by Mr. Morgan, who is at the peak of his form. . . . An elegant production, with striking settings and handsome costumes. Mr. March, his physiognomy decorated with a pointed beard, is called upon to do feats of agility which are like some of the tricks done by Douglas Fairbanks in silent films. . . . The dialogue is smartly written.

Robert J. Landry in *Variety:*
Diverting light comedy . . . a triumph of directorial legerdemain. It deals with adultery and no amount of lacquer can quite hide the fact. . . . In order to get the story passed [by the Hays office] the studio has done some slick surgery. That the picture bears some scars and is intermittently weak and pallid is incontrovertible. What emerges is a thin layer of comedy over a hot story and upon which a clever cast weaves curlicues without breaking through. It's all impersonalized and spoofed. Frank Morgan runs away with the film . . . Fredric March behind a goatee is plausible if historically incredible, as the gifted liar-libertine-murderer-genius. . . . Picture as a whole manages to be gay and entertaining although whipped up synthetically like circus ice cream.

The Barretts of Wimpole Street

Metro-Goldwyn-Mayer / 1934

THE PLAYERS

Mr. March was *Robert Browning* in a cast that included: Norma Shearer *(Elizabeth Barrett)*; Charles Laughton *(Edward Moulton Barrett)*; Maureen O'Sullivan *(Henrietta Barrett)*; Katherine Alexander *(Arabel Barrett)*; Una O'Connor *(Wilson)*; Ian Wolfe *(Harry Bevan)*; Marion Clayton *(Bella Hedley)*; Ralph Forbes *(Captain Surtees Cook)*; Vernon Downing *(Octavius Barrett)*; Neville Clark *(Charles Barrett)*; Matthew Smith *(George Barrett)*; Robert Carleton *(Alfred Barrett)*; Alan Conrad *(Henry Barrett)*; Peter Hobbes *(Septimus Barrett)*; Ferdinand Munier *(Dr. Chambers)*; Leo Carroll *(Dr. Ford-Waterlow)*.

THE CREATORS

Sidney Franklin *(director)*; Claudine West, Ernest Vajda and Donald Ogden Stewart *(screenplay)*; adapted from the play by Rudolph Besier; William Daniels *(photography)*; Herbert Stothart *(musical score)*.

Opened at the Capitol Theatre, New York, September 28, 1934. Running time when released, 110 minutes.

THE PICTURE

March was reunited with Norma Shearer, with whom he had made the widely admired *Smilin' Through*, in *The Barretts of Wimpole Street*, the MGM film version of the Rudolph Besier play in which Katharine Cornell had made an enormous 1931 hit. Charles Laughton was also on hand for *his* second picture with March, and Sidney Franklin, always a sensitive and perceptive director of romantic pieces, guided his stars with painstaking care. The screenplay was faithful to its original, and gifted cameraman William Daniels, who had produced magical effects with Garbo, photographed Miss Shearer to exceptional advantage.

The well-known story of the invalid poetess Elizabeth Barrett, confined to a room in her father's London townhouse circa 1845 with her books and her dog, and sadly resigned to the loss of any meaningful love relationship as forty approaches, suited the refined sensibilities of Miss Shearer to a T, and Charles Laughton, as her tyrannical father, Edward Moulton Barrett, was at his most hair-raisingly horrific, delivering full-force in the florid

Laughton style his fans expected, indeed demanded. March was forthright and reasonably robust as Browning, but this is not one of his more felicitous assignments, and his two co-stars outplayed him.

Elizabeth's growing love for Browning, whose visits revitalize her being, brings her gradually back to health, and her enraged and frustrated father, who rules his brood with rigid authoritarianism, attempts to prevent her recovery, his subconsciously incestuous fixation on her, suppressed by a heavy-handed religiosity, being best served by her invalidism and consequent dependence. But when Elizabeth eventually realizes the true source of her father's obsessive protectiveness, she at last heeds Browning's plea that she go away with him, and leaves her father's house forever.

Sidney Franklin was to direct still another MGM version of ''The Barretts,'' released twenty-three years later, in 1957 with Jennifer Jones as Elizabeth, Bill Travers as Browning and John Gielgud as Edward Moulton-Barrett. I have studied both versions carefully, and prefer the 1957 film. For one thing, there is very little use of mood music in the 1934 version, in a story that cries out for it, and the story is static, at times even leaden, though Miss Shearer was splendid, superior to Miss Jones in the later version which was, however, handsomely mounted in CinemaScope and Technicolor, beautifully and affectingly scored, and better paced, with more dramatic elan and romantic power. And for my money, Bill Travers, a greatly underrated actor, made a more attractive, ardent and vigorous Browning than Franklin had permitted March to be in 1934. Moreover, the 1957 version boasted a cast that was almost entirely English, the settings were authentic London, and the flavor was somehow more true. Sir John Gielgud was absolutely brilliant as Edward Moulton Barrett, giving a

With Norma Shearer

performance filled with bitter complexities and subtle self-churnings only Gielgud could have generated.

THE REVIEWERS
Richard Watts, Jr. in the *New York Herald Tribune:*
The screen has been handsomely loyal to [the play] and, admirably acted by Miss Norma Shearer, Fredric March and, in particular, by Charles Laughton, the celebrated stage drama of Victorian family tyranny and love among the artists reaches the screen as a distinguished and loyal motion picture.... [Laughton's] portrayal of the stern, repressed family tyrant is nothing short of a masterpiece of power and understanding and sheer dramatic

*With Charles Laughton and
Norma Shearer*

With Norma Shearer

With Norma Shearer

With Charles Laughton (holding his Oscar for Henry VIII)
and Norma Shearer

effectiveness.... Miss Shearer is admirable as Elizabeth Barrett, providing a genuinely lovely portrayal of strength and understanding. Mr. March is splendid as Robert Browning, a part that fits him as have few of his recent screen roles.

Andre Sennwald in *The New York Times:*
Sidney Franklin has filmed a drama of beauty, dignity and nobility. There will be applause for Norma Shearer's Elizabeth, Fredric March's Robert Browning and Charles Laughton's Mr. Barrett, but for the high-minded aspirations which went into its production, there can be nothing less than a shout of benediction. Hollywood could make no more fitting answer to her critics than this.... Miss Shearer's Elizabeth is a brave and touching piece of acting and she is successful in creating the illusion of a highly sensitive and delicate woman who beats her luminous wings in vain against the chains which bind her. Charles Laughton is, of course, superb as the stubborn, selfish and pious father. Fredric March makes a healthy and virile Browning, although his performance will impress the critical as a highly competent job by a versatile actor rather than an inspired portrayal of the great poet.

With Norma Shearer

Time:
There are big chunks of dialog which, in spite of all Norma Shearer, Fredric March and director Sidney Franklin can do, remain just talk. The adapters, instead of squeezing in the accordion-folds of the play, have pulled them out, injected a number of scenes which pad the continuity but add nothing to the plot.

Abel Green in *Variety:*
March's bravado style of juvenility is well suited to the role of the ardent Browning... Miss Shearer is at all times sincerely compelling... Laughton's relentless, abnormal assignment is played to the hilt and the auditor will walk out hating the character and admiring the art which makes the antipathy so vivid.

With Anna Sten

We Live Again

Samuel Goldwyn   United Artists / 1934

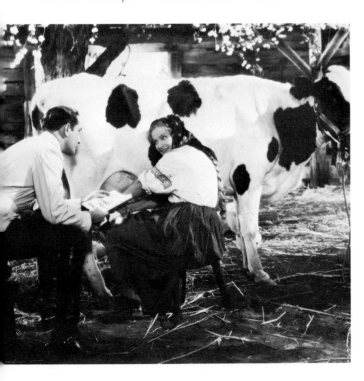

THE PLAYERS
Mr. March was *Prince Dmitri Nekhilyudov* in a cast that included: Anna Sten *(Katusha Maslova)*; Jane Baxter *(Missy Kortchagin)*; C. Aubrey Smith *(Prince Kortchagin)*; Ethel Griffies *(Aunt Marie)*; Gwendolyn Logan *(Aunt Sophia)*; Jessie Ralph *(Matrona Pavlovna)*; Sam Jaffe *(Simonson)*; Cecil Cunningham *(Theodosia)*; Jessie Arnold *(Korablova)*; Fritzi Ridgeway *(the redhead)*; Morgan Wallace *(the colonel)*; Davison Clark *(Tikhon)*; Leonid Kinskey *(Kartinkin)*; Dale Fuller *(Botchkova)*; Michael Visaroff *(judge)*; Edgar Norton *(judge)*.

THE CREATORS
Rouben Mamoulian *(director)*; Preston Sturges, Maxwell Anderson and Leonard Praskins *(screenplay)*; adapted from Leo Tolstoy's novel *Resurrection*. Gregg Toland *(photography)*; Sergei Soudeikin *(settings)*; Alfred Newman *(music)*; Robert Lee *(assistant director)*.

Opened at Radio City Music Hall, November 1, 1934. Running time when released, 85 minutes.

With Anna Sten

123

THE PICTURE

Rouben Mamoulian, who had done so well with March in *Dr. Jekyll and Mr. Hyde*, next joined him under Samuel Goldwyn's auspices for a third film version of Tolstoy's "Resurrection," which had been given a whirl as a silent with Dolores Del Rio and Rod LaRocque and an early talkie with Lupe Velez and John Boles. When he wrote it at the end of the nineteenth century, Tolstoy had become more obsessed with social reform than with art, and in its egalitarian idealism the novel anticipates the great Russian Revolution, then a score of years in the future.

This third film version had more depth and dignity than its predecessors and was produced with more care. Mamoulian gave it the benefit of his best directorial inspirations; Greg Toland's photography was evocative and in some instances inspired; there was a plethora of Russian atmosphere, including a lengthy Easter Mass sequence reportedly chock-full of genuine Russian *emigré* extras; care and taste were written all over it. Seen again some thirty-six years after its original showings, *We Live Again* (as Goldwyn retitled it) impressed me as a handsome and conscientiously wrought production, and the slow pace of which the 1934 critics had complained seemed right and warranted, in order to establish the characters firmly in their setting. It also reaffirmed Anna Sten's luminous beauty and solid acting proficiency. Samuel Goldwyn at this point was doing his utmost to promote Miss Sten into a major starring niche in such carefully-mounted productions as the one with March, *Nana* and *The Wedding Night* with Gary Cooper. But for some reason no one to this day has successfully fathomed, she didn't "take" with American audiences.

Sten and March played together extremely well. His performance was sincere, thorough and carefully thought out. Somewhat underrated in its own day, *We Live Again* seen in 1971 holds up as a fine, carefully paced, beautifully composed work, though granted that Tolstoy's tendency to sacrifice art to polemics in his later period makes some of it seem stodgy and dated.

With Anna Sten

The well-known story deals with a Russian prince raised in the country on equal terms with a peasant servant; they have an innocent romantic idyll; then he departs to become an officer; grown jaded, dissipated and de-sensitized by his officer's existence in the capital (where wine and women figure heavily with soldiers of his class), he returns to the estate years later to visit his relatives, lusts after the girl, who is now in full bloom, seduces her, then callously leaves in the morning after sending her money. The heartsick girl, who is sincerely in love with him, gives birth later to an illegitimate baby who dies. She is gradually reduced by misfortune to the status of a cabaret wanton, and years later in the capital the Prince, by accident, encounters her as the defendant in a murder-and-robbery trial.

Realizing that he was initially responsible for the downward path his childhood love had taken, he tries to make amends, maneuvers for an acquittal (she is innocent), but fails because of rigid legal procedures. He then visits her in prison; she scorns him contemptu-

ously. Realizing that he has been reborn as a truly human spirit, the Prince sells his possessions, gives away his lands to his retainers, and joins the girl in her Siberian exile. Now convinced that her Prince is again the boy she once loved, and realizing that he has sacrificed everything for her, she starts off joyously with him to meet their mutual fate.

THE REVIEWERS

"Beverly Hills" in *Liberty:*

One of the important stories of the year . . . filmed with painstaking care and sheer photographic beauty. Miss

Sten looks like a peasant and acts like one . . . she is at all times the betrayed housegirl, simple, sentimental, tragic, bitter, and she demonstrates a solid and sound grasp of emotion. . . . Fredric March gives his best screen performance; in a role that might easily have been theatric and unbelievable, he is sure and telling in his effects. . . . [Toland's] photography is lovely . . . a polished, dramatic film.

Eileen Creelman in the *New York Sun*:
Fredric March, although somewhat subdued by the ubiquitous loveliness of Miss Sten, gives a sincere and effective impersonation of the boyish prince. . . . He is perhaps less credible as the heedless officer. . . . As the

somewhat impractical idealist of the last reels he is again back in his stride.

Edwin Schallert in the *Los Angeles Times*:
March's work in the picture is variable. His voice seems ill pitched at times, mainly in those sequences in the middle of the picture. Brilliant indeed is his work at the beginning, and [he is] forcefully emotional toward the close.

The Times (London):
Mr. Fredric March, though at the beginning one feared that he might find it hard to be sufficiently Russian, undergoes Prince Dmitri's more elaborate emotions with remarkable competence.

Les Miserables

20th Century   United Artists / 1935

THE PLAYERS

Mr. March was *Jean Valjean* in a cast that included: Charles Laughton *(Javert)*; Cedric Hardwicke *(Bishop Bienvenu)*; Rochelle Hudson *(Big Cosette)*; Marilyn Knowlden *(Little Cosette)*; Frances Drake *(Eponine)*; John Beal *(Marius)*; Jessie Ralph *(Madame Magloire)*; Florence Eldridge *(Fantine)*; Ferdinand Gottschalk *(Thenardier)*; Jane Kerr *(Madame Thenardier)*; Eily Malyon *(Mother Superior)*; Vernon Downing *(Brissac)*; Lyons Wickland *(Lamarque)*; John Carradine *(Enjolras)*; Charles Haefeli *(Brevet)*; Leonid Kinskey *(Genflon)*; John Bleifer *(Chenildieu)*; Harry Semels *(Cochepaille)*; Mary Forbes *(Madame Baptiseme)*; Florence Roberts *(Toussaint)*; Lorin Baker *(Valain)*; Perry Ivins *(M. Devereux)*; Thomas Mills *(L'Estrange)*; Lowell Drew *(Duval)*; Davidson Clark *(Marcin)*; Ian McClaren *(head gardener)*.

THE CREATORS

Richard Boleslawski *(director)*; Darryl F. Zanuck *(pro-ducer)*; adapted from the novel by Victor Hugo; W. P. Lipscomb *(screenplay)*; Gregg Toland *(photography)*; Alfred Newman *(musical director)*; Barbara McLean *(film editor)*.

Opened at the Rivoli Theatre, New York, April 20, 1935. Running time when released, 109 minutes.

THE PICTURE

March then began on his second picture under his 20th Century deal. Richard Boleslawski guided him through one of the finest performances of his career, as Jean Valjean in Victor Hugo's classic, *Les Miserables*. W. P. Lipscomb wrote a compressed 109-minute script in which all the intrinsic values of the novel were retained as much as cinema-capsulizing allowed—in this case, surprisingly, a great deal. Acclaimed as one of the best films of its year, it holds up, thirty-six years later, as a

With Florence Eldridge

With Eily Malyon and Rochelle Hudson

moving and intelligent work, expertly paced, with an emotional immediacy and a gripping intensity that command respect.

The novel has been filmed several times—including a primitive, superficial silent and a three-hour French version of 1936, but none matched the intrinsic quality, or caught the true spirit, of the 1935 Hollywood version. The secret of its success, as seen today, was its intelligent selectivity of incident and its telling highlighting of the basic points Hugo was trying to make. Like Tolstoy,

Hugo was a humanitarian greatly concerned with social reform, but unlike Tolstoy in his later period, Hugo never sacrificed entertainment value to preaching, and his 1862 novel, *Les Miserables*, became one of the world's best-loved classics.

Jean Valjean, sentenced to years of cruel prison punishment for stealing a loaf of bread, finally emerges from his incarceration as a hardened, desensitized derelict, but he is redeemed by the kindness of a Bishop (admirably played by Sir Cedric Hardwicke) who refuses to turn him in for stealing silver. Valjean is deeply moved by this exceptional instance of Christian compassion, and determines to reform and rebuild his life. Through self-discipline and hard work, he becomes a successful

businessman in another French town and is eventually chosen Mayor. His police administrator Javert (played with superb incisiveness by Charles Laughton) is a letter-of-the-law administrator, rigid, unyielding and pitiless, his fanatic adherence to legalistic principles the result of his early hurt over having a convict parent.

Javert and Valjean clash when Valjean comes to the aid of Fantine, another social outcast (admirably played by Florence Eldridge) and Javert begins investigating Valjean's past, especially after he is struck by the mayor's strength in lifting a wagon during an accident—a strength he associates with remembered convict-labor. Javert through assiduous investigations uncovers Valjean's past, but becomes confused as to whether he has the right man when a befuddled prisoner closely resembling him (also played by March) goes on trial as the supposed Jean Valjean in another town. Though silence will keep him safe, Valjean declares his identity, then takes his adopted child and escapes to Paris.

Meanwhile his daughter, now grown, has fallen in love with Marius, a student and revolutionary who advocates prison reform. Javert, who has been assigned to subvert the revolutionaries, encounters Valjean and proceeds to dog him all over again. Valjean rescues Marius during an uprising, then, resigned to surrendering to Javert, he leaves the young people to their life together and goes to meet his old enemy. But Javert, moved despite himself by compassion for Valjean, a compassion that untenably affronts his rigid legalistic principles, has drowned himself in the Seine. Valjean, now blessedly free at last, lifts his eyes to the heavens. (In the original novel, Valjean later died).

THE REVIEWERS

Irene Thirer in the *New York Evening Post:*
A superlative effort, a thrilling, powerful, poignant picture, produced on a tremendous scale, yet retaining all the color, passion and intimacy of Hugo's fiercely dra-

With Charles Laughton

matic tale of nineteenth-century France. Fredric March's interpretation of the convict Jean Valjean is a creditable addition to his histrionic repertoire. He surrenders himself completely to the role, which covers a period of thirty years ... a singularly worthy production, one which will certainly be included in the lineup of the best pictures of 1935.

Eileen Creelman in *The New York Sun:*
A picture so fine that it will be many years before anyone dares attempt another production of the Hugo classic ... this is no film to be cheerfully applauded for colorful costuming and pretty performances. It is a story, at least as powerful as any ever attempted on the screen, of two human beings and, through them, of most of

With Frances Drake

humanity. It is also grand entertainment. . . . Mr. March's Jean Valjean is a superb piece of work. Throwing away any vestiges of the matinee idol, he plays with new tenderness and depth . . . [the film] has drama enough for a dozen pictures. Somehow it flows along easily, subordinating its background of melodrama and elaborate costumes to the undiscussed, never forgotten central theme . . . a picture of power and hope.

William Boehnel in the *New York World-Telegram:*
Many thick and famous books that have been literary masterpieces and thunderbolts have turned out to be just so many cream puffs when they reached the screen. Stripped of the bitterness, irony, power and truth of their printed pages . . . they have come to life in shadow form not as giants but as puny weaklings. Not so with [Zanuck's] screen version of [Hugo's] immortal *Les*

Miserables . . . which is deserving of rank among the cinema's finest achievements. . . . As the hounded Valjean Fredric March is splendid, giving a performance that is rare for its sincerity and comprehension. As Javert Charles Laughton is feline and subtly hateful in a superb manner . . . a profound and disturbingly true film.

Variety:
March makes the screen Jean Valjean a living version of the panegyrical character. He is the same persecuted, pursued, pitiable but always admirable man that all readers of the book must visualize. There is studied acting in the March performance but none of it tends to sacrifice Valjean for flashy histrionics. . . . Laughton is equally powerful and always believable. . . . Florence Eldridge, in one of her infrequent screen appearances, makes the betrayed Fantine amount to something.

With Basil Rathbone and Greta Garbo

Anna Karenina

Metro-Goldwyn-Mayer / 1935

THE PLAYERS

Mr. March was *Vronsky* in a cast that included: Greta Garbo *(Anna Karenina)*; Freddie Bartholomew *(Sergei)*; Maureen O'Sullivan *(Kitty)*; May Robson *(Countess Vronsky)*; Basil Rathbone *(Karenin)*; Reginald Owen *(Stiva)*; Reginald Denny *(Yashvin)*; Phoebe Foster *(Dolly)*; Gyles Isham *(Levin)*; Buster Phelps *(Grisha)*; Ella Ethridge *(Anna's maid)*; Joan Marsh *(Lili)*; Sidney Bracey *(Vronsky's valet)*; Cora Sue Collins *(Tania)*; Joe E. Tozer *(butler)*; Guy D'Ennery *(tutor)*; Harry Allen *(Cord)*; Mary Forbes *(Princess Sorokino)*; Ethel Griffies *(Madame Kortasoff)*; Harry Beresford *(Matve)*; Sarah Padden *(governess)*.

THE CREATORS

Clarence Brown *(director)*; David O. Selznick *(producer)*; Clemence Dane and Salka Viertel *(screenplay)*; S. N. Behrman *(dialogue)*; adapted from the novel by Count Leo Tolstoy; Herbert Stothart *(musical director)*; Marguerite Wallmann, Chester Hale *(dances)*; Russian Symphony Choir *(choral effects)*; William Daniels *(photography)*; Count Andrei Tolstoy *(story consultant)*; Robert J. Kearn *(film editor)*.

Opened at the Capitol Theatre, New York, August 30, 1935. Running time when released, 85 minutes.

THE PICTURE

As Vronsky in *Anna Karenina*, March gave a highly effective performance, stalwart yet sensitive, direct yet subtly intuitive, and his and Greta Garbo's styles and chemistries meshed to compelling effect. The Tolstoy novel had been filmed eight years before as the silent *Love* with John Gilbert as Garbo's Vronsky, but the 1935 version was couched in more mature terms and was more carefully produced, with authentic costumes in careful settings. (The 1927 version had been primarily designed as a vehicle for the lovemaking of Garbo and Gilbert at the height of their well-publicized romance, and had even been played in modern dress.)

Some critics thought the film dull, heavy and slow in spots, but Garbo and March drew excellent personal notices. Though he was thirty-seven at the time he made *Anna Karenina*, March succeeded in getting across the impetuous ardor and youthful self-centeredness that was the essence of the handsome officer Vronsky, who lures the lonely and bored Madame Karenina, languishing in a loveless marriage to stuffy bureaucrat Karenin, into a passionate extra-marital affair that flouts the rigid, albeit hypocritical, conventions of Russian society of a century ago. Electing to feel rather than to think, the emotional, love-hungry Anna, after some initial hesitancy, leaves her husband and small son for a life with her lover.

With Greta Garbo

With Greta Garbo and Freddie Bartholomew

They go to Italy for a time and are fleetingly happy.

But Vronsky, whose approach to the affair is more immature than Anna's, tires of her gradually and plots to escape back into the army. Anna tries to see her son, which she does, fleetingly, but is then ordered from the house by her enraged husband. Social pressures force Vronsky into an eventual all-out desertion, and when Anna tries to find him at the station where he is leaving for the Turkish-Serbian war, she discovers him engaged with his mother and a young princess to whom the mother wishes him affianced.

Realizing that she has lost everything and that she is without refuge emotionally, Anna throws herself under the wheels of a train.

David O. Selznick gave the picture a sumptuous production gloss, and Clarence Brown's direction extracted all possible values. *Anna Karenina* was made again in 1948 with Vivien Leigh, but it was not as successful,

With Reginald Owen (at March's left) and cabaret employees

With Greta Garbo

With May Robson

THE REVIEWERS

Richard Watts, Jr. in the *New York Herald Tribune*: Miss Garbo has never looked lovelier nor played more beautifully . . . an admirably managed example of heavily brooding and slightly ponderous sentimental drama. . . . She portrays the role . . . with insight, compassion and a tragic beauty that demonstrates once more her magnificence as an actress. . . . Although the photoplay is entirely Miss Garbo's there are some excellent portrayals. . . . Mr. March plays the unfeeling hero with spirit and skill and there is a splendid performance by Basil Rathbone as the chill husband.

though the 1948 version contained plot elucidations and psychological nuances not present in the 1935 version. Garbo's performance gives the earlier version the edge, though Leigh's portrayal was not without its merits.

With Basil Rathbone, Greta Garbo, Ethel Griffies and Constance Collier

With Greta Garbo

With Greta Garbo

The Times: (London)
There is about the picture a somber greyness which at times becomes almost oppressive. It reaches no great heights of tragedy or drama but rather moves forward relentlessly and a little coldly. Miss Garbo's is a delicate and restrained performance, at first a little disappointing because its subtleties are not at once apparent. There is an infinite tenderness under this reserve. Mr. Fredric March [is] stalwart and determined, but always more of the soldier than the lover.

Andre Sennwald in *The New York Times:*
Miss Garbo, the first lady of the screen, sins, suffers and perishes illustriously in the new, ably produced and comparatively mature version of the Tolstoy classic... and dignified and effective drama.... Familiar as [the film] is in outline, it is freshly touching in its description of a great romance which is slain by the very elements that gave it birth.... Miss Garbo, always superbly the apex of the drama, suggests the inevitability of her doom from the beginning.... Bouncing with less determination than is his custom, Mr. March gets by handsomely as Vronsky.

With Reginald Denny

With Merle Oberon

The Dark Angel

Samuel Goldwyn   United Artists / 1935

THE PLAYERS
Mr. March was *Alan Trent* in a cast that included: Merle Oberon *(Kitty Vane)*; Herbert Marshall *(Gerald Shannon)*; Janet Beecher *(Mrs. Shannon)*; John Halliday *(Sir George Barton)*; Henrietta Crosman *(Granny Vane)*; Frieda Inescort *(Ann West)*; Claude Allister *(Lawrence Bidley)*; George Breakston *(Joe)*; Fay Chaldecott *(Betty)*; Denis Chaldecott *(Ginger)*; Douglas Walton *(Roulston)*; Sarah Edwards *(Mrs. Bidley)*; John Miltern *(Mr. Vane)*; Olaf Hytten *(Mills)*; Lawrence Grant *(Mr. Tanner)*; Helena Byrne-Grant *(Hannah)*; Ann Fielder *(Mrs. Gallop)*; David Torrence *(Mr. Shannon)*; Cora Sue Collins *(Kitty as a child)*; Jimmy Baxter *(Alan as a child)*; Jimmy Butler *(Gerald as a child)*; Randolph Connolly *(Lawrence as a child)*.

THE CREATORS
Sidney Franklin *(director)*; Samuel Goldwyn *(producer)*; Lillian Hellman and Mordaunt Shairp *(screenplay)*; adapted from the play by Guy Bolton; Gregg Toland *(photography)*; Alfred Newman *(musical direction)*; Hugh Boswell *(assistant director)*.

Opened at the Rivoli Theatre, New York, September 5, 1935. Running time when released, 105 minutes.

THE PICTURE
Samuel Goldwyn beckoned March again, and this time

With Herbert Marshall

With Herbert Marshall and Merle Oberon

under the aegis of sensitive, perceptive, tasteful Sidney Franklin, with whom he had worked in *The Barretts of Wimpole Street*, March did *The Dark Angel*, a remake of the silent film Goldwyn had done in 1925 with Ronald Colman. Lillian Hellman and Mordaunt Shairp prepared an excellent screenplay that extracted all the dramatic values inherent in the piece. The mounting and production were impeccable, as in all Goldwyn films, and March's performance proved one of his most popular to date. Merle Oberon, who had developed from a sloe-eyed exotic into a sensitive and feelingful actress, was co-starred along with Herbert Marshall, and both gave excellent accounts of themselves.

Adapted from the play by Guy Bolton, the story dealt with three childhood friends in the England of World War I. The two boys, Alan and Gerald, both love the girl, Kitty, but Kitty chooses Alan, and spends the night with him just before he must leave for France and the front. It seems that they had been frustrated in securing the marriage license they had both badly wanted, and loneliness and impending separation had overwhelmed them.

Alan and Gerald are in the same outfit, with Gerald his commanding officer. Gerald has taken Kitty's choice in sportsmanlike fashion, but when he learns of the incident between Kitty and Alan, the two men quarrel.

With Herbert Marshall, Merle Oberon and Janet Beecher

135

With Merle Oberon

Feeling that Alan has betrayed Kitty, Gerald sends him out on a dangerous mission, from which he does not return. Later in England, Gerald and Kitty presume Alan is dead, and make plans to marry, though Kitty still loves Alan. Alan meanwhile has been wounded and blinded, and when he recovers he asks his friend Sir George Barton (John Halliday) to conceal the fact that he is still alive, because he does not want to burden Kitty with his affliction.

Alan goes back to live in England under an assumed name, and in time becomes a best-selling author of children's stories. Sir George reads in the paper that Kitty and Gerald are to be married, and feeling that Kitty should know that the man she loves is still alive, he informs her and Gerald of Alan's whereabouts. When Alan learns that they are coming, he memorizes every detail of his drawing room so that his movements and general demeanor will disguise his blindness. At first Kitty and Gerald are deceived. Later Kitty realizes the true state of affairs and the lovers are reunited.

Seen today, the film has its trite aspects, and the romantic situation seems forced, overly sentimental, artificial. The excellent acting and sincere direction, as well as the aforementioned tasteful production values, however, make the sum total more than attention-holding, if no longer as moving as it once was.

THE REVIEWERS
The Times: (London)
The film makes a systematic and often very skillful appeal to those untrustworthy emotions which may suddenly cause the most hardened intellects to dissolve before the most obvious sentimentality. The assault on the emotions is cunning and varied. . . . Mr. Fredric March and Mr. Herbert Marshall are masters of the art of parading their feelings while apparently concealing them.

Liberty:
Impeccably mounted and suavely presented, [the film] is quite the loveliest of the new movie season's lachrymose offerings . . . superior entertainment in all its departments. Gregg Toland's photography is superb; the musical score is consistently effective in heightening the mood of the scenes; and Sidney Franklin's direction, though slow, sharpens the poignancy of the film's well-mannered sentimentality. Merle Oberon—no longer an exotic but a fresh and appealing English girl—is not only the most fetching eyeful to hit the screen in some time but gives a performance of blended warmth and restraint that marks her for a glittering future. As her rival suitors, Herbert Marshall and Fredric March are properly noble and romantic. March, especially, unburdened with costumes, is at his best in the juiciest role he has ever had.

Kate Cameron in the *New York Daily News:*
A tenderly sentimental film that has been produced and directed with care. It is acted by an excellent cast with restraint and sympathetic understanding. Fredric March is impressive as the blind hero, Merle Oberon is beautiful in a new and refreshing makeup as the girl March left behind him, and Herbert Marshall plays the rival suitor with his customary competence.

*With Katharine Hepburn
during the shooting*

Mary of Scotland

RKO Radio / 1936

THE PLAYERS
Mr. March was the *Earl of Bothwell* in a cast that included: Katharine Hepburn *(Mary Queen of Scots)*; Florence Eldridge *(Elizabeth I of England)*; John Carradine *(David Rizzio)*; Douglas Walton *(Lord Darnley)*; Robert Barrat *(Morton)*; Ian Keith *(Moray)*; Gavin Muir *(Leicester)*; Moroni Olsen *(John Knox)*; Ralph Forbes *(Randolph)*; William Stack *(Ruthven)*; Alan Mowbray *(Throckmorton)*; Frieda Inescort *(Mary Beaton)*; Donald Crisp *(Huntley)*; David Torrence *(Lindsay)*; Molly Lamont *(Mary Livingston)*; Anita Colby *(Mary Fleming)*; Lionel Pape *(Burghley)*; Jean Fenwick *(Mary Seton)*; Alec Craig *(Donal)*; Mary Gordon *(nurse)*; Monte Blue *(messenger)*; Brandon Hurst *(Avian)*; Leonard Mudie *(Maitland)*; D'Arcy Corrigan *(Kirkcaldy)*; Wilfred Lucas *(Lexington)*; Doris Lloyd *(fisherman's wife)*; Lionel Belmore *(fisherman)*; Cyril McLaglen *(Faudoncide)*; Frank Baker *(Douglas)*; Bobby Watson *(fisherman's son)*; Robert Warwick *(Sir Francis Knellys)*; Walter Byron *(Sir Francis Walsingham)*; Wyndham Standing *(sergeant)*; Earle Foxe *(Duke of Kent)*; Paul McAllister *(Du Croche)*; Gaston Glass *(Chatelard)*; Neil Fitzgerald *(nobleman)*; Ivan Simpson, Lawrence Grant, Nigel De Brulier, Murray Kinnell, Barlowe Borland *(the five judges)*.

THE CREATORS
Pandro S. Berman *(producer)*; John Ford *(director)*; Dudley Nichols *(screenplay)*; based on the play by Maxwell Anderson; Joseph H. August *(photography)*; Van Nest Polglase *(art direction)*; Carroll Clark *(associate art director)*; Jane Loring *(editor)*; Darrell Silvera *(set decorations)*; Robert Parrish *(assistant editor)*; Hugh McDowell, Jr. *(sound)*; Nathaniel Shilkret *(music)*; Maurice de Packh *(orchestration)*; Walter Plunkett *(costumes)*; Mel Burns *(makeup)*; Vernon L. Walker *(special photographic effects)*; Edward Donahue *(assistant director)*.

Opened at Radio City Music Hall, New York, July 30, 1936. Running time when released, 123 minutes.

THE PICTURE
March next co-starred with Katharine Hepburn in *Mary of Scotland*, at RKO under John Ford's direction. The film will never go down in the books as one of the all-time greats, but it did display Hepburn's arresting and distinctive personality in a role that called upon all her acting resources—and she revealed herself as an actress of greater range than was believed. Ford gave the picture careful directorial handling, and it was handsomely

With Katharine Hepburn

fears the threat the Scottish queen represents, as she is next in line for the English throne. Mary, a Catholic, runs up against the Protestant leaders and the power-hungry, recalcitrant lords. To insure the succession to the throne and enhance her position, Mary marries the weakling Lord Darnley, whom she does not love.

The dashing Earl of Bothwell proves her staunch ally against her enemies, and love grows between them. The Lords murder Mary's secretary, the foreigner David Rizzio, before her eyes because they resent his influence on her; Darnley is taken in by the nobles and betrays Mary before he, too, dies in a mysterious explosion at his house. Mary marries Bothwell, but there is much dissension in the Kingdom over the alliance, and Bothwell is forced to leave the country, after exacting from the Lords the promise that they will maintain Mary on the throne.

However, the perfidious nobles imprison Mary; subsequently she escapes and flees to England, where her jealous rival Elizabeth puts her under close surveillance. Since she will not sign away her claim to the English throne, Elizabeth's counsellors drum up treason charges against her, and she is put to death. Before the end the two women meet (as in the Maxwell Anderson play on which the film is closely modeled, but without the play's blank verse. In real life they never met). In a flashingly dramatic and at times poignant scene, Mary reminds Elizabeth that Mary's son will one day reign over England, and Elizabeth stalks out in a rage. Bothwell has meanwhile fled to Denmark, where he is detained, and dies in prison. Mary is brought to trial for treason, at first puts up a spirited resistance, protesting her innocence, but when she hears of Bothwell's death she resigns herself to the inevitable. She goes to the scaffold calm and dignified.

mounted in all departments. March garnered excellent reviews as the bold and dashing Bothwell.

The story is well known; Mary, onetime consort of the young French king, who has died prematurely, comes to Scotland, where she is the rightful monarch. To the south, her cousin Elizabeth, Queen of England,

With Katharine Hepburn

With Katharine Hepburn

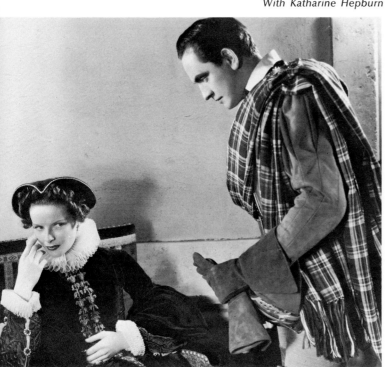

With Katharine Hepburn

Helen Hayes had played Mary to great acclaim on Broadway. In the film Florence Eldridge played Queen Elizabeth (Bette Davis among others had coveted the role) and gave a superior account of herself depicting the contradictory elements in one of history's most enigmatic and fiery sovereigns.

THE REVIEWERS
Variety:
Fredric March as Miss Hepburn's vis-a-vis in the role of the swashbuckling Bothwell is a natural and excellent choice, playing the slapdash Earl to the hilt. Florence Eldridge as Elizabeth . . . turns in a fine acting job.

Kate Cameron in the *New York Daily News:*
Fredric March's Bothwell is a forceful and finely executed performance.

Richard Watts, Jr. in the *New York Herald Tribune:*
The tragedy of the most alluring of the Stuarts, which has fascinated dramatic poets from Schiller to Maxwell Anderson and every other sensible romantic since her reign, reaches the cinema in a moving, eloquent and distinguished transcription. Although Dudley Nichols, who made the screen adaptation of Mr. Anderson's excellent blank-verse play, has changed the poetry of the dialogue to prose. He has written speech that is both graceful and powerful, thus maintaining the lyric, as well as the theatrical, effectiveness of the drama. . . . Fredric March has never been finer.

The Road to Glory

20th Century-Fox / 1936

With Lionel Barrymore and Theodore Von Eltz

THE PLAYERS

Mr. March was *Lieutenant Michael Denet* in a cast that included: Warner Baxter *(Captain Paul La Roche)*; Lionel Barrymore *(Papa La Roche)*; June Lang *(Monique)*; Gregory Ratoff *(Bouffiou)*; Victor Killian *(Regnier)*; Paul Stanton *(relief captain)*; John Qualen *(Dufious)*; Julius Tannen *(Lieutenant Tannen)*; Theodore Von Eltz *(major)*; Paul Fix *(Rigaud)*; Leonid Kinskey *(Ledoux)*; Jacques Vanoire *(courier)*; Edythe Raynore *(nurse)*; George Warrington *(old soldier)*.

THE CREATORS

Howard Hawks *(director)*; Darryl F. Zanuck *(producer)*; Joel Sayre and William Faulkner *(screenplay)*; from a story by Joel Sayre and William Faulkner; Gregg Toland *(photography)*; Hans Peters *(art direction)*; Thomas Little *(settings)*; Louis Silvers *(music)*; Edward Curtiss *(editor)*; Ed O'Fearna *(assistant director)*.

Opened at the Rivoli Theatre, New York, August 5, 1936. Running time when released, 103 minutes.

THE PICTURE

Director Howard Hawks, an expert at blending action

and romance in equally entertaining parts, guided March, Warner Baxter and Lionel Barrymore through a well-paced, carefully mounted World War I battle film, *The Road to Glory*, which boasted a script by William Faulkner and Joel Sayre in a fashion that was relatively realistic for romantic, swashbuckling 1936. The Darryl F. Zanuck production was reportedly a remake of an earlier French film, *Croix du Bois* ("Wooden Crosses") which had never been released in America. Some of the French film's battle footage, which was highly realistic and reportedly a product of the World War I French archives, had been used in other Fox war films. *The Road to Glory* did not use this footage, according to some experts, because the 1936 print was too fresh and clear throughout.

However that may be, war is shown as an adventurous but hardly glamorous pursuit. Warner Baxter is a notoriously underrated and neglected actor—lest we forget, he won one of the first Oscars, for *In Old Arizona*. He was splendid as the Captain of the 39th Regiment of the French Army, a regiment founded by Napoleon, as he reminds each fresh contingent of replacements, half of whom get lost in action and have to be replaced all over again. Baxter got across brilliantly the bone-weariness and cruel tension that accrue to a commander in such a position.

March was also fine as his lieutenant, who begins as a relatively dapper and carefree young officer and ends a sober-spirited, realistic-minded combat veteran. Lionel Barrymore, in one of his last roles before the physical misfortunes which confined him permanently to a wheelchair, was moving as the patriotic, romantic-spirited old Franco-Prussian war veteran, Baxter's father, who enlists under an assumed name as a private in his son's regiment.

With June Lang and Edythe Raynore

Of course, as per 1936 movie custom, there is a girl around somewhere, and this time it's nurse June Lang, a fresh and lovely newcomer to films who was long on looks but short on emoting, but delivered adequately enough in her love scenes with March. March and Baxter, again as per 1936-style triangle movies, are both in love with her but it is March she prefers, though she is fond of Baxter and does not wish to hurt him.

Meanwhile, on patrol the elderly Barrymore has lost

With Paul Stanton and Warner Baxter

With Warner Baxter

his courage at a crucial moment, resulting in loss of lives, and Baxter, who had not wanted him in the outfit in the first place, is chagrined. Eventually Baxter is blinded in action, and is returned to a field hospital, from which, later, with the contrite Barrymore's help, he manages to get back to an outpost where he and his father both sacrifice their lives while directing French artillery fire. Which, of course, leaves March with Miss Lang, for better or worse.

The picture is replete with fine little vignettes: a group of soldiers listening in terror to the tap-tap of enemy tunnelers planting mines beneath them that will eventually blow them to smithereens; Baxter putting out of his misery a soldier who is dying in agony on the barbed wires; Baxter's sad little speeches to each fresh wave of recruits. The film was produced with great care, and everyone connected with it seemed to approach the project with a sincere, respectful, no-nonsense attitude. March contributed a naturalistic, relaxed, underplayed performance that is among his most creditable.

THE REVIEWERS

Abel Green in *Variety:*
Baxter as the nervewracked captain and March as his equally efficient lieutenant are capital as are Barrymore and Ratoff . . . the Sayre-Faulkner screenplay is competently, often brilliantly, transmuted to the screen by Howard Hawks, whose direction is tip-top.

The Times: (London)
Mr. March and Mr. Baxter act as though they believe in it all, but Miss Lang does little more than pose for a series of photographs. [The film] is devious, sometimes inglorious, and always romantic.

Literary Digest:
A grim, terrifying, straightforward cinema report of what war is like, war anywhere. . . . A thumping triumph in objectivity.

Regina Crewe in the *New York American:*
A grim and gripping drama of the great war. The direc-

tion of Howard Hawks is fully in keeping with the excellence of the picture. Fredric March [is] the debonair hero, who grows in depth and stature under fire.

William Boehnel in the *New York World-Telegram:*
The film is at its best when it sketches swiftly and sharply the characters of the enlisted men and their valiant services at the frontline trenches. . . . The battle scenes, too, are realistic and gory enough to make one limp and perhaps realize just how monstrous war is. . . . The acting reveals an admirable integrity. Fredric March, Warner Baxter and Lionel Barrymore as his father, bring a force and validity to their characterizations.

With Lionel Barrymore, Warner Baxter and June Lang

Anthony Adverse

Warner Bros. / 1936

THE PLAYERS

Mr. March was *Anthony Adverse* in a cast that included: Olivia de Havilland *(Angela Guessippi);* Edmund Gwenn *(John Bonnyfeather);* Claude Rains *(Don Luis);* Anita Louise *(Maria)* Louis Hayward *(Denis Moore);* Gale Sondergaard *(Faith Paleologue);* Steffi Duna *(Neleta);* Billy Mauch *(Anthony Adverse, age 10);* Donald Woods *(Vincent Nolte);* Akim Tamiroff *(Carlo Cibo);* Ralph Morgan *(Debrulle);* Henry O'Neill *(Father Xavier);* Pedro de Cordoba *(Brother François);* George E. Stone *(Sancho);* Luis Alberni *(Tony Guessippi);* Fritz Leiber *(Ouvrard);* Joseph Crehan *(Captain Elisha Jorham);* Rafaela Ottiano *(Signora Bovino);* Rollo Lloyd *(Napoleon Bonaparte);* Leonard Mudie *(De Bourienne);* Marilyn Knowlden *(Florence as a child);* Mathilde Comont *(Cook Guessippi);* Eily Malyon *(Mother Superior);* J. Carroll Naish *(Major Dounet);* Scotty Beckett *(Anthony as a small boy);* Paul Sotoff *(Ferdinando);* Frank Reicher *(coach driver to Paris);* Clara Blandick *(Mrs. Jorham);* Addison Richards *(Captain Matanoza);* William Ricciardi *(coachman in Leghorn);* Grace Stafford *(Lucia);* Boris Nicholai *(courier).*

THE CREATORS

Mervyn LeRoy *(director);* Sheridan Gibney *(screenplay);* adapted from the novel by Hervey Allen; Tony Gaudio *(photographer);* Erich Wolfgang Korngold *(music);* Leo Forbstein *(musical director);* Dwight Franklin *(technical*

With Olivia de Havilland

With Olivia de Havilland

licly expressing concern as to the screen result. He need not have worried. *Anthony Adverse* was a magnificent film, considerably underrated, at the time of its original release, by the critics. Seen recently on television, it has sweep, magnificence, enormous vitality, admirable pacing, fine acting, and a score by Erich Wolfgang Korngold that is one of the loveliest and most stirring that gifted man ever wrote.

The novel had been excessively long, and talented director Mervyn LeRoy had his work cut out for him in packing it all into a fast, pageant-style 140 minutes of movie—no easy task, even with the benefit of Sheridan Gibney's taut screenplay which extracted every possible dramatic and characterizational value from its source. The end product was a sterling example of what Hollywood at its zenith could do, with lavish, painstaking production mounting, beautiful sets, absorbing characterizations, a pace that never slackened, and a kind of tragic elan about the story and the individual episodes.

The famous tale deals with Anthony Adverse, the love-child of a Spanish grandee's unhappy young wife and the soldier who is murdered by the grandee (Claude Rains) in a duel-fluke. After its mother's death, the nobleman drops the newborn baby at a girl's convent near Leghorn, Italy, where the child is raised as the school's only male. Befriended by a kindly priest, he is brought to the home of John Bonnyfeather, a Scottish-born merchant operating out of Leghorn.

Bonnyfeather is inexplicably moved by the boy's countenance, as well he should be, as it is his own grandson, the child of his unfortunate daughter. (So skillful was the storytelling that even this coincidence seemed natural.) The boy grows to manhood and falls in love with Angela (Olivia de Havilland) child of one of the domestics. Their brief idyll is interrupted when Angela's father moves elsewhere and Bonnyfeather sends Anthony across the seas to check on some of his investments abroad.

With Olivia de Havilland

consultant on eighteenth-century customs and costumes).

Opened at the Strand Theatre, New York, August 26, 1936. Running time when released, 140 minutes.

THE PICTURE
In 1933 novelist Hervey Allen published a book, *Anthony Adverse*, that proved a smash best-seller and was translated into eighteen foreign languages. Allen sold the rights to Warner Bros. a short time later, while pub-

144

In Cuba and later in Africa, Anthony almost succumbs to native decadence but is rescued by a kindly priest; he returns home just in time to prevent Bonnyfeather's associate, Faith (Gale Sondergaard), with whom Anthony has never been on friendly terms, from inheriting Bonnyfeather's property, the now-dead merchant's will stating that all is to go to Anthony if he reappears within a certain time. Faith is meanwhile involved with the old nobleman who had killed Anthony's soldier father (superbly played by Claude Rains) and later she becomes his wife.

Rains and Faith know Anthony's origin and try to destroy him, but he circumvents their plans. In Paris, Anthony, who still dreams of Angela, his first and only love, finds her, now a famous opera singer. Later he learns to his disenchantment that she is Napoleon's mistress. Angela had borne him a son and though she still loves Anthony, she realizes that life has permanently separated them and sends the boy to him. Anthony and his son set out for a new life in America, and in one of the screen's most movingly summational closing scenes, the saddened Anthony and the eager child talk of making their mutual name, "Anthony Adverse" (chosen years before by Bonnyfeather because he believed the boy truly a child of adversity) mean something good and permanent in the new land.

The absorbing plot, despite its coincidences and telegraphed situations, was a stirring one by any standards of storytelling and moviemaking, and the superb performances of Miss Sondergaard, Rains, Gwenn and others helped to give it much human immediacy. March was quite fine in the role of Anthony, underplaying gracefully so as to keep the characterization moving forward easily through the numerous episodes of the film (not an easy feat in pageant-style epics like this) and although his approach was misunderstood by the 1936 critics and got a mixed reaction, as seen in 1971

With Olivia de Havilland

With Steffi Duna

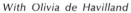

With Olivia de Havilland

the star's skill and restraint can be more fittingly respected and appreciated.

The picture was an excellent example of the better type of buoyant historical epic that so distinguished mid-1930s cinematic output at its best. The direction and cutting were sharply disciplined, and many films of the period radiated creative elan and excitement and the painstaking enthusiasm of a host of creative folk in all categories. *Anthony Adverse*, though appreciated at

Haranguing the natives (Pedro de Cordoba is priest at left)

present only by a small coterie of admirers, deserves wider recognition as a masterpiece of its kind, a film made with enormous gusto, and indeed with that commitment that is the sincerest form of love and that so rarely is evinced in films today. And the genius Korngold's heart-stopping recapitulation of his superb musical leitmotifs in the closing scene will leave you in a glow.

With J. Carroll Naish

The Times: (London)
There is much efficient entertainment here, though it would be much better if it were not all collected in one film, since apart from all other reasons, the connections between the incidents are taken more slowly than the incidents themselves, and the movement of the whole is continuously checked. . . . The crowd scenes are well-designed, and there is a mass of local colour, which is apparently the result of prodigious research. The architecture, interiors and dresses are often interesting, and there is a remarkable reconstruction of an opera by Monteverde which might well have lasted much longer, for in this context his music has a wonderful effect on the spirits. Mr. Fredric March in the part of Anthony is every inch a hero, and Miss Olivia de Havilland has great charm.

Punch (London):
Probably it was a mistake to try to make a picture of so diffuse a book as *Anthony Adverse*. It must have been extremely difficult to compress the story even within its present limits of two hours and twenty minutes—and that is about forty minutes too long. Fredric March is, of course, extremely competent.

Howard Barnes in the *New York Herald Tribune:*
The inevitable screen transcription of Hervey Allen's mammoth best-seller . . . has been accomplished in a handsome and spectacular production. Populated with a huge cast and bulging with picaresque adventure and romance, it richly deserves one of Hollywood's favorite adjectives—colossal. . . . The show is fairly glutted with plot and counter-plot and is apt to make one feel that one is witnessing a serial run off continuously at a single performance. Sheridan Gibney's adaptation has been adroit, considering the problems in conversion and the frowns of the censors. . . . Fredric March, in the title role, is rather baffled by the exigencies of a characterization which had scant dimensions even in the novel. He plays the part for its color and excitement rather than attempting to make it credible or sympathetic.

Frank S. Nugent in *The New York Times:*
The fault, in my opinion, is less with the mammoth dimensions of the novel—which admittedly offered a problem to the screen adapters—than with the complete aimlessness with which the Warners effected their transcription. Scene after scene is presented almost as Mr. Allen described it, but the people in them are substanceless as dreams. Things happen, changes come, subtitles assure us that Anthony is at the crossroads, but somehow we are not convinced that a real crisis impends. Our faith is less in Mr. Allen than in Mervyn LeRoy and the Warners; we know that Anthony's soul is on the alkaline side. . . . Fredric March is a thoroughly spiritless Anthony the Man.

With Janet Gaynor, Adolphe Menjou,
Lionel Stander and Vince Barnett

A Star Is Born

Selznick-International   United Artists / 1937

THE PLAYERS
Mr. March was *Norman Maine* in a cast that included:
Janet Gaynor (*Esther Blodgett-Vicki Lester*); Adolphe
Menjou (*Oliver Niles*); May Robson (*Lettie*); Andy De-
vine (*Danny McGuire*); Lionel Stander (*Libby*); Elizabeth
Jenns (*Anita Regis*); Edgar Kennedy (*Pop Randall*); Owen
Moore (*Casey Burke*); J. C. Nugent (*Theodore Smythe*);
Clara Blandick (*Aunt Mattie*); A. W. Sweatt (*Esther's
brother*); Peggy Wood (*Miss Phillips, a clerk*); Adrian
Rosely (*Harris*); Arthur Hoyt (*Ward*); Guinn (Big-Boy)
Williams (*posture coach*); Vince Barnett (*Otto Friedl*);
Paul Stanton (*Academy Awards speaker*); Franklin Pang-
born (*Billy Moon*).

THE CREATORS
William A. Wellman (*director*); David O. Selznick (*producer*); Dorothy Parker, Alan Campbell and Robert Carson (*screenplay*); from a story by William A. Wellman
and Robert Carson; Max Steiner (*music*); color by Technicolor; Eric Stacey (*assistant director*); Lansing C. Holden (*color designer*); W. Howard Greene (*photography*);
Lyle Wheeler (*art direction*); Omar Kiam (*costumes*);
James E. Newcom (*film editor*); Edward Boyle (*interior
decoration*); Natalie Kalmus (*color supervision*).

With Janet Gaynor at court

With Janet Gaynor

With Janet Gaynor

Opened at Radio City Music Hall, New York, April 22, 1937. Running time when released, 98 minutes.

THE PICTURE

So much has been written about the 1937 *A Star Is Born* that protracted comment on it at this late date seems almost superfluous. March regards it as one of the best films he ever made. It is certainly one of his "top three" favorites, the others reportedly being *The Best Years of Our Lives* (1946) and *Laughter* (1930). He was nominated for the 1937 Academy Award for *A Star Is Born*

but lost out to Spencer Tracy, whose *Captains Courageous* performance won that year. Many feel the Oscar should have gone to March. Certainly he was never finer, that year he reached forty, than as the fading screen star who comes upon an unsure young girl, Janet Gaynor, who is trying to get a foothold in Hollywood, helps her to acting fame and then has to stand by in the shadows of his own fading stardom while she climbs to the heights.

The idea wasn't exactly a novel one, but the treatment redeemed it. Reportedly the picture was based on the careers of both John Barrymore and silent star John Gilbert, who had died the year before, 1936, after a career that had gone downhill when his speaking voice failed to impress talkie fans. Barrymore, who had the best voice of any actor in Hollywood, was the victim of another problem: drink, plus poor health. He lingered until 1942, but his stardom had ended by 1934. In the Gilbert case there was an interesting parallel to *A Star Is Born*. The young wife he had divorced in 1934, Virginia Bruce, had by the time of his death become a rising star.

But enough of parallels, and back to the film, which was one of the most piercing and true ever made about Hollywood. There was throughout an authentic feel about it, and a bitter reality that was at all times present, for all its tender romanticism and poignant drama. David O. Selznick provided it with a glossy and painstaking production mounting, and its creators in all departments delivered in superior style, from director William Wellman on down. Max Steiner contributed one of his most eloquent scores, Dorothy Parker, Alan Campbell and Robert Carson got across a sense of the real, behind-the-scenes film capital in their taut, well-written and expressive screenplay, and the Technicolor process, supervised by Natalie Kalmus, reproduced handsomely and complemented the action well. (A sad note was struck when onetime famed silent director Marshall Neilan was featured in a bit part in a scene where March

With Janet Gaynor

is humiliated and punched by his scornful former publicity aide.)

Miss Gaynor in early 1937 was in real life on the verge of starring in her own private drama, labeled *A Star Is Dying,* for this onetime (1928) Oscar-winner and Fox Films luminary of the early thirties had not had a good picture in several years, and her screen appearances had grown infrequent. Her own ups-and-downs careerwise may have helped her in giving her finest screen performance.

March was never more natural, never more sincere, never more *right* as tragic Norman Maine, a man of fundamentally decent instincts ruined by his hedonism and self-destructive tendencies. As his young wife's star ascends, he slips to all-out has-been status; she rescues him from a jail term for drunken driving, and when he overhears his former producer (Adolphe Menjou in a fine performance) telling his wife that he has become only a shell of what he once was, he gets up, puts on one final, smiling, reassuring scene for his worried wife, and then walks into the sea in a famous scene that for thirty-four years has been the most discussed among the many well-discussed scenes of this movie masterpiece.

The film was remade in 1954 with Judy Garland and James Mason, and while both were excellent, the public's chief affection is still reserved for the 1937 version, one of those that will go down in Hollywood and film buff annals as a milestone in fine cinema.

THE REVIEWERS

Howard Barnes in the *New York Herald Tribune:*
Hollywood has turned brilliantly introspective in [this film].... The photoplay has its fabulous aspects, but through it runs a core of honesty that makes it the most remarkable account of picture making that has yet reached the stage or screen. The authors have achieved narrative substance and fidelity of detail.... William Wellman has directed the script superbly, employing Technicolor without affectation and bridging a variety of moods triumphantly. With Fredric March, Janet Gaynor and the supporting players handling their roles with restrained intensity, the work becomes an exciting document of the world's biggest showbusiness, and an exciting entertainment. It has been clothed in such rich language, telling performances and splendid directorial handling that the tale and the few people in it become a vital and revealing cross-section of the motion picture capital.... Mr. March has the difficult assignment of acting an actor whose acting days are ended, but he does it with flair and versatility. It is a cruel, authoritative and perfectly modulated portrait that he draws.... [Miss Gaynor's] is a true and moving performance that holds the show together emotionally.

Frank Nugent in *The New York Times:*
A Hollywood story of, by and for its people ... the most accurate mirror ever held before the glittering, tinseled, trivial, generous, cruel and ecstatic world that is Hollywood.... Here are violence and understanding in [the]

With Janet Gaynor

writing, a feeling for telling detail, and a sympathy for the people they are touching. It is not a maudlin picture ... Janet Gaynor's movie-struck Esther Blodgett is not a caricature. Fredric March's waning Norman Maine is not an outrageous ham.... Capitally played all down the line. Its script is bright, inventive and forceful. Mr. Wellman's direction is expert.

Kate Cameron in the *New York Daily News:*
[The film] gives Miss Gaynor an opportunity to display her considerable talents as a comedienne, and as an emotional actress, too.... Her co-star, Fredric March, gives one of the best performances of his career as the glamorous, irresponsible, impulsive and generous screen star Norman Maine.... The appeal is not in its originality of plot but in its brilliantly written dialogue, its human delineation of character, the excellence of William Wellman's direction and the superb work of the cast, particularly that of the two principal players.

Ivan Spear in *Boxoffice:*
A fine and workmanlike performance has come to be expected from Fredric March in any part he undertakes and, as Janet Gaynor's husband, he doesn't disappoint. In fact, he adds new laurels to his reputation as one of pictures' finest actors by showing that he is a master of light comedy in the film's early footage.

Nothing Sacred

Selznick-International   United Artists / 1937

THE PLAYERS
Mr. March was *Wally Cook* in a cast that included: Carole Lombard *(Hazel Flagg)*; Charles Winninger *(Dr. Downer)*; Walter Connolly *(Stone)*; Sig Rumann *(Dr. Eggelhoffer)*; Frank Fay *(master of ceremonies)*; Maxie Rosenbloom *(Max)*; Margaret Hamilton *(drug store lady)*; Troy Brown *(Ernest Walker)*; Hattie McDaniel *(Mrs. Walker)*; Olin Howland *(baggage man)*; George Chandler *(photographer)*; Claire Du Brey *(Miss Rafferty)*; John Qualen *(Swede fireman)*; Charles Richman *(mayor)*; Alex Schoenberg *(Dr. Kochinwasser)*; Monte Woolley *(Dr. Vunch)*; Alex Novinsky *(Dr. Marachuffsky)*; Aileen Pringle *(Mrs. Bullock)*; Hedda Hopper *(dowager)*; Dick Rich *(Moe)*; Katherine Shelton *(Dr. Downer's nurse)*; A. W. Sweatt *(office boy)*; Clarence Wilson *(Mr. Watson)*; Betty Douglas *("Helen of Troy")*; Eleanor Troy *("Catherine of Russia")*; Monica Bannister *("Pocahontas")*; Jinx Falkenberg *("Katinka")*; Margaret Lyman *("Salome")*; Shirley Chambers *("Lady Godiva")*.

THE CREATORS
William A. Wellman *(director)*; David O. Selznick *(producer)*; Ben Hecht *(screenplay)*; from a story by James H. Street; W. Howard Greene *(photography; color by Technicolor;* Natalie Kalmus *(color supervision)*.

Opened at Radio City Music Hall, New York, November 25, 1937. Running time when released, 75 minutes.

THE PICTURE
Seeking to vary his pace and image after his major dramatic triumph in the poignant *A Star Is Born*, March reteamed with director William Wellman for the second of the two pictures under his Selznick deal—this time in a screwball comedy, and one of the best of its genre. The film revealed March as one of the most proficient farceurs around and indicated that Cary Grant had better look to his laurels. On hand to keep March's comic moods sharp, fancy, and pointed was Carole Lombard, who had appeared with March (and Grant) in 1933's *The Eagle and the Hawk*. It will be recalled that in that film Grant was a dour lad indeed and Lombard was on hand for two sexy scenes, then dismissed. Grant and Lombard had since climbed to the top of the screwball-comedy heap. Lombard, commencing with *Twentieth Century* in 1934, had demonstrated a surprisingly apt comic sense and the year before *Nothing Sacred* had brought her a sensational success in *My Man Godfrey*.

   March and Lombard complemented each other very well indeed in *Nothing Sacred*, a pot-pourri of shrewdly

Socking Carole Lombard

With Carole Lombard

put together zaniness from the typewriter of Ben Hecht (who could deliver in fine style when not forced to tamper with Noel Coward originals, as in *Design for Living*.)

The hilarious plot dealt with a Vermont working girl who is told by her doctor that she has radium poisoning and only a short time to live. Later her doctor tells her he was wrong and that she is perfectly sound, but meanwhile reporter March has gotten wind of her case. March is a circulation-crazy newsman on a New York tabloid of the more hysterical kind presided over by dyspeptic managing editor Walter Connolly, who has just demoted him for trying to pass off a New York Negro as the ''Sultan of Marzipan'' who reportedly will donate $500,000,000 for an art institute. When the Negro's wife and kids expose him before a dignified gath-

ering at a banquet, March is demoted to writing obits.

Anxious to get out of his rut, March seeks to parlay Lombard's radium poisoning into a headline-attracting tear jamboree. Hazel is brought by the paper to New York with much fanfare, wined and dined and given a banquet where sob sisters drool over her and she passes out from drunkenness. March and Connolly inform the concerned gathering of notables that her illness has reasserted itself and carry her sepulchrally from the hall. At Madison Square Garden and other public places, people weep at sight of her and hold ''minutes of respect'' for the soon-to-be departed.

When the editor gets suspicious as to Hazel's true condition, he demands that a team of doctors examine her. This leads to the famous fight scene, in which March (whom she has cued in on her radiant health by

With Walter Connolly and Mike Mazurki

With Olin Howland

151

With Carole Lombard

now) roughs her up and then punches her right on the snoot to get her in the proper physical condition for her medical examination.

Meanwhile a delegation of prominent citizens come to visit Hazel. They learn the truth: that she will not die after all, and beg her to "die" and then quietly disappear, so as to save her "sponsors" faces. Hazel and her reporter are now in love with each other and she has lost all interest in continuing the hoax. Hazel's "death" is therefore properly announced and duly mourned while the lovebirds sneak off for a honeymoon. Ben Hecht, of *Front Page* fame, knew his newspapers and newspapermen backwards and forwards, and the journalistic scenes are fast-paced and filled with authentic atmosphere. The film's seventy-five-minute running time is well-edited for brisk, terse results and the laughs never flag. The film was photographed in Technicolor, in this case a superfluity, but some handsome shots did prove that the new color process was going to be a major asset to the screen.

Nothing Sacred was reincarnated in 1953 as a Broadway musical called *Hazel Flagg*, and later as a Martin and Lewis film romp, *Living It Up*, that was inferior by miles to its source.

THE REVIEWERS

Photoplay:
Aided by color, an extremely smart Ben Hecht script and the competent direction of William Wellman, Carole Lombard and Fredric March have turned in a wild comedy drama that for this reviewer tops *My Man God-*frey. It may seem unbelievable to say that a plot featuring Carole and Fred punching each other on the chin has a delicate theme, but it really has. Seriously dramatized, the plot might be grim indeed, but, satirized, it is packed with irrepressible laughter, novelty and strange tenderness. . . . Miss Lombard is at her most scintillating and her darkened hair becomes her. March has not been so delightfully cast since *The Royal Family*. Winninger and Walter Connolly contribute much to the picture's importance and the wrestling match, the Frank Fay tableaux honoring heroines of history, and the Sultan's dinner are brilliant nonsense. It's among the ranking laugh films of all time.

Life:
Acted with finesse by an unbeatable pair of light comedy experts, Carole Lombard and Fredric March.

Bland Johaneson in the *New York Mirror:*
An extravagant burlesque of [the] newspaper business . . . [a] hilarious comedy. . . . Mr. Hecht, long famed as the roguish lambaster of the business which developed him, builds a fantastic tale. Incredible, it is good fun, providing slapstick mirth for the fans, inside chortles for the press. It is blessed with the exuberant presence of Fredric March and Carole Lombard, Walter Connolly and Maxie Rosenbloom. Lively direction, witty dialogue, handsome mounting, effective Technicolor photography combine to lend it distinction. . . . Miss Lombard and March excel in playing such lunatic comedy and they give their fans their rousing best.

With Walter Connolly

Regina Crewe in the *New York Journal-American:*
Carole and Fred carry the complete burden of the picture on their competent shoulders, for it is they who sustain the rapid-fire story all the way with expertly paced performances that never falter. . . . William Wellman has added to his copious credits with keen, thrusting direction of the satire. And there must be laurel leaves, too, for the screen storyteller, Ben Hecht.

With Carole Lombard

The Buccaneer

Paramount / 1938

THE PLAYERS

Mr. March was *Jean Lafitte* in a cast that included: Franciska Gaal *(Gretchen);* Margot Grahame *(Annette de Remy);* Akim Tamiroff *(Dominique You);* Walter Brennan *(Ezra Peavey);* Anthony Quinn *(Beluche);* Ian Keith *(Senator Crawford);* Douglas Dumbrille *(Senator Claiborne);* Beulah Bondi *(Aunt Charlotte);* Robert Barrat *(Captain Brown);* Fred Kohler *(Gramby);* Hugh Sothern *(Andrew Jackson);* John Rogers *(Mouse);* Hans Steinke *(Tarsus);* Stanley Andrews *(collector of port);* Spring Byington *(Dolly Madison);* Montagu Love *(Admiral Cockburn);* Louise Campbell *(Marie de Remy);* Eric Stanley *(General Ross);* Gilbert Emery *(Captain Lockyer);* Evelyn Keyes *(Madeleine);* Holmes Herbert *(McWilliams);* Francis J. McDonald *(Camden Blount);* Frank Melton *(Lieutenant Shreve);* Jack Hubbard *(Charles);* Richard Denning *(Captain Reid);* Lina Basquette *(Roxane);* John Patterson *(young blade);* Other cast members: Reginald Sheffield, Barry Norton, John Sutton, Mae Busch, Philo McCullough, Ralph Lewis, E. J. Le Saint, Ed Brady, Charlotte Wynters, Crauford Kent, James Craig, Stanhope Wheatcroft, Charles Morton, Ethel Clayton, Maude Fealy, Jane Keckley.

THE CREATORS

Cecil B. De Mille *(producer and director);* William LeBaron *(executive producer);* William H. Pine *(associate producer);* Edwin Justus Mayer, C. Gardner Sullivan, Harold Lamb *(screenplay);* adaptation by Jeanie MacPherson of Lyle Saxon's *Lafitte the Pirate;* George Antheil *(music);* Victor Milner *(photography);* Anne Bauchens *(film editor);* Boris Morros *(musical director);* Farciot Edouart and Dewey Wrigley *(special effects);* Edwin Maxwell *(dialogue supervision);* Harry Lindgren *(sound).*

Opened at the Paramount Theatre, New York, February 16, 1938. Running time when released, 124 minutes.

In his dressing room on the set

THE PICTURE

Cecil B. De Mille and March, in their first picture together since 1932's *The Sign of the Cross*, teamed up for a lively depiction of the adventure, on sea and land, in war and love, of colorful privateer Jean Lafitte, who helped the Americans win the War of 1812 against the British. March went through the scenes with verve, though his French accent was criticized for what was alleged to be its lack of authenticity. His performance was also faulted by some critics as artificial, mannered, and overdone. Viewed after several decades, his portrayal holds up quite well, and indeed gives every evidence of being well thought out and cleverly shaded. What is evident after the passage of so many years is that March was obviously experimenting with new approaches. With the instincts of the artist he was, he was searching for new wellsprings of creative vitality and imaginative character-delineation. The 1938 critics, who were accustomed to seeing him project a certain personality with only minor variations were understandably puzzled by his Lafitte. It must also be kept in mind that De Mille was partly responsible for the performance; whether for better or worse remains a moot point.

Certainly the film was lavishly produced, and it introduced new actress Franciska Gaal (who later, a la Anna Sten, drifted into obscurity). Margot Grahame was fine as another of March's loves, and sterling character actors

With Franciska Gaal, Akim Tamiroff and Anthony Quinn

like Gilbert Emery, Beulah Bondi, Walter Brennan and Akim Tamiroff made more than their usual contributions. Of course, De Mille being De Mille, the picture emphasized action, excitement, pageantry, DeMille-style heroics; events move at such speed and with such De-Millean dispatch that the wonder is that March got to experiment with characterization at all.

The rambling, confused and episodic story (the play was *not* the thing in this particular movie) covered the adventures of the brazen Lafitte, who from his lair near New Orleans preys on the ships of every nation except the United States. He rescues Miss Gaal from a vessel he has ransacked, and she falls in love with him; he, however, loves a New Orleans belle, Margot Grahame. Lafitte proves himself a good friend of the Americans when war breaks out between the United States and Great Britain, his earthy, adventurous, underdog temperament being more attuned to their cause than to that of the British, whom he considers rigid, stuffy and authoritarian. Lafitte aids General Jackson at the Battle of New Orleans, but when it is learned that he had burned a boat in which the New Orleans belle's sister had been a passenger, there are complications and soon he is back to his pirating activities in the bayous. There is talk of a pardon from President Madison, and other episodic plot strands get entangled in the skein. As in all good De-Mille pictures, however, the plot strands and variegated romancing played second fiddle to the swashbuckling.

THE REVIEWERS
Photoplay:
With a stirring story woven from the fabric of our country's history, a cast of exceptional attainments, lavish production and some incredibly beautiful photography, C. B. De Mille once again proves his magic in the art of

With Franciska Gaal

picturing action on the screen. From the opening sequence with the burning and gutting of the White House at Washington to the climax in the heroic battle of New Orleans, it is stunning drama, and nothing Mr. De Mille has directed since 1913 can touch it.... There are so many splendid performances it is hard to know where to begin to give credit.... March puts over a fine job;

Margot Grahame does well in a sympathetic role; Walter Brennan as (General Jackson's) orderly is a standout, as is Akim Tamiroff as Lafitte's sidekick. Our plaudits go to Mr. De Mille himself, however, for one of the most impressive screen documents toward entertainment and patriotic education ever presented.

Howard Barnes in the *New York Herald Tribune:*
Mr. March, who has given some uncommonly good performances recently, is disappointing as Lafitte. He assumes a French accent awkwardly and plays the part in a quasi-swashbuckling manner that is far from persuasive. Always he is too palpably Mr. March in 1812 costumes.

Archer Winsten in the *New York Post:*
The piratical swashbuckling, the scenes of battle and the historical sets have been treated in the Cecil B. De Mille manner, which is to say lavishly and with plenty of action.... It would be difficult to think of anyone who would better fit the role of Lafitte than March. His French accent may not be all that the French could require, but it suffices, and for the rest, he is the very devil of a patriotic bold fellow.

Rose Pelswick in the *New York Journal-American:*
A grand show, an exciting blood-and-thunder entertainment packed with enough action and color to suit the most avid of adventure-yarn enthusiasts. It was filmed on a large and impressive scale. The historical background is as accurate as any fictionalized account could be, and the story is expertly played by a troupe of players who seem to have had as much fun making the picture as audiences will have enjoying it. March, who assumes a French accent for the role, [is] outstanding.

With Gilbert Emery, Akim Tamiroff and Franciska Gaal

With Virginia Bruce

There Goes My Heart

Hal Roach   United Artists / 1938

THE PLAYERS
Mr. March was *Bill Spencer* in a cast that included: Virginia Bruce *(Joan Butterfield)*; Patsy Kelly *(Peggy O'Brien)*; Nancy Carroll *(Dorothy Moore)*; Alan Mowbray *(Pennypacker)*; Eugene Pallette *(editor Stevens)*; Claude Gillingwater *(Cyrus Butterfield)*; Arthur Lake *(Flash Fisher)*; Harry Langdon *(minister)*; Etienne Girardot *(secretary)*; Robert Armstrong *(Detective O'Brien)*; Irving Bacon *(floorwalker)*; Irving Pichel *(attorney)*; Sid Saylor *(Robinson)*; Mary Field *(Mrs. Crud)*.

THE CREATORS
Norman Z. McLeod *(director)*; Milton H. Bren *(producer)*; Jack Jevne and Eddie Moran *(screenplay)*; based on an original story by Ed Sullivan; Norbert Brodine *(photography)*; Marvin Hatley *(musical director)*; William Terhune *(editor)*.

Opened at Radio City Music Hall, October 13, 1938. Running time when released, 91 minutes.

THE PICTURE
After appearing briefly on the New York stage, March went back to Hollywood and resumed picture-making, signing with Hal Roach for a rather weak imitation of *It Happened One Night*. Virginia Bruce played opposite

With Virginia Bruce

With Virginia Bruce

him. Titled *There Goes My Heart,* the film limped its way through an hour and a half with much scurrying about and very little spontaneous fun. The plot was so close to the original that the critics harped on the matter when the film was released, nor were the production standards up to those of the earlier film or Norman Z. McLeod's direction up to Frank Capra's. Nor did Virginia Bruce's comedy duplicate that of Claudette Colbert in the earlier film or March's that of Gable, granting that it was a tough act to follow.

Again we have the one about the headstrong, bubble-headed heiress who is bored with her riches and wants to see what life is like and via first-hand experience among the lower classes. She disappears from the yacht of her grandfather, department store tycoon Claude Gillingwater, and there is a Niagara of publicity about it. Of course, a reporter (March) is assigned by his editor to track her down and get the story straight from the mare's mouth; also of course, he falls in love with her gradually and she with him.

There's also the bit about the reporter writing an exposé of the heroine's life and adventures, then tearing it up due to the proddings of conscience—and love, but back at the paper, the shark editor pieces it together and publishes it anyway, whereupon a slew of fresh misunderstandings are let loose.

The heiress meanwhile has acquired a humble job in her grandfather's department store under an assumed name. Here she is befriended by another shopgirl, Patsy Kelly, who according to some critics of 1938 stole the show. (She is still doing it, as witness her recent Tony award.) Naturally the reporter trails the heiress to the department store and there are more complications, and (to make an end of the business) the in-love-but-pridefully-stubborn couple are duped by similar telegrams from interested friends into going to the same place at the same time—where they are forthwith married by Parson Harry Langdon.

March was not at his best here, not that he had that much to work with; nor was Miss Bruce. The character actors did best: Miss Kelly, Pallette, Gillingwater. Nancy Carroll was seen in a small part, although seven years before, she had *co-starred* with March. The role did nothing to restore her lost filmic eminence. Recent viewings reveal the film as far below March's previous standards in its production, direction and general mounting, and as eminently forgettable in 1971 as it was in 1938—more so, in fact.

With Virginia Bruce

With Eugene Pallette

With Nancy Carroll

THE REVIEWERS

Photoplay:

The failure of this sometimes amusing, sometimes embarrassing film must be assigned to the miscasting of Fredric March and to the dated story. Surely by now you're tired of seeing the *It Happened One Night* formula; and surely March has never been more unhappy in a role. He plays the news reporter who tracks down Virginia Bruce, runaway heiress who is bored with riches and wants to live as the People do. She is befriended by Patsy Kelly, a shopgirl—and here Patsy is in her element. She gets most of the laughs and manages to lift the show from the elegant Miss Bruce and the bewildered Fredric. Eugene Pallette shouts and worries as the editor, Nancy Carroll returns to the screen as another shopgirl but she does not Come Back. If you are still a devotee of the "mad mad fun" school, you will probably enjoy this.

Frank S. Nugent in *The New York Times:*

It cannot be mere coincidence that Hal Roach's first production this year, *Merrily We Live*, had all the earmarks of *My Man Godfrey*, and that his second, *There Goes My Heart*...is *It Happened One Night* without the transcontinental bus. If Mr. Roach is in the market for other choice originals, we should be glad to suggest *Mr. Deeds*, *Mutiny on the Bounty*, and *Ruggles of Red Gap*. Frankly, though, we prefer our revivals straight and with the original casts; imitations so seldom do justice to the source work.... Give the boys credit: they know a good comedy when they see one. It's the next best thing to knowing a good comedy when they write one.... Fredric March and Virginia Bruce play it rather more soberly than Clark Gable and Claudette Colbert did and the script—in its few moments of originality— is not half so resourceful as the classic Robert Riskin- S. H. Adams job.... This admittedly is a prejudiced report; we can't help being prejudiced against copycats.

Howard Barnes in the *New York Herald Tribune:*

While the plot structure remains familiar and feeble, there is enough incidental nonsense to take your mind off it a good deal of the time. The clowning is random, but it is generally refreshing.... Virginia Bruce and Fredric March are pleasant performers, but they don't even begin to make the characters plausible.... A moderately beguiling show.

With Virginia Bruce and Alan Mowbray

159

Trade Winds

Walter Wanger   United Artists / 1939

THE PLAYERS
Mr. March was *Sam Wye* in a cast that included: Joan Bennett *(Kay Kerrigan)*; Ralph Bellamy *(Blodgett)*; Ann Sothern *(Jean)*; Sidney Blackmer *(Thomas Bruhm II)*; Thomas Mitchell *(Chief of Detectives)*; Robert Elliott *(Detective Faulkner)*; Patricia Fair *(Peggy)*; Wilma Francis *(Judy)*; Phyllis Barry *(Ruth)*; Dorothy Tree *(Clara)*; Kay Linaker *(Grace)*; Linda Winters *(Ann)*; Walter Byron *(Bob)*; Wilson Benge *(butler)*; Harry Paine *(captain)*.

THE CREATORS
Tay Garnett *(director)*; Walter Wanger *(producer)*; Dorothy Parker, Alan Campbell, Frank R. Adams *(screenplay)*; based on a story by Tay Garnett; Rudolph Mate *(photography)*; James B. Shackleford *(special photography)*; Dorothy Spencer, Walt Reynolds *(editors)*.

Opened at Radio City Music Hall, January 12, 1939. Running time when released, 93 minutes.

With Joan Bennett, Ralph Bellamy and Ann Sothern

With Joan Bennett

THE PICTURE

This film had its origin in a trip around the world director Tay Garnett had taken several years before on his yacht. En route he photographed Japanese street scenes, Singapore dives, Bombay dwellings and assorted views of Shanghai and other Oriental scenic wonders. He then decided to make professional use of this "process-screen" potential, and dreamed up a story to put in front of it. He enlisted the services of Dorothy Parker, Alan Campbell, and Frank R. Adams, who presented him with a screenplay that was witty, fast-paced, and

With Ethelreda Leopold

verbally and situationally sparking. For stars he got Fredric March and Joan Bennett, with Walter Wanger producing.

Though a great deal of the Garnett travel footage was used as background, there was still enough left over for him and March to consider doing still another travel-oriented screenplay. This, however, never materialized,

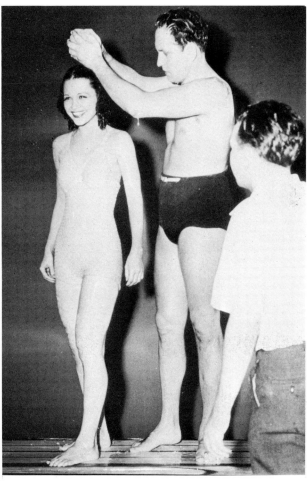

Mineral oil is used as "imitation water" because it photographs "wet." Here March gives a cast member an oil bath while property man assists.

primarily because *Trade Winds* was far from a boxoffice wow, despite its merits. Not that it was flawless; one critic, at a loss as to how to characterize the odd result, which was neither romance, melodrama, mystery nor travelogue (or at least none of these in pure, unadulterated, recognizable form), came up with a term: "a travestory comi-romance—or dramalogue of travesty."

March was at his best as the outwardly callous but inwardly human criminal investigator from San Francisco who rushes halfway across the world trailing an exotic and elusive woman (Joan Bennett) with a racy past in 'Frisco. Seems she is wanted for murder. During the chase Miss Bennett dyes her hair from blonde to brunette (thus giving *Trade Winds* publicity mileage on her "Hedy Lamarr look-alike" gimmick—and to be fair,

161

With Ralph Bellamy and Joan Bennett

she *did* look like Lamarr in her brunette sequences).

There is much scurrying and chasing and reverse-chasing, all interlarded with comic travesty and sparkling wise-talk, with March, of course developing an ever-increasing affection for his quarry. Naturally, it turns out that the blonde-brunette charmer didn't kill that guy back in San Francisco at all. But, as one critic so aptly noted, the murder-mystery stuff wasn't even up to the Charlie Chan level, and the picture was forced to rely for its primary substance and entertainment value on that brittle, brilliant Parker-Campbell-Adams dialogue, of which there was plenty—ably abetted by March's and Bennett's fast-paced, sharp performances; and the authentic Garnett location shots were no handicap.

With Joan Bennett

THE REVIEWERS

The New Yorker:
There is . . . not only this nice supply of travel, romance, and crime but an unusual sparkle to the lines, a wicked and spry turn of phrase.

William Boehnel in the *New York World-Telegram:*
Admirably interpreted by Fredric March. . . . Amusing as the script is, I wish it had a more convincing ending and that such fine acting, writing and directing talent weren't wasted on such a formularized plot. But apparently the best thing to do is to take no chances in these stories of banter and murder. This latest imbroglio, brash and bold as its many predecessors, moves ingeniously in the old zig-zag grooves.

Bland Johaneson in the *New York Mirror:*
Hollywood's most ancient and revered device for generating suspense, "the chase," reaches its full flower in [this film]; a breezy little comedy, it features most attractive players, provides them with exotic backgrounds, jaunty enough dialogue. The story, however, is one of those "you chase me—now I'll chase you" affairs in which the grinding of the plot machinery can be heard plainly, above the artificial tumult it creates. . . . [The stars] are such substantial favorites that their fans will enjoy [this film] which undeniably does build to a whirlwind finish.

Kate Cameron in the *New York Daily News:*
There isn't the hilarious slapstick element to [this flim] that distinguished "Nothing Sacred," but March's performance . . . is on a par with his work as the reporter in the earlier comedy. . . . He speaks the wittily-written dialogue with as great an appreciation of its comic intent as though he had written it himself. . . . An absorbing and thoroughly entertaining adventure film.

With Joan Crawford

Susan and God

Metro-Goldwyn-Mayer / 1940

THE PLAYERS
Mr. March was *Barrie Trexel* in a cast that included: Joan Crawford *(Susan Trexel)*; Ruth Hussey *(Charlotte)*; John Carroll *(Clyde)*; Rita Hayworth *(Leonora)*; Nigel Bruce *(Hutchie)*; Bruce Cabot *(Michael)*; Rita Quigley *(Blossom)*; Rose Hobart *(Irene)*; Constance Collier *(Lady Wigstaff)*; Gloria De Haven *(Enid)*; Richard O. Crane *(Bob)*; Norma Mitchell *(Paige)*; Marjorie Main *(Mary)*; Aldrich Bowker *(Patrick)*.

THE CREATORS
George Cukor *(director)*; Hunt Stromberg *(producer)*; Anita Loos *(screenplay)*; based on the play by Rachel Crothers; Robert Planck *(photography)*; Cedric Gibbons *(art direction)*; Herbert Stothart *(music)*; Adrian *(costumes)*; William H. Terhune *(editor)*.

Opened at the Capitol Theatre, New York, July 11, 1940. Running time when released, 117 minutes.

THE PICTURE
After a year and a half off the screen, March returned to Hollywood to co-star with Joan Crawford in Metro-Goldwyn-Mayer's *Susan and God*, adapted from the play by Rachel Crothers, which had starred Gertrude Lawrence on Broadway. George Cukor directed the stars with his customary incisiveness and the film not only signalled an advance in Miss Crawford's acting expertise

(Cukor helped her to deepen her projection and broaden her range over several pictures in this period) but also gave March a winning and likeable part which he got across with his customary naturalness and charm.

As Barrie Trexel, a society figure who has been driven

With Joan Crawford

163

to drink as an escape from his frivolous and insensitive wife, Susan (Crawford), he finds himself initially hopeful of a change in their barren and neglect-ridden marital status when Susan comes home from Europe agog over a new religious fad she has discovered, one that involves a fancy variety of do-goodism. She tries to foist her newfound spiritual approach on her bored society friends but they are too jaded and preoccupied with their own worldly problems to take her seriously.

Barrie himself comes to realize that this is just the latest manifestation of Susan's novelty-chasing, to fend off the essential ennui of her nature. Susan's friends become annoyed when her stupid meddling interferes with whatever shaky order-structures they have achieved in their jaded lives, and meanwhile her shy and withdrawn daughter, who has been neglected while her mother chases faddish butterflies, and her husband, both of whom stand in real need of her affection and attention, are compelled to stand forlornly on the sidelines.

Barrie asks Susan for a deal: a trial reconciliation; if it fails after a certain period she can have the divorce she wants. Susan, feeling that he won't live up to his promises of "reform" agrees. They resume their marriage, and gradually Susan comes to realize that her daughter badly needs her, that her husband needs her even more, and that charity truly begins at home.

After a couple of prior films that were only so-so,

Fredric March, left

With Rose Hobart and Ruth Hussey

topped with a protracted absence from the screen, March found that *Susan* helped him off to a flying start in a get-reacquainted campaign with his still-loyal audience. Though not one of his best-remembered films, it proved worthwhile for this reason, especially with MGM distributional clout thrown in, plus the lavish production mounting and Cukor's tasteful direction. This was the one and only picture March ever made with Joan Crawford. Cukor's painstaking directorial guidance, plus the inspiring presence of March, one of the most accomplished actors around, helped Miss Crawford to give one of her best performances in one of those pictures that heralded the polished (and later Oscar-winning) actress Crawford who gradually replaced the personality-star Crawford of the thirties.

THE REVIEWERS
Archer Winsten in the *New York Post:*
Not very successful. Apparently there is a field of brittle satire that can be exploited on the stage without great loss of audience belief. The same thing, or something close to it, becomes silly when viewed under the more penetrating focus of the camera.... Fredric March retains his sincerity.

Herbert Cohn in the *Brooklyn Eagle:*
The Susan Trexel of *Susan and God* is the kind of a woman that even the meekest male would be driven to spank. Joan Crawford is responsible for that. She might easily have made her so obnoxious and meaningless that one wouldn't consider the spanking worth the effort. Miss Crawford made her a nuisance and yet reserved for her a modicum of sympathy. She made her seem misguided and curable.... With Miss Crawford's wisdom [and] the assistance of a thoroughly capable cast under George Cukor's guidance, *Susan and God* is an enticing play.... Fredric March, as Susan's unhappy husband, [gives] a delightful and sometimes moving performance.

With Rita Quigley and Joan Crawford

Bosley Crowther in *The New York Times:*
Mr. March is strangely listless in an aggravating role.

Lee Mortimer in the *New York Daily Mirror:*
Continuing her startling metamorphosis from a glamor girl into a versatile, volatile screen actress of Academy Award proportions, Joan Crawford's first appearance as a stellar comedienne is a spectacular success... the superior and imposing cast so ably supporting the splendid co-starring team of La Crawford and Fredric March, a feast of talent and a famine of story.... Miss Crawford rises far above the limitations imposed on her by stuffy dialogue and a tedious plot.... It is a joy to watch her rip into this new sort of part.

Victory

Paramount / 1940

THE PLAYERS
Mr. March was *Hendrik Heyst* in a cast that included: Betty Field *(Alma)*; Sir Cedric Hardwicke *(Mr. Jones)*; Sig Rumann *(Mr. Schomberg)*; Margaret Wycherly *(Mrs. Schomberg)*; Jerome Cowan *(Ricardo)*; Fritz Feld *(Signor Makanoff)*; Rafaela Ottiano *(Madame Makanoff)*; Lionel Royce *(Pedro)*; Chester Gan *(Wang)*.

THE CREATORS
John Cromwell *(director)*; Anthony Veiller *(producer)*; John L. Balderston *(screenplay)*; based on the novel by Joseph Conrad; Leo Tover *(photography)*; William Shea *(editor)*; Joseph Youngerman *(assistant director)*.

Opened at the Rivoli Theatre, New York, December 21, 1940. Running time when released, 77 minutes.

THE PICTURE
The works of Joseph Conrad have always proved difficult to put on the screen. His novels, written with a florid intensity and possessed by a complex, moody inner-life of their own, do not adapt themselves to the more direct, more surface-y techniques of photographic delineation. Nonetheless March and director John Cromwell decided to put Conrad's *Victory* to the test, with a John Balderston screenplay that unfortunately watered down Conrad's philosophical points and added a happy ending.

One of Conrad's pervading themes was an ironical pity for human beings caught up in the unpredictabilities and sudden treacheries of a fate that is beyond their control; he also went in for melodramatic approaches to his plots. The melodrama is to be found in the film version, but precious little of the philosophy. Though Balderston was doubtless trying to cinematize the tale in order to assure its success, his efforts were not appreciated by one critic, who implied that Balderston had reduced Conrad's melodramatic devices to dime-novel proportions.

March did well as Hendryk Heyst, who has become a virtual recluse on a Dutch East Indies island because he had found through bitter personal experience that his father's warnings to him of the treachery of his fellow men had proven correct. On a brief business trip to a neighboring island, he rescues a forlorn girl (a member of a theatrical troupe that left her stranded) from the advances of a lecherous innkeeper and takes her back with him to his island.

An attachment grows between them, but in line with his pessimistic views, he contemplates sending her away when he realizes he is falling in love. The innkeeper, to take revenge, tells a preposterous tale to three crooks: the fiction highlights the hidden riches Heyst is supposed to have. The three blackguards proceed to invade the hero's sanctuary.

With Betty Field

With Betty Field

How he outwits his three enemies forms the substance of the plot (his eventual triumph over them constituting the "Victory" of the title). Cedric Hardwicke was highly praised for his acting as the leader of the evil threesome, misogynistic, cunning, unscrupulous. As the story progresses Heyst comes to realize increasingly that he can no longer live as an isolated human unit trammeled morally by impractical, theoretical applications of the Golden Rule, but must show courage in the face of evil if life is to be worth living. The three villains, Hardwicke's cynic, Lionel Royce's halfwit, and Jerome

Cowan's knife-wielding woman-chaser, prove the reverse-catalysts for Heyst's emergence into the open air of full adulthood and human understanding. And when he realizes that he and the girl are united by a genuine love and that, now that he has faced down and conquered evil, he has a future of happiness and fulfillment to look forward to, his spiritual journey is complete.

THE REVIEWERS
C. J. Bulliet in the *Chicago Daily News:*
The Conrad "cult," I imagine, will register disappoint-

With Betty Field and Jerome Cowan

With Betty Field

Going to see the "rushes" with Betty Field

ment. Joseph Conrad wrote fervidly and floridly, conjured up strange, exotic, feverish creatures, men and women, roaming the seas, particularly in the tropics. It's hard for any actor or actress of flesh and blood to match psychologically the images in the memories and minds of the "cult" . . . a weird and intense story told on the screen, as in the novel, with intensity.

Elsie Finn in the *Philadelphia Record*:
There's power and beauty in the screen version of Joseph Conrad's *Victory*. The story—one of Conrad's best—is told with stark, forceful simplicity that captures the mood of this strange tale of romance and adventure in the South Seas. . . . A cast of vivid characters, well defined in the script and sharply etched by excellent players. Fredric March . . . has respect and understanding for Hendryk Heyst, the recluse he portrays. . . . *Victory* is not a film of flamboyant hues. Its merits don't hit with a bang. But the production has quality, weight and—more important—compelling drama.

William Boehnel in the *New York World-Telegram*:
A mood of impending doom and horror . . . more than makes up for its slow and deliberate action. . . . This new version alters Conrad's story considerably, but the changes have resulted in a fine and penetrating motion picture melodrama. For while speed is a vital characteristic of melodrama, it is not the only essential, as its creators have here proved. Character and atmosphere, the creation of a mood and making it motivate the things the characters say and do—these are things

which are important too. And these are the things which the picture contains. . . . Throughout you also get a feeling of Conrad's penetrating irony, of his pity and tolerance for people caught up in a fate beyond their understanding . . . not only is Cromwell's direction of a superior quality but the acting also is of the highest order. Fredric March is Heyst to perfection. . . . Betty Field can hardly be improved upon as the girl he befriends.

With Betty Field

With Frances Dee

So Ends Our Night

Loew-Lewin   United Artists / 1941

THE PLAYERS

Mr. March was *Josef Steiner* in a cast which included: Margaret Sullavan *(Ruth Holland)*; Frances Dee *(Marie Steiner)*; Glenn Ford *(Ludwig Kern)*; Anna Sten *(Lilo)*; Erich Von Stroheim *(Brenner)*; Allan Brett *(Marcel)*; Joseph Cawthorn *(Patzlock)*; Leonid Kinskey *(The Chicken)*; Alexander Granach *(The Pole)*; Roman Bohnen *(Mr. Kern)*; Sig Rumann *(Ammers)*; William Stock *(Professor Meyer)*; Lionel Royce *(Barnekrogg)*; Ernst Deutsch *(Dr. Behr)*; Spencer Charters *(Swiss policeman)*; Hans Schumm *(Kabel)*.

THE CREATORS

John Cromwell *(director)*; David L. Loew and Albert Lewin *(producers)*; Talbot Jennings *(screenplay)*; based on the novel *Flotsam* by Erich Maria Remarque; William Daniels *(photography)*; Louis Gruenberg *(music)*; Stanley Kramer *(production assistant)*; William Reynolds *(editor)*.

Opened at Radio City Music Hall, New York, February 27, 1941. Running time when released, 120 minutes.

THE PICTURE

So Ends Our Night was a worthy, serious effort at significant and meaningful film-making, produced conscientiously by David L. Loew and Albert Lewin and di-

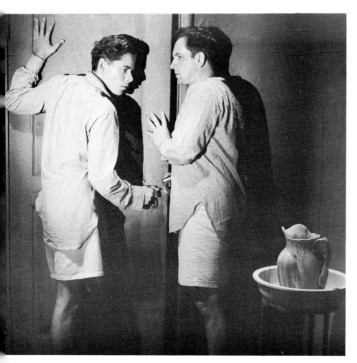

With Glenn Ford

rected painstakingly by John Cromwell. Based on the novel *Flotsam*, by Erich Maria Remarque, the film undoubtedly had its heart in the right place, reflecting the sincere commitment of all involved in it. But critical opinion tended to be divided. The movement of the story was on the sluggish, episodic side; in fact the story itself amounted to very little. March, Margaret Sullavan, and especially young Glenn Ford, then at the beginning of his career, were praised lavishly for their sensitive, penetrating characterizations, but a film that should

have possessed a tragic universality seemed ponderous and at times downright dull.

The main fault lay in the story, which Talbot Jennings could salvage from the novel only to a point. Remarque's power lay in his characterizations and his shrewd establishment of mood, well captured by him on paper but difficult to transpose successfully to cinema. What story there was dealt with a group of refugees from Nazi Germany at the beginning of World War II who are driven from country to country due to the denial of

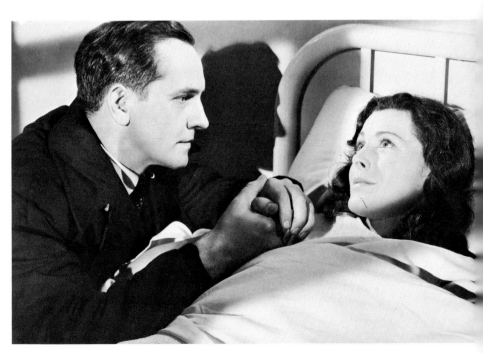

With Frances Dee

With Nazis

passports by a Hitler regime that persecutes, hounds and pursues them.

March plays an upright, conscientious German who cannot accept the Nazi regime. Denied a passport, he joins the other displaced pilgrims in wandering the face of Europe, meeting assorted forms of persecution wherever he goes. He meets up with a lonely, disoriented young nineteen-year-old refugee (Ford) and they strike up a friendship. Ford falls in love with Margaret Sullavan and their touching romance, played-out with consummate simplicity and sincerity by both, is responsible for some of the finest sequences in the film.

March has left his wife, Frances Dee, back in Germany; when he hears she is ill, he returns to her, sacrificing his freedom, and presumably his life, in the process. Ford and Sullavan, on the other hand, find happiness together; they along with the other refugees, or some of them anyway, will manage, it is implied, to fight their way through to peace and happiness somewhere, somehow.

Despite attempts to leaven the heavygoing proceedings with humor, the net result was drab, even pedestrian, the total relieved only by the exceptionally fine acting, with March in the vanguard. The film also provided a boost to the career of Glenn Ford, then twenty-four, who was to become one of the biggest stars in films within five years.

THE REVIEWERS
Archer Winsten in the *New York Post:*
It ought to be a great picture but it isn't. It moves in a lackadaisical fashion through episodes of refugees without passports being sent from one country to another. Such experiences ought to be heartbreaking. Intellectually it is easy enough to realize that hearts are breaking, but the picture talks, repeats, and talks again until the fine edge of sympathy is blunted. . . . Fredric March is at the top of his form. . . . [The film] can be labeled as the worthiest effort of the week, and like many worthy things, not too thrilling.

William Boehnel in the *New York World-Telegram:*
A decidedly uneven film, in which there are just about twice as many bad things as there are good. It is long; it is episodic; it lacks sustained suspense and interest and at times it is altogether unconvincing. . . . If the narrative is spotty and the direction less than inspired, the acting at least is excellent. Fredric March gives a fine, penetrating performance as Steiner. Frances Dee is lovely and persuasive as his wife. Margaret Sullavan and Glenn Ford, who play the two young lovers, are capable beyond praise.

Leo Mishkin in the *New York Morning Telegraph:*
Neither Mr. March nor Miss Sullavan let us down. They are both excellent in their roles, as fine as they have ever been, realizing in every shade, every nuance, the full tragedy of what they depict.

John Beaufort in the *Christian Science Monitor:*
The film brings to the screen the starkness of Mr. Remarque's narrative, its tension, and the manifold implications of circumstances and character. . . . Mr. March gives one of his finest performances.

One Foot In Heaven

Warner Bros. / 1941

THE PLAYERS

Mr. March was *William Spence* in a cast that included: Martha Scott *(Hope Morris Spence)*; Beulah Bondi *(Mrs. Lydia Sandow)*; Gene Lockhart *(Preston Thurston)*; Elizabeth Fraser *(Eileen Spence at eighteen)*; Harry Davenport *(Elias Samson)*; Laura Hope Crews *(Mrs. Preston Thurston)*; Grant Mitchell *(Clayton Potter)*; Moroni Olsen *(Dr. John Romer)*; Ernest Cossart *(John E. Mavis)*; Jerome Cowan *(Dr. Horrigan)*; Hobart Bosworth *(Richard Hardy Case)*; Frankie Thomas *(Hartzell Spence at seventeen)*; Nona Bruant *(Mrs. Morris)*; Carlotta Jelm *(Eileen Spence at eleven)*; Peter Caldwell *(Hartzell Spence at ten)*; Casey Johnson *(Fraser Spence at ten)*; Casey Johnson *(Fraser Spence at seven)*; Virginia Brissac *(Mrs. Jellerson)*; Olin Howland *(Zake Harris)*; Roscoe Ates *(George Reynolds)*; Clara Blandick *(Sister Watkins)*; Paula Trueman *(Miss Peabody)*; Harlan Briggs *(druggist MacFarlan)*.

THE CREATORS

Irving Rapper *(director)*; Casey Robinson *(screenplay)*; based on the biography by Hartzell Spence; Dr. Norman Vincent Peale *(technical advisor)*; a Hal B. Wallis Production; Max Steiner *(music)*; Charles Rosher *(photography)*; Hugh MacMullin *(dialogue director)*; Warren Low *(editor)*.

Opened at Radio City Music Hall, November 13, 1941. Running time when released, 106 minutes.

THE PICTURE

In a warm and winning film in which he was never in better acting form, March played a minister, the Rev. William Spence. *One Foot in Heaven* was based on newsman Hartzell Spence's biography of his father, an obscure midwestern clergyman of unique stripe and solid integrity. The Rev. Spence was also a deeply human and compassionate individual, with an instinctive knowledge of what made people tick, and although he maintained certain standards of life and conduct and adhered to them all his life, he was the kind of man who deserved memorializing precisely because of his down-to-earth approach.

Irving Rapper directed the film, and a fine cast, headed by Martha Scott as Mrs. Spence, included such

With Martha Scott

172

excellent character performers as Beulah Bondi, Gene Lockhart, Harry Davenport and Laura Hope Crews. The story begins in Canada, where young Spence switches from medical studies to the ministry, and takes his young bride, Miss Scott, to Iowa, where they find themselves forced to start from scratch in a poor community with a rundown parsonage. They cope with poverty, difficult parishioners (March warns his wife never to dress better than the parishioners lest they think she's putting on airs) and of course the children come one by one.

From parish to parish they go, in one state after another, over the next twenty years. There are warm vignettes of family life; the oldest boy converts his father to moviegoing by taking him to a right-triumphs-over-evil William S. Hart film, and the previously anti-movie clergyman delivers his next Sunday sermon on the subject of the potentiality of movies for good. Later March takes issue with snobbish Beulah Bondi, who objects to her minister having tea with one of her servants.

When a choir of substantial citizens with aging, out-of-tune voices proves too much for March to bear, he tactfully substitutes the clear sweet tones of the parish children. This maneuver predictably wins the ire of Laura Hope Crews and Gene Lockhart, two town fat-cats who proceed to spread lies about his oldest son, winningly played by Frankie Thomas, who is forthwith expelled from school because of gossip over a girl he allegedly "got in trouble" and who left town with her family.

Meanwhile March, who is a builder not an exploiter, keeps refusing prosperous parishes because his stand-

ards will not allow him to profit from the labors of his predecessors; always he is endeavoring to get improvements in his own rundown church, despite the parsimony of well-heeled parish members. Offered, eventually, a fine parish in California, he turns down the post and determines to stick it out in the midwestern town where his independent stances have made him enemies.

He exposes the lie about his son and the girl to the gossipmongers concerned and threatens to broadcast it to his flock; then, applying a bit of shrewd "white blackmail" he gets from the rich woman who had instigated the gossip the funds for a fine new church and the carillon and a stained glass window from a contrite Miss Bondi, who wants to be where the fashionable action is. Those who tried to stain his son's reputation unjustly are thus given their come-uppance, and in a constructive way characteristic of Mr. Spence.

But when the new church is built, plus a handsome new parsonage, and he and his family are at last secure after years of struggle, he hears of a little parish in Iowa that needs refurbishing and building-up. Though he and his wife are getting on in years, she, ever faithful and compliant, agrees to go there with him. In a rather theatrical and sentimental closing sequence, Spence plays the carillon and the whole town comes flocking to the church to listen with uplifted faces and tears in their eyes.

The entire film is rich in human incident; the wife, Miss Scott, who from the beginning has followed the "whither thou goest I will go also" Biblical principle, is endlessly self-sacrificing; the children put up with the strictures of being ministerial offspring, recalling their father's injunction that the family has "one foot in heaven and the other on earth." In one incident early in the picture, the minister, pressed for supper money for his family, does a bit of delightful finagling to lure two-dollar-license-fee-paying couples from the justice of the peace to the parsonage. The wife finds she is forced, during their humbler parish phase, to keep unattractive objects, like a wildcat's stuffed head, on the wall be-

With Martha Scott

With Elisabeth Fraser, Casey Johnson, Martha Scott, and Frankie Thomas

cause the parishioner who contributed the thing dotes on it. The entire life of a minister in the 1904-1924 period is offered here, a warm, loving, utterly sincere depiction of the kind of man and the kind of life that seem now so regrettably extinct in our American culture. March was never finer, and the other members of the cast, especially the warm and womanly Martha Scott were right there with him every moment. The film garnered unanimously favorable reviews and was one of the best-liked Hollywood offerings of the year. The famed Dr. Norman Vincent Peale served as technical advisor. March later repeated his role of William Spence on the radio, with Miss Eldridge in the Martha Scott role.

THE REVIEWERS

Donald Kirkley in the *Baltimore Sun:*
Rich in warm emotional values . . . [the film] illuminates an American household wherein is found the virtues, foibles and problems which make up the warp and woof of the family life of this nation. It has the ring of truth about it, there is a great deal of incidental comedy arising from the interplay of the characters, and even the sad, troubled episodes are lightened by the sympathy of the writer for his people and the communication of that benevolent feeling to the spectator. . . . Fredric March and Martha Scott are ideally cast.

Richard Peters in *The Cleveland Press:*
A fine, sentimental story of a practical parson—beautifully acted and sympathetically directed. . . . Fredric March is perfect as the parson whose one foot was per-

haps in Heaven but whose other foot was usually in hot water.

William Boehnel in the *New York World-Telegram:*
That so much of the man Spence, as well as the inspired preacher, comes through, is due to Fredric March's brilliant acting in the part. March, one of the finest actors on the screen, tempers his severity with drollness, his religious convictions with worldly wisdom. . . . He makes William Spence a breathing, vital person.

Cecilia Ager in *PM:*
It takes more courage to make a clean, sweet, decent picture like *One Foot in Heaven* than to sneak a hot mattress past the drooping eyelids of the Hays office. . . . A movie about religion without sanctimony. It doesn't bedevil you with misplaced piety. It portrays a preacher without gushing over him, it presents him as no more than a man doing his job, which job requires the constant cooperation of his whole family, without always constant or commensurate rewards. This is not the sort of material that provides obvious movie excitement. It has no thrills; it can evoke only admiration for its integrity as a movie, give insight into a kind of life not heretofore mulled over much, and yield an over-all gentle warmth from the basic goodness of its subject matter.

John Rosenfield in the *Dallas Morning News:*
In this role Fredric March gives the performance by which he should be remembered. It bristles with vitality and an intelligent consistency. The pattern of a parson's histrionics fits perfectly the grandiloquence that is Mr. March's histrionics. . . . When it is over you will like your minister better and think more highly of your church. You may even donate a copper to fix the plumbing in the parsonage.

With Dr. Norman Vincent Peale on the set. Dr. Peale was technical advisor representing nationwide Protestant denominations.

Bedtime Story

Columbia / 1942

THE PLAYERS
Mr. March was *Lucius Drake* in a cast that included: Loretta Young *(Jane Drake)*; Robert Benchley *(Eddie Turner)*; Allyn Joslyn *(William Dudley)*; Eve Arden *(Virginia Cole)*; Helen Westley *(Emma Harper)*; Joyce Compton *(Beulah)*; Tim Ryan *(Mac)*; Olaf Hytten *(Alfred)*; Dorothy Adams *(Betsy)*; Clarence Kolb *(Collins)*; Andrew Tombes *(Pierce)*.

THE CREATORS
Alexander Hall *(director)*; B. P. Schulberg *(producer)*; Richard Flournoy *(screenplay)*; based on a story by Horace Jackson and Grant Garrett; Joseph Walker *(photography)*; William Mull *(assistant director)*; Viola Lawrence *(editor)*.

Opened at Radio City Music Hall, March 19, 1942. Running time when released, 85 minutes.

THE PICTURE
At Columbia March did an amiable, but hardly epoch-making, comedy with Loretta Young called *Bedtime Story*. Alexander Hall, one of the more clever comedy directors, gave the proceedings a highly professional gloss, Richard Flournoy's screenplay kept things moving at a brisk pace and such dependable supporting players as Robert Benchley, Allyn Joslyn, Eve Arden and Helen Westley did their best to help March and Miss Young keep the fun bubbling. Sometimes it did, and sometimes it didn't, but a number of laughs were gleaned from the frenetic proceedings (Hall didn't let up for a moment on the pace) and March, though forced by the vapidities of the plot to overplay a bit (some critics noted that his overplaying was a necessity in the circumstances) proved a thoroughly adept farceur.

Despite the title, there is little of the bedtime stuff, and that very peripheral, though Miss Young manages

With Loretta Young

175

With Loretta Young

to look continually enticing in a series of breathtaking negligees, gowns and what-not. March this time around is an eccentric playwright whose wife, Miss Young a First Lady of the Theatre, wants to retire permanently to their farm. But March has a new play in mind, and he proceeds to inveigle her by any means that comes to hand into trying yet another Broadway appearance. His methods, in view of his wife's determined resistance, are decidedly underhanded, and when Miss Young finds that his promises and reassurances mean nothing and that he has secretly sold the farm and bought a new theatre, she huffs out and gets a divorce.

Then she marries a stuffy banker who will be (she imagines) safe and predictable, albeit on the dull side. Of course the persistent March isn't taking any of this lying down, and he turns the banker's and Miss Young's

With Loretta Young

176

With Helen Westley and Robert Benchley

honeymoon night into a farcical hotel fiasco, what with alerting plumbers, exterminators and electricians to the suite's allegedly bad facilities and creating other embarrassments of an ingenious kind, all of which make for much confusion and flying feathers in the honeymoon quarters of Miss Young and Joslyn.

It then develops that through a fluke Miss Young's divorce and remarriage are not valid and after more complications, all engineered skillfully by March, it is he, not the banker, who gets to tell Miss Young bedtime stories. The doings border on the hysterical at times, what with everyone trying so hard for a Cary Grant-Irene Dunne-style smasheroo (which doesn't develop, regrettably). Though Miss Young is March's straight woman for much of the running, she does work in some sly wit at times, and Miss Westley, Joslyn and Benchley deliver amusing moments with their usual dependability. But none of it was calculated to give Grant or Dunne any gray hairs worrying about March-Young competition.

THE REVIEWERS
Eileen Creelman in *The New York Sun:*
Amiable and often amusing.... Fredric March, an experienced farceur, has a tendency to overplay his scenes. This may be as well. [The film] latest in a long line of domestic comedies, cannot be hurt by overemphasis. It is not a subtle subject.

Leo Mishkin in the *New York Morning Telegraph:*
The farcical antics of Mr. March give [the film] its greatest strength... A first-rate actor... March makes the most of his opportunities on this occasion, and manages to turn in a highly engaging performance.

Kate Cameron in the *New York Daily News:*
Loretta Young and Fredric March respond to Al Hall's persuasive direction with an engaging awareness of the picture's comedy values.

Herbert Cohn in the *Brooklyn Eagle:*
It is a terrifying chore to overcome the emptiness of the film, and though the players toil with moderate success, the laughs they win are more from sympathy than genuine gayety. It is hard to be glum when Young, March, Hall and Company try so hard to please.

With Loretta Young

With Veronica Lake

I Married a Witch

Cinema Guild   United Artists / 1942

THE PLAYERS
Mr. March was *Wallace Wooley* in a cast that included: Veronica Lake *(Jennifer)*; Robert Benchley *(Dr. Dudley White)*; Susan Hayward *(Estelle Masterson)*; Cecil Kellaway *(Daniel)*; Elizabeth Patterson *(Margaret)*; Robert Warwick *(J. B. Masterson)*; Eily Malyon *(Tabitha)*; Robert Greig *(town crier)*; Helen St. Rayner *(vocalist)*; Aldrich Bowker *(Justice of the Peace)*; Emma Dunn *(his wife)*.

THE CREATORS
René Clair *(director)*; Robert Pirosh and Mark Connelly *(screenplay)*; based on a story by Thorne Smith completed by Norman Matson; a René Clair Production; Ted Tetzlaff *(photography)*; Eda Warren *(editor)*.

Opened at The Capitol Theatre, New York, November 19, 1942. Running time when released, 82 minutes.

THE PICTURE
March then found himself paired—abrasively it turned out—with Veronica Lake, Paramount's bright new star with the hair-over-one-eye trademark—in the film version of Thorne Smith's unfinished fantasy-tale, *The Passionate Witch*, which Norman Matson had completed.

Retitled *I Married a Witch* it was the first of a projected series of films produced by Paramount but sold for release to United Artists.

It concerned the love of a mischievous seventeenth-century New England witch, reincarnated in blonde, full-bosomed Miss Lake, of course, for a descendant of the man who had ordered her burned at the stake. A blend of such elements as the "Topper" tales and such fantasies as the 1936 *The Ghost Goes West*, which had starred Robert Donat and been directed by René Clair, *I Married a Witch* had an amusing premise amusingly executed. Clair directed the fey romp, which was replete with witch-oriented jokes—lightning flashes, puffs of smoke, taxis driven by sorcerers which float in the air, spirits imprisoned in bottles, hex-induced hurricanes, and what-not. Clair imparted to the film many of the light, fey, subtle nuances for which he was justly famed, but Production Code tempering dictated the watered-down approach to potentially sexy situations which dampened some of the gifted Clair's inspirations. (He was yet another of that talented group of European directors who found Hollywood ways hampering.)

In her recent book, *Veronica*, Miss Lake claims that

With Veronica Lake

With Veronica Lake

Clair had originally thumbed her down for the role, later hired her upon Preston Sturges' insistence, and even later apologized and told her he had been mistaken and that she *was* a good comedienne. As for Fredric March, Miss Lake claims that they did not get along well during the shooting, that March had a low opinion of her abilities, and that she disliked him soundly and got back at him via small annoyances any way she could. March adherents claim that his reported exasperation with Miss Lake during the shooting may well have been justified, as her inexperience (she had been a star at that point for exactly one year and had had little experience prior to that) did chalk up rather starkly against March's then twenty-two-year experience on stage and screen. The gist of the dispute between them was, March aficionados feel, the polished professionalism of a major talent expressing its impatience with amateur approaches.

Miss Lake, in all fairness, did rather well in the film, and some critics liked her very much; others had reservations. March garnered his usual respectful reviews, for the most part. The film opens in 1690 in New England where Cecil Kellaway and his daughter, Miss Lake, are burned by March's ancestor; the two witches lay a curse on the family: that no male of the breed will ever find happiness in marriage. Some dozen generations of unhappy marriages later, the witchburner's descendant, March, is a candidate for governor, and he is set to marry the daughter of the influential publisher who is backing him. Lightning strikes a tree where the sorcerer and his daughter are imprisoned, they materialize (at first) as puffs of smoke and then take human form, set-

ting out to wreak direct vengeance on March, which Miss Lake proceeds to do with all the fey and impish resources at her command, culminating with a hex-induced hurricane at March's wedding.

When the bride-to-be later finds him in an amorous clinch with Miss Lake, she walks out on him. March and the Witch realize they are in love and she realizes she cannot continue her campaign against him. Her father opposes her, so she contrives to shut him up in a bottle. Several years later the now married March and Lake find themselves with a daughter who wears her hair over one eye and rides a broomstick as to the saddle born, which gives them pause, to put it mildly.

THE REVIEWERS
Alton Cook in the *New York World-Telegram & Sun*:
Section after section of Thorne Smith's fantastic novel

With Cecil Kellaway, Veronica Lake and Robert Benchley

was cast into the righteous fires of Hollywood censorship before filming began. In their stead, Robert Pirosh and Marc Connelly have conjured up episodes certainly as mirthful and just about as mischievous as the original. ... If you have been one of the faction wondering what constitutes the allure of Veronica Lake, this picture may solve your dilemma. You never saw a more hexy display from any witch. Fredric March is present with one of the stalwart and good performances standard with him.

Leo Mishkin in the *New York Morning Telegraph:*
It seems that Fredric March must be marked down as this season's foremost exponent of fantasy and wonderful nonsense. ... Miss Lake ... in turning out to be a first-rate movie comedienne, in addition to being one of the sultriest ladies on the screen, and when you get a combination like that, in a figure like Miss Lake's— brother, you've got a handful. ... M. Claire's Gallic sense of humor has been kept in some restraint by the conventions of the Hays office ... but on the whole he has managed to convey a delightful sense of oddity and enchantment.

Eileen Creelman in the *New York Sun:*
Hollywood seems to have flattened the piquancy of Clair's film. [The film] entertains only moderately by its tricks. The picture's main fault may lie in the performance of Veronica Lake, who plays the witch. Miss Lake's sulky prettiness permits her to look the part. She has more difficulty in playing it. Her high little voice is far from exotic. She never brings a sparkle to the comedy nor a hint of real emotion to the drama. It is a monotonous performance that kills the attempts at light laughter. ... Fredric March is happier in his role. He plays ... an amiable, sober-minded New Englander. ... Occasionally this is pleasant nonsense. Most of the time it is

heavy-handed fantasy without either the René Clair or Thorne Smith sparkle.

John T. McManus in *PM:*
Jennifer (the witch character) was really quite lucky, as it turns out, to find a body like Veronica Lake's to cache herself in, and so noted a cinema spiritist as René Clair (*The Ghost Goes West*) to manage her earthly career. Because, embodied in Veronica's very vital externals, and by virtue of René Clair's sly camera conjuring, Jennifer's inspired fling at witchery makes up in prankery what it lacks in point.

With Veronica Lake

With Veronica Lake

Fredric March

The Adventures of Mark Twain

Warner Brothers / 1944

THE PLAYERS

Mr. March was *Samuel Clemens (Mark Twain)* in a cast that included: Alexis Smith *(Olivia Langdon)*; Donald Crisp *(J. B. Pond)*; Alan Hale *(Steve Gillis)*; C. Aubrey Smith *(Oxford chancellor)*; John Carradine *(Bret Harte)*; William Henry *(Charles Langdon)*; Robert Barrat *(Horace E. Bixby)*; Walter Hampden *(Jervis Langdon)*; Joyce Reynolds *(Clara Clemens)*; Whitford Kane *(Joe Goodwin)*; Percy Kilbride *(Billings)*; Nana Bryant *(Mrs. Langdon)*; Jackie Brown *(Sam Clemens at twelve)*; Dickie Jones *(Sam Clemens at fifteen)*; Russell Gleason *(Orrin Clemens)*; Joseph Crehan *(General Grant)*; Douglas Wood *(William Dean Howells)*.

THE CREATORS

Irving Rapper *(director)*; Jesse L. Lasky *(producer)*; Alan LeMay *(screenplay)*; Alan LeMay and Harold M. Sherman *(adaptation)*; Harry Chandlee *(additional dialogue)*. All biographical material based on works owned or controlled by the Mark Twain Company and the play *Mark Twain* by Harold M. Sherman. Sol Polito, Laurence Butler, Edwin Linden, Don Siegel, James Leicester *(photography)*; Max Steiner *(music)*; Herschel Daugherty *(dialogue director)*; Leo F. Forbstein *(music director)*; Bernaud Kaun *(arrangements)*; Ralph Dawson *(editor)*.

With Alexis Smith

181

With Robert Barrat and William Henry

Opened at the Hollywood Theatre, May 3, 1944. Running time when released, 130 minutes.

THE PICTURE

March's role as Samuel Clemens (Mark Twain) in the lengthy, episodic, lavishly produced 1944 Warner film, is one of his best-remembered characterizations. He got himself up to look remarkably like that fabulous man whose life (1835-1910) spanned the years of America's coming of age, and who left his country and the world such immortal works as *Tom Sawyer* and *Huckleberry Finn.* Irving Rapper, who had worked so successfully with the star in *One Foot in Heaven,* was again on hand to direct. The Alan LeMay and Harold M. Sherman screenplay, given careful production mounting by Jesse L. Lasky, tended to stress a series of transitional montages and to simplify the facts of Twain's complicated and stress-ridden seventy-five years, reducing this many-

sided personality to a simplistically-motivated individual. The character of his wife, played by Alexis Smith, also was Hollywoodized into an unconvincing saccharinity. The complex Twain life-struggles were all covered over with a pat, sugary, surfacey gloss that made it difficult to know and understand what manner of man this was under the heavily made-up, colorful and expansive exterior.

All the facts of Twain's celebrated life are, it is true, paraded for review: his life as a boatman on the river, his days as a reporter, his adventurings in the goldrush West. Literary fame hit Twain with the publication of his jumping-frog tales; the great books follow, incidents of his courtship and marriage are offered, his friendships with the great of the world, his variegated dealings with his publisher, his fellow-adventurers, all are given a work-out, sometimes in overly perfunctory fashion, in the course of the 130 minutes running time.

Viewed today, the film impresses one as episodic,

With Alan Hale

montaged to a bewilderingly frequent extent, and superficial in its attempts to depict what made this complicated man and artist tick.

Twain's disastrous financial adventures also are related, including the bankruptcy that follows ill-advised publishing ventures and a cataclysmically abortive investment in a typesetting machine. All of which tends to prove that artists and businessmen are two different breeds of cat. Eventually (as in the lamentable instance of Sir Walter Scott) Twain is forced to write to the point of nervous exhaustion in order to pay off his creditors.

Later years are replete with honors, at Oxford University and elsewhere, and famed contemporaries like Bret Harte and William Dean Howells parade in and out of his life in pageant style. March's performance, given the heavy makeup and the episodic confusions of the plot, was excellent—so fine in fact that it managed to tower above all the sound and fury at certain points—which, in a film like this, is some achievement. Alan Hale, John Carradine, Donald Crisp, all are effective in their roles, with Miss Smith being given little to do other than enact the ever-faithful spouse. While the film was regarded in its day as colorful, ambitious and lavish,

With Alexis Smith

THE REVIEWERS
David Lardner in *The New Yorker*:
It's not that [the film] is much worse than most cinematized biographies, because it does have its good moments. It's just that once more biographical inaccuracy is rampant, and once more the best dramatic possibilities have been overlooked, so it's hard to think of anything new, in the line of protest, to say.

With Alexis Smith and Walter Hampden

and in many individual scenes highly effective, more than one critic emphasized the necessity of achieving characterizational depth and correct motivation when delineating lives of artists. This pat portrait had serious deficiencies; nonetheless many in the 1944 audience admired it—and March's portrayal—enormously.

With Donald Crisp

Wanda Hale in the *New York Daily News:*
As Samuel Clemens, Fredric March dominates this interesting, amusing and touching comedy drama. The star's performance is one of his best. He makes you feel that he *is* Mark Twain, the lovable, cynical, disarming humorist. The fact that he gets better as the character grows older compensates for the film's one shortcoming, the too-deliberate presentation.

Fileen Creelman in *The New York Sun:*
Fredric March, looking startingly like all the familiar photographs of Twain, plays the character with respect and understanding.

Abel Green in *Variety:*
The discriminating film audience will recognize in *The Adventures of Mark Twain* something that is more than a little sentimentally close to their hearts. The stars, notably, perform their assignments with extraordinary compassion and understanding, particularly March in the title role. Director Irving Rapper has accomplished an intelligent job in the general direction; the stage technique serves in good stead here. The scripting is likewise topnotch.

Archer Winsten in *The New York Post:*
A tribute must be paid to Fredric March's excellent makeup and sincere performance. He looks remarkably like Mark Twain and there is no reason to doubt that he talks and acts like him ... [the film] is a reminder of a great man rather than an inspiring and lusty recreation of his career. The obvious conclusion to be drawn from *The Adventures of Mark Twain* is that Hollywood had better fight shy of literary heroes until it can summon up the courage, analytical acumen, respect for absolute accuracy, and subtlety to do them full justice.

Alton Cook in the *New York World-Telegram:*
The glow of a lovable character is the happy quality this picture spreads through an audience. . . . Near the finish cutting might have been judicious. But with material so ingratiating reluctance to discard is understandable. It is hard to part with any moment of Fredric March's characterization of Mark, a magnificent creation in the grand style, painstakingly detailed and sweepingly forceful. As you watch the picture you lose awareness of admiration for the achievement of Fredric March. You are laughing with and revering Mark Twain.

With Betty Field

Tomorrow the World

Lester Cowan   United Artists / 1944

THE PLAYERS
Mr. March was *Mike Frame* in a cast that included: Betty Field *(Leora Richards)*; Agnes Moorehead *(Jessie)*; Skippy Homeier *(Emil Bruckner)*; Joan Carroll *(Pat Frame)*; Edith Argold *(Frieda)*; Rudy Wissler *(Stan)*; Boots Brown *(Roy)*; Marvin Davis *(Dennis)*; Patsy Ann Thompson *(Millie)*; Mary Newton *(school principal)*; Tom Fadden *(mailman)*.

THE CREATORS
Leslie Fenton *(director)*; Lester Cowan *(producer)*; Ring Lardner, Jr., and Leopold Atlas *(screenplay)*; adapted from the play by James Gow and Armand D'Usseau.

Opened at the Globe Theatre, New York, December 21, 1944. Running time when released, 86 minutes.

THE PICTURE
Tomorrow the World was based on a hit Broadway play that starred Ralph Bellamy and Shirley Booth. Lester Cowan produced and Leslie Fenton directed the 1944 film version with Fredric March, Betty Field and the amazing child actor Skippy Homeier (when he grew up, he shortened it to Skip) who repeated his viciously trenchant stage portrayal of the Nazi-indoctrinated twelve-year-old, Emil, and in the process stole the picture. The consensus of reviewer opinion was that while March and Field were dignified, sincere, and earnest in their portrayals, the picture constituted in effect a one-boy tour-de-force.

    March plays a professor in a small college town; he

With Skippy Homeier

With Skippy Homeier

brings to America his nephew, Homeier, who has been orphaned in Germany. His parents have died in a concentration camp because of his father's ardent anti-Nazi intellectualism. Emil is the typical brainwashed young Nazi; he hates his dead father for what he considers his craven defection from the Nazi cause.

Once installed in March's household, he makes constant trouble; he fosters unrest among the children at school; he develops a hostility toward his widower-

uncle's schoolteacher fiancee, Miss Field, because she is of Jewish blood, he makes friends with a Chinese boy he mistakenly believes to be a "Jap," and he is intent on learning the plans his uncle is working on in secret for the War Department.

When his hatred of his surroundings finally gets really out of hand, he almost kills his young girl cousin, for whom by degrees, and in spite of himself, he has been developing a fondness. This brings on a manhunt of sorts, with the neighborhood out looking for him. Belatedly (and to many viewers, inexplicably) he realizes the error of his ways and is chastened. There was some criticism of his insufficiently motivated change of heart, a questioning of the psychological validity of this dyed-in-the-wool young Nazi's switch-about. Let's face it, when Emil was bad he was very very bad (*and* exciting), but when he turned good he was something of a wash-out, what they would call today a cop-out. Of course in 1944, when the picture was made, we were fighting a vicious war with the Nazis and it was fashionable to give psychological realities the go-by if chauvinistic purposes could be served. And in 1944 what audiences wanted to see an *un*redeemed Nazi child? Though Homeier was duly "redeemed," there was added criticism of his performance's stagey overemphases before the far more intimate camera eye. There was some weakening of the message, such as it was, in the transition from stage to screen; moreover the professor was not the showiest role March had ever had, with the nominal star and Miss Field, the nominal co-star, playing distinct second fiddle to Homeier.

THE REVIEWERS
Frank Leyendecker in *Film Bulletin:*
Fredric March gives an intelligently restrained performance.

With Betty Field

The *New York Herald Tribune:*
[The stage] explosion . . . has been considerably muf-
fled in the film version. . . . Skippy Homeier, the talented
youth who acted Emil on Broadway and plays it on the
screen . . . hasn't been able to reduce the volume of his
performance to the magnifying glass of the screen close-
up and so his portrayal of Emil often seems badly exag-
gerated. Fredric March, as the professor who adopts
Emil and Betty Field as the Professor's schoolteacher
bride-to-be, walk through the piece as a pair of foils for
Emil's malice. But even this acid has been diluted for
screen presentation; there is very little left of *Tomorrow
the World* except the curious oil-and-water mixture of a
Nazi among Americans.

Variety:
Fredric March and Betty Field are starring in the roles
played originally on Broadway by Ralph Bellamy and
Shirley Booth and both give dignity to the parts of the
Professor and his bride-to-be. But the main accolade
must go to Skippy Homeier, the young Nazi.

T.M.P. in The New York Times:
A sincere if not completely satisfying attempt . . . in film
form no more conclusive than it was as a play. It mirrors
in terms often more theatrical than realistic, the problem
that will confront the Allies in purging Nazi-poisoned
minds after the battle is won. The picture does not
convincingly put across its theory that patience, kindness and education in the principles of Democracy will
do the trick. Skippy Homeier's portrayal of the deceitful
youth . . . is frighteningly vicious . . . the film is generally
well-acted and directed. Fredric March is always believable, if too easygoing, as the small midwestern town

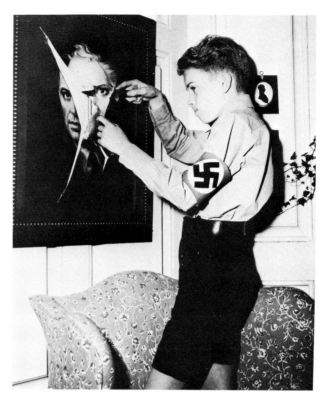

Skippy Homeier waxing destructive

college professor and widower who is completely baffled
by his obnoxious nephew. Betty Field is a bulwark of
tolerance and sympathetic understanding as the fiancee-
schoolteacher. . . . Leslie Fenton's direction is generally
excellent.

*On the set with Betty Field and a visitor, Theron Bamberger,
producer of the stage version of* Tomorrow the World

*On the studio lot with Skippy Homeier, producer Lester
Cowan, Joan Carroll and Betty Field*

With Myrna Loy

The Best Years of Our Lives

Samuel Goldwyn   RKO / 1946

THE PLAYERS
Mr. March was *Al Stephenson* in a cast that included: Myrna Loy *(Milly Stephenson)*; Dana Andrews *(Fred Derry)*; Teresa Wright *(Peggy Stephenson)*; Virginia Mayo *(Marie Derry)*; Harold Russell *(Homer Parrish)*; Cathy O'Donnell *(Wilma Cameron)*; Hoagy Carmichael *(Butch Engle)*; Gladys George *(Hortense Derry)*; Roman Bohnen *(Pat Derry)*; Ray Collins *(Mr. Milton)*; Steve Cochran *(Cliff)*; Minna Gombell *(Mrs. Parrish)*; Walter Baldwin *(Mr. Parrish)*; Dorothy Adams *(Mrs. Cameron)*; Don Beddoe *(Mr. Cameron)*; Erskine Sanford *(Bullard)*; Marlene Ames *(Luella Parrish)*; Michael Hall *(Rob Stevenson)*; Charles Halton *(Prew)*; Howland Chamberlin *(Thorpe)*.

THE CREATORS
William Wyler *(director)*; Samuel Goldwyn *(producer)*; Robert E. Sherwood *(screenplay)*; from the novel *Glory For Me* by MacKinlay Kantor; Gregg Toland *(photography)*; Daniel Mandell *(editor)*; Joseph Boyle *(assistant director)*; George Jenkins, Perry Ferguson *(art directors)*; Julia Heron *(set decorator)*; Hugo Friedhofer *(music)*; Emil Newman *(music director)*; Sharaff *(costumes)*.

Opened at the Astor Theatre, New York, November 21, 1946. Running time when released, 165 minutes.

THE PICTURE
March won his second Academy Award for his role in *The Best Years of Our Lives* and deservedly. Much has been written about this great motion picture, impeccably produced by Samuel Goldwyn and directed with consummate discernment and disciplined, highly-selec-

With Dana Andrews

With Dana Andrews, Teresa Wright and Myrna Loy

and milieu. Never had a group of topflight actors pooled their talents to such exceptional advantage. Released in late 1946, the picture caught the postwar mood and attitude of the American public with pinpoint accuracy. The identification quotient was one of the highest in film-audience history, as its story, dealing with the problems of returned veterans and those who knew and loved them, had a universal appeal, being close to the experience of most people viewing it.

March was never more sincere or quietly forceful as the banker-turned-soldier who returns to his wife, son and daughter and finds that a subtle change has taken place, not in their mutual love but in their attitudes and approaches toward each other. To dispel his self-conscious unease he takes his wife and daughter out for a wild night on the town, carousing and getting drunk in a superbly played series of scenes. While March has been away, his daughter (Teresa Wright) has matured

tive craftsmanship by the brilliant William Wyler. Reportedly the idea for it originated in 1944, when Goldwyn read a news item about a returning veteran's adjustment to civilian life. He commissioned writer MacKinlay Kantor to do a "treatment"; this resulted in a novel—in blank verse—by Kantor which was published as *Glory for Me*. Robert E. Sherwood was called in to do the screenplay; when Goldwyn had passed on this, the production personnel were assembled and March, Dana Andrews, Myrna Loy, Teresa Wright and other accomplished performers were signed on. One of the more interesting castings was that of Harold Russell, who had lost both hands during Navy service. Along with March he was to win an Oscar, for the best supporting actor of 1946.

The finished film was long (165 minutes after editing) but continuously absorbing, and Gregg Toland photographed it superbly in a new deep-focus technique which gave unparalleled verisimilitude to the characters

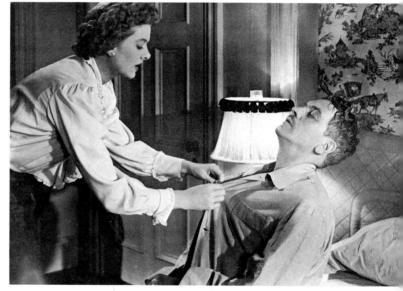

With Myrna Loy

from teenager to young lady, and his son (Michael Hall) has matured into a lad with decided opinions of his own. When he returns to his job at the bank March's patience is tested when his smug play-it-safe overlords demur at giving loans to ex-GIs. He succeeds in convincing them that there is no better investment than in human beings of good will who are willing to work.

Another returning veteran, Dana Andrews, finds his family shiftless and impoverished as always; he also discovers that he has nothing in common any more with his garish, blatant blonde wife (Virginia Mayo) nor does he relish returning to his job as a soda jerk. Andrews and Miss Wright meet and gradually fall in love but March breaks them up because he does not want his daughter hurt by an involvement with a married man.

With Hoagy Carmichael and Harold Russell

With Dana Andrews

With Charles Halton and Ray Collins

Russell, the sailor, has problems with his over-solicitous family because of the loss of his hands, and he fears that his girl (Cathy O'Donnell) no longer loves him but feels only pity. In one of the film's most moving scenes, he tests her feeling by allowing her to help him when he doesn't have his hooks on. Convinced then that it is love, not sympathy, that holds her to him, he marries her.

Meanwhile Andrews has arranged to divorce his wife, and in the final scene, at Russell's wedding, it is indicated that he and March's daughter may yet find happiness together.

The secret of the film's enormous success, of course, lay in its preoccupation with intimate aspects of the human condition in the surging peacetime backlash of a society exhausted by the stresses and strictures of war. Though perhaps some of it dates, the quality of 1946 American life differing from that of 1971 in a number of crucial respects, it still retains most of its humanity and universality, and as a mirror of what our country was thinking and feeling in 1946 it is heartwrenchingly accurate and true. Sherwood's dialogue was naturalistic and absolutely right for the individual characters; the acting was certainly of the highest order; all in all a film of which anyone connected with it (or anyone viewing it) can be proud, in that era, this or any other era. The picture won for various individuals involved with it the total of nine Academy Awards: for best actor, best picture, best supporting actor, best director, best screenplay, best scoring and film editing, the Irving Thalberg award and another, special award.

THE REVIEWERS
James Agee in *The Nation*:
This is one of the very few American studio-made movies in years that seems to me profoundly pleasing, moving and encouraging ... this is a most unusually good screenplay. Although the dialogue has a continuous sheen of entertainment slickness, it is also notably well-differentiated, efficient, free of tricks of snap and punch and over-design, and modest in its feeling for how much weight it should carry on the screen; and most of the time there is an openness about the writing which I don't doubt every good screen writer tries for but which few achieve. By openness I mean simply that the scenes are so planned, and the lines so laid down, that every action and reaction, every motion and everything that is seen, is more centrally eloquent than the spoken lines. The movie thus has and takes its chance to be born in front of the camera, whereas the general run of screenplays force what takes place before the camera to

With Michael Hall, Teresa Wright and Myrna Loy

be a mere redigestion of a predigestion. With a director and cameraman in charge so gifted as Messrs. Wyler and Toland it is impossible to guess which of them, or Mr. Sherwood, is most to be thanked for the great force, simplicity and beauty of some of the scenes and countless of the camera set-ups. . . . William Wyler has always seemed to me an exceedingly sincere and good director; he now seems one of the few great ones. He has come back from the war with a style of great purity, directness and warmth, about as cleanly devoid of mannerism, haste, superfluous motion, aesthetic or emotional over-reaching, as any I know. . . . [Mr. Wyler got] new and better things out of professionals than they had ever shown before. . . . March is far outside his normal habits, and very good indeed. . . . It is easy, and true to say that [the film] suggests the limitations which will be inevitable in any Hollywood film, no matter how skillful and sincere. But it is also a great pleasure, and equally true, to say that it shows what can be done in the factory by people of adequate talent when they get, or manage to make themselves, the chance.

With Myrna Loy and Teresa Wright

Abel Green in *Variety:*
Inspired casting has newcomer Harold Russell, a real-life amputee, pacing the seasoned trouper, Fredric March, for personal histrionic triumphs. . . . March's forthright stance as banker, father and free-and-easy bourbon-drinker makes his performance easily one of the year's cinematic outstanders. Given a v.p. title and a returning war hero's salary boost as the bank's officer in charge of small loans to GIs, he tells off the smug, doubletalking bankers about "secure collateral" by exercising innate judgment, predicated on human values and faith in the American future. In a couple of scenes, which by their very underplaying hit hard, he scores a single-handed thespic triumph. . . . Not a line or scene is spurious. . . . The people live; they are not mere shadow etchings on a silver sheet. The realism is graphic; the story compelling; the romantic frailties and the human little problems confronting each of the group are typical of the headlines in stressing postwar readjustment and faith in the future.

With Harold Russell and Dana Andrews

Another Part of the Forest

Universal-International / 1948

THE PLAYERS

Mr. March was *Marcus Hubbard* in a cast that included: Ann Blyth *(Regina Hubbard)*; Edmond O'Brien *(Ben Hubbard)*; Florence Eldridge *(Lavinia Hubbard)*; Dan Duryea *(Oscar Hubbard)*; John Dall *(John Bagtry)*; Donna Drake *(Laurette)*; Betsy Blair *(Birdie Bagtry)*; Fritz Leiber *(Colonel Isham)*; Whit Bissell *(Jugger)*; Don Beddoe *(Penniman)*; Wilton Graff *(Sam Taylor)*; Virginia Farmer *(Clara Bagtry)*; Libby Taylor *(Cora)*; Smoki Whitfield *(Jake)*.

THE CREATORS

Michael Gordon *(director)*; Jerry Bresler *(producer)*; Hal Mohr *(photography)*; Vladimir Pozner *(screenplay)*; from a play by Lillian Hellman; Daniele Amfitheatrof *(music)*; Milton Carruth *(editor)*.

Opened at the Rivoli Theatre, New York, May 18, 1948. Running time when released, 106 minutes.

THE PICTURE

In 1948 the Marches were seen in two excellent pictures under Universal-International auspices, both under the direction of the talented and painstaking Michael Gor-don. Both received fine reviews, and they were well-deserved. The first was *Another Part of the Forest*, adapted from Lillian Hellman's play by Vladimir Pozner. It dealt with the notorious, albeit fascinating, Hubbard family of *Little Foxes* fame as they were twenty years before the action of *Foxes* began, and traces the origins of the amoral Regina and her vicious brothers Oscar and Ben.

The patriarch Marcus Hubbard (March in one of his best performances) has profiteered in salt during the Civil War, ruthlessly exploiting his fellow Southerners for gain. Fifteen years later, in 1880, he is hardly popular around town but is grudgingly respected because he has money. His sons, the surly Ben and the weakling Oscar, hate him, and his daughter uses him for her own purposes, she being his one Achilles heel. His gentle and long-suffering wife (sensitively played by Miss Eldridge) has for years protected him from the consequences of a terrible secret: he had contributed to the deaths, at the hands of the enemy, of some seventeen young Confederate soldiers, sons of the community.

Marcus is conscienceless, insensitive, interested only in money and the power it will bring. Coming from

With Dan Duryea

With Ann Blyth

humble "poor white" origins, he is typical of the New South which rose to power through sharp business practices. Marcus condescends insultingly to the offspring of now-impoverished aristocrats who had once condescended to *him*. He ignores his wife, treats his sons tyrannically, makes fun of Confederate war heroes. When his eldest son takes issue with him on various matters, he orders him from the house, but his wife comes to the son's defense and reveals the secret of the Civil War betrayal. With this the son blackmails the father into handing over the family fortune.

His brother Oscar, a craven coward who is always on the side of the winner, sides with the now-triumphant Ben against their humbled father, as does Regina, who like a true fledgling opportunist goes where the power lies. The only member of the family with positive, decent instincts is the mother, and at the end she tells her entire family that she doesn't like them and talks of going somewhere where people are decent and affirmative.

Michael Gordon directed with perception and keen insight, the Marches were in top form, as were Edmund

With Edmond O'Brien

O'Brien, Dan Duryea and Ann Blyth as the bear's sharp-teethed cubs. It was a fitting follow-up to March's *Best Years of Our Lives* triumph and also reminded his admirers that he could project evil as well as beneficence in his performances with equally felicitous results.

THE REVIEWERS
Frank Leyendecker in *Boxoffice*:
Fredric March is superb as the self-styled demigod who amassed a fortune in the South profiteering during the Civil War.

Whit. in *Variety*:
Picture is sparked with list of top names headed by Fredric March who make this a field day for superb characterization, and from a production standpoint film is outstanding on all counts . . . the type of film audiences will leave the theatre talking about, and continue pointing out as a prime example of how a highly dramatic piece may still spell entertainment. From bitter drama, pace frequently swings to near whimsical humor, with result spectator is left in constant state of expectancy, with never a dull moment. . . . March delivers to tremendous effect as the father. . . . Miss Eldridge makes her portrayal count. . . . Michael Gordon's direction is topflight, catching nuances of every scene at right pitch.

Look:
The film commands interest in its unpleasant people and belief in its melodrama through excellent writing, acting and direction. . . . March makes the father a masterpiece of cynicism and arrogance and O'Brien matches it as the scheming son. Florence Eldridge as the innocent and bedeviled mother is also superb.

Edwin Miller in *Seventeen*:
Clothed in bitter wit, [the film] affords you an arresting

With Betsy Blair and John Dall

insight into one kind of people who were part of American history. The atmosphere in this crackling piece about a Southern family bristles with excitement . . . the movie presents, and presents enthrallingly, a subject too often left to the theatre or to books, namely people who do not abide by the golden rule and who go on to make their materially successful mark in the world. . . . Michael Gordon continually stresses movement, cutting rapidly and pacing the dialogue to move the picture along at top speed. March, Blyth, O'Brien, Duryea, Florence Eldridge and the others, are excellent.

With Ann Blyth, Florence Eldridge, Dan Duryea and Edmond O'Brien

Live Today for Tomorrow

Universal-International / 1948

THE PLAYERS

Mr. March was *Judge Calvin Cooke* in a cast that included: Florence Eldridge *(Catherine Cooke)*; Geraldine Brooks *(Ellie Cooke)*; Edmond O'Brien *(David Douglas)*; Stanley Ridges *(Dr. Walter Morrison)*; John McIntire *(Judge Ogden)*; Frederic Tozere *(Charles Dayton)*; Will Wright *(Judge Jim Wilder)*; Virginia Brissac *(Mrs. Russell)*; Francis McDonald *(Mr. Russell)*; Mary Servoss *(Julia)*; Don Beddoe *(Peterson)*; Clarence Muse *(Mr. Pope)*.

THE CREATORS

Michael Gordon *(director)*; Michael Blankfort and Robert Thoeren *(screenplay)*; based on the novel *The Mills of God* by Ernst Lothar; Jerry Bresler *(producer)*; Hal Mohr *(photography)*; Daniele Amfitheatrof *(music)*; Ralph Dawson *(editor)*.

Opened at Loew's Criterion Theatre, New York, December 5, 1948. Running time when released, 91 minutes.

THE PICTURE

The second of the two Universal-International pictures directed by Michael Gordon and starring the Marches was *Live Today for Tomorrow* which was retitled after its initial release, *An Act of Murder*, doubtless to stimulate boxoffice returns. (It is surprising that sales-conscious Universal executives had not adopted a surefire title like *Act of Murder* in the first place.) Again the Marches had themselves a fine picture, the result being that rare phenomenon for any actor: three excellent pictures in a row. Of the pictures in which he appeared with Miss Eldridge, this is reported to be March's favorite, and it is easy to understand why, for it is a mature and meaningful drama with excellent in-depth roles for both, to which they do full justice.

It is about a judge who finds out his wife is dying of an incurable and excruciatingly painful ailment. To spare her further suffering he drives their car over an embankment; he survives, but she does not. Being a "letter-of-the-law"-style jurist, he applies to his own case the same rigid principles that he would apply to a stranger before him in his courtroom, and insists on turning himself in, claiming he has been guilty of murder.

The matter of euthanasia becomes a subject of court debate. The judge insists that he is guilty, but the young lawyer who is in love with his daughter is determined

With Florence Eldridge

to free him, and eventually it is discovered that March's wife had died of an overdose of a self-administered drug and had been dead at the time of the crash. (She had learned the truth of her condition a while before.)

Even though March is acquitted, he insists to the court that while legally innocent he was morally guilty, and declares that the trial and the questions it raised have given him new insights into the law and that a man must be judged according to his heart as well as his actions. Highly intelligent, beautifully directed, sincerely acted, especially by Miss Eldridge who is poignant and true in the finest screen work she had ever done, *Live Today for Tomorrow* (or *Act of Murder*—take your choice) is a most creditable picture that holds up beautifully when viewed twenty-three years later on the TV screen. Moreover, it is that rare item—in 1948 or any other year—a picture that makes thoughtful observations in entertaining fashion, and leaves the audience intellectually as well as emotionally catharsized.

Director Michael Gordon wrote the author concerning the Marches: "That they were enormously gifted actors is common knowledge—what may be less known about them is the conscientiousness and dedication with which they approached their work. They were not merely 'movie stars,' they were mature and responsible artists who had an abiding respect for their craft, their material, their public, and of course, for their performances. Their meticulous concern for the quality of their performances

With Geraldine Brooks

was readily apparent to anyone who saw them. But the extent and depth of their preparation, their relentless and exhaustive search into the characters they were portraying (note the striking differences in both style and content between [Mr. March's] Marcus Hubbard and Calvin Cook) could be fully appreciated only by those of us who were privileged to work with them. My respect for them as co-workers and my affection for them as people is deep and enduring."

THE REVIEWERS
Lawrence J. Quirk in *Movies in Boston*:
If you want to see a film that showcases two superb artists at the height of their disciplined creativity and intuitional excellence, make a beeline for the Fredric Marches' latest effort, a mature, adult, sensitively directed and well-mounted drama that deals with the

With Florence Eldridge

With Geraldine Brooks

With Florence Eldridge and Stanley Ridges

With Florence Eldridge

subject of euthanasia, and covers all bases with discernment, compassion, and a wise objectivity that eventually elects for an anti-mercy killing stance. Fredric March and Florence Eldridge, married now for over two decades, make a compelling acting team. . . . Compelling, mature and attention-holding though the theme certainly is, the chief pleasure for this reviewer was watching these superior performers, Fredric and Florence Eldridge March, delivering in top-notch style in one of those rare thought-provoking and professionally-wrought films in which Hollywood should take humble pride whenever they surface. Michael Gordon's direction is brilliant.

Variety:
As adult and well-handled a picture as any that have come out of Hollywood in recent months. Universal

went far out on a limb with this one by putting the subject of euthanasia, or mercy-killing, squarely up to the audience and then taking a negative stand on the problem. Film, consequently is very close to documentary in theme, although it's given straight dramatic treatment. . . . Fine thesping turned in by all members of the cast under the adept direction of Michael Gordon. March, Edmond O'Brien, Florence Eldridge (who incidentally plays her real-life counterpart as March's wife), and Geraldine Brooks are standout, with Miss Eldridge, in particular, turning in a notable performance. . . . The screenplay maintains the best aspects of the novel but lightens the grim aspects of the film substantially for top audience reaction. . . . March's portrayal of the judge runs the full gamut of thesping and is consistent throughout. He's very slightly overshadowed by Miss Eldridge, who has the difficult part of the suffering wife down pat. O'Brien's splendid work, particularly in the final courtroom scene, should materially boost his boxoffice rating.

Photoplay:
Definitely on the somber side, this emotion-charged drama poses the question: Is a "mercy-killing" ever justified? March . . . turns in a noteworthy performance. . . . Miss Eldridge poignantly portrays a doomed woman; O'Brien and Brooks make a fine young couple . . . stirring human drama.

With Mary Servoss and Florence Eldridge

With Geraldine Brooks

Christopher Columbus

J. Arthur Rank   Universal-International / 1949

THE PLAYERS
Mr. March was *Christopher Columbus* in a cast that included: Florence Eldridge *(Queen Isabella of Spain)*; Francis L. Sullivan *(Francisco de Bobadilla)*; Kathleen Ryan *(Beatriz)*; Derek Bond *(Diego de Aranas)*; Nora Swinburne *(Joanna de Torres)*; Abraham Sofaer *(Luis de Santangel)*; Linden Travers *(Beatriz de Peraza)*; James Robertson Justice *(Martin Pinzon)*; Dennis Vance *(Francesco Pinzon)*; Richard Aherne *(Vincente Pinzon)*; Felix Aylmer *(Father Perez)*; Francis Lister *(King Ferdinand of Spain)*; Edward Rigby *(Pedro)*; Niall McGinnis *(Juan de la Cosa)*; Ralph Truman *(captain)*; David Cole *(Columbus' son)*.

THE CREATORS
David MacDonald *(director)*; A. Frank Bundy *(producer)*; Cyril Roberts and Muriel and Sydney Box *(screenplay)*; a Sydney Box Production and a Gainsborough Picture; Stephen Dade and David Harcourt *(photography)*; V. Sagovsky *(editor)*; color by Technicolor.

Opened at the Victoria Theatre, New York, October 12, 1949. Running time when released, 104 minutes. (Originally opened at the Odeon, London, June 14, 1949.)

With Nora Swinburne

With David Cole and Felix Aylmer

With Kathleen Ryan

THE PICTURE

The Marches then went to England to appear for J. Arthur Rank in *Christopher Columbus*. Unfortunately, their splendid luck with their two previous pictures did not hold. Certainly the film would seem to have all the earmarks of a promising enterprise—March's first centuries-past costume picture in some years, an exciting, glamorous historical subject, Miss Eldridge as Queen Isabella, scads of extras, lavish production mounting, loads of fifteenth-century atmosphere, beautiful photography in color processes carefully antiqued, authenticity in settings and furnishings and so on. Yet the net result was disappointing. What should have emerged from the screen as buoyant and exciting proved pedestrian, slow-moving, flat, elephantine of pace, and the characters never seemed to come alive. Too much time was given in the first half of the film to Spanish court intrigue, and rather dull intrigue at that, and by the time everybody got around to the discovery of America the audience interest had slackened to the point of no return.

March did well enough, all things considered, though he was not in his best form here, and even Miss Eldridge, sterling artist that she is, and who could usually be relied upon for a distinctive performance, managed to be no more than dignified and stately as the monarch who, at long last, sent Columbus voyaging.

The picture opens with Columbus and his son arriving in Spain, where they ask Father Perez (Felix Aylmer), the queen's former confessor, to get them introductions at court. Here Francis L. Sullivan proves to be March's implacable foe as he tries to persuade the Spaniards to raise sufficient capital for his exploratory voyage to the West. Much palaver goes on, in stiffish tableaux-style sequences, as Sullivan, who has his own fish to fry, insists that the idea is foolish and visionary. The Queen shilly-shallies, but when Columbus decides all is lost

and departs in despair, he is (as in all such films) recalled post-haste by a messenger from the Queen, and eventually gets his ships.

On to the famous voyage, with the *Nina*, *Pinta* and *Santa Maria*, as one film critic so unkindly noted, bobbing about like toy ships in a bathtub, while Columbus March copes with mutinous sailors, adverse weather and what-not. America is duly discovered, Columbus returns home in triumph, knows a brief period of glory and acclaim, and then it's another voyage, catastrophic disgrace and a return in chains, then the slide to obscurity.

The sad tale is the stuff of historical legends now—but the critics joined in wonderment at the failure of David MacDonald, the director, to take full advantage of his sweeping, actionful, panoramic subject—actionful, that is, in theory. The Marches strove valiantly, but the negatives of the enterprise vitiated whatever positives they doubtless sought to inject, and even March's performance was castigated by one critic as dour and solemn and the film was compared by another reviewer to a series of handsomely colored but essentially lifeless picture postcards.

THE REVIEWERS

Lawrence J. Quirk in *Movies In Boston*:
In this earnest but slow-paced and rather soporific costume-drama about that most famed of explorers, Fredric March, Florence Eldridge, Francis L. Sullivan and some other gifted mimes are as professional and vital as the direction and screenplay permit them to be. It would be pleasant to report that they triumph over the adversities implicit in the below-par contribution of director and writers, but the sad truth is that the finest actors need something minimal to work with—and a succession of extremely-well-photographed but intrinsically lifeless tableaux, with stilted dialogue and presentation, can

defeat the best. The Marches and Mr. Sullivan, being superior craftsmen, indeed artists, are not exactly defeated, but they are, shall we say, neutralized by overwhelming odds. But after those two excellent pictures contributed by the Marches last year . . . they can afford an occasional miss.

The New Yorker:
The scriptwriters have managed to transform some fine historical material into a film about as stimulating as a trip through the Hudson tubes. The business lumbers along in Technicolor, constantly contriving tableaux that

On the set with visiting Dennis Price

show off characters sweating under old Spanish costumes, and it takes Columbus so long to get the *Nina,* the *Pinta* and the *Santa Maria* under way that by the time they put to sea one half expects him to meet Lindbergh coming in the other direction. As Columbus, Fredric March is about the most dour mariner I've ever laid eyes on, and as Queen Isabella, Florence Eldridge seems a bit less lively than Her Majesty was reported to have been. Francis L. Sullivan is the expansive villain, but even his impressive talents are pretty well lost in this overstuffed picture.

Time:
[The film] turns an exciting bit of history into a series of dull tableaux in antiqued color. Even ten-year-olds, at whom this British-made movie is plainly aimed, will find it about as thrilling as an afternoon spent looking at Christmas cards. The discovery of the New World is practically shoved out of the movie by listless court intrigue directed against Columbus by a palace hanger-on (Francis L. Sullivan) who is trying to protect some real estate holdings in the Canary Islands. Columbus' Atlantic journey, viewed mainly by a camera in a fourth boat, shows the *Pinta, Nina* and *Santa Maria* in silhouette, bobbing around like toy boats in a bathtub. Columbus' men, weighted down by thick makeup, jewelry and rented fancy-dress costumes, do little but grouse about their historic mission and sit around waiting for San Salvador to bump into them. [The film] seems to be trying for the pageantry of *Henry V* but no one thought to get a script as good as the one Laurence Olivier got from Shakespeare.

With Derek Bond

With Francis Lister and Florence Eldridge

Death of a Salesman

Columbia / 1951

THE PLAYERS

Mr. March was *Willy Loman* in a cast that included: Mildred Dunnock *(Linda Loman);* Kevin McCarthy *(Biff Loman);* Cameron Mitchell *(Happy Loman);* Howard Smith *(Charley);* Royal Beal *(Ben);* Don Keefer *(Bernard);* Jesse White *(Stanley);* Claire Carleton *(Miss Francis);* David Alpert *(Howard Wanger);* Elisabeth Fraser *(Miss Forsythe);* Patricia Walker *(Letta).*

THE CREATORS

Laslo Benedek *(director);* Stanley Roberts *(screenplay);* based on the play by Arthur Miller; a Stanley Kramer Company Production; Frank F. Planer *(photography);* Alex North *(music);* Morris Stoloff *(musical director);* William Lyon *(editor).*

Opened at the Victoria Theatre, New York, December 20, 1951. Running time when released, 115 minutes.

THE PICTURE

Two years went by while March busied himself with stage work. When he finally elected to do a picture, it was an auspicious choice, for he took the role of Willy Loman in the screen version of Arthur Miller's trenchant play, *Death of a Salesman.* This had been a tremendous

Broadway hit in 1949, and the debacle of *Christopher Columbus* had set March to looking before he leaped when it came to film ventures. He gave one of his greatest all-time performances in this forceful film, made from an admirable play, about a man whose whole life has been given to crass self-deception and tawdry escapism. For this March won still another Academy Award nomination but lost to Humphrey Bogart (in *The African Queen).* Certainly in this film March was never displayed to better advantage; his sincerity, humanity, understanding of human nature, were in superb evidence as he skillfully limned the buried life of a man who lacked the spiritual resiliency and depth of spirit to improve his inner and outer circumstances.

Willy Loman's tragedy consists, among other things, of his escapist tendencies; they have blinded him to his own consummate mediocrity, his essential smallness of spirit. Now in his early sixties, he has been fired by the company for which he has worked for thirty years; his brand of selling is outdated and his energies have waned. He has raised his sons Biff and Happy on false, warped values tinctured with chicanery and petty ruthlessness.

Though both had worshipped him in their ingenuous

201

With Mildred Dunnock

With Mildred Dunnock, Cameron Mitchell and Kevin McCarthy

adolescence, they have become disillusioned with their father and no longer take him seriously. Though Willy's son Happy does fairly well in business, his spirit is withered. Biff, whom Willy wants to believe is a success, despite all evidence to the contrary, also gets fired from his job, and Willy dimly perceives that his son's and his long-suffering, tolerant wife's lives have been warped by his own shortcomings as well as by the Fates.

In a flashback it is revealed that he contributed to his son Biff's failure by searing the boy's mind and emotions with a memory: the sight of his father and another woman in a hotel room, where Biff caught them on an

unexpected, unannounced visit to Willy. At the play's close, Willy realizes that he has cashed in whatever paltry and tawdry spiritual dividends he has, and commits suicide, leaving a bereft wife who has just made the final payment on the house after a quarter of a century. March never plumbed deeper aspects of human reality than he did in this sterling performance. At many moments he seemed to actually blend himself into the tragic mystique of Willy, becoming one with the character, but always with the sure objective control of the artist he was. *Death of a Salesman* must rank with the finest work of March's career in any medium.

THE REVIEWERS
Bosley Crowther in *The New York Times:*
A nigh-exact translation of Mr. Miller's play, both in its psychological candor and its exhibit of a bleak, bourgeois

With Mildred Dunnock, Kevin McCarthy, Cameron Mitchell

With Royal Beal

With Kevin McCarthy, Don Keefer and Cameron Mitchell

the fatal flow of success-and-popularity-worship at first unbalances and then destroys him. March plays a little man's agony with the enormous passion that expands him into a symbol of humanity and therefore a tragic figure, and the contrast of his numerous escapes into visions of the past, where he was a hero to his lithe, promising sons, is a sharp one which is greatly moving.

Variety:
Fredric March [gives] one of the great film performances of the year . . . perhaps the greatest performance of his career. It is a particularly notable portrayal because at no time during the unreeling does it seem incredible for March to play a character so disparate from his former romantic roles. It is a physically and mentally exhausting part that demands his presence in almost every scene and he has set the pace for an excellent cast of supporting players. . . . Laslo Benedek has done a nifty job of directing, especially in the "dissolves" bridging reality and fantasy . . . a memorable if exhausting film experience.

milieu. . . . Mr. March's performance does a lot to illuminate the broader implications of the drama for it fills out considerably the lack of humanity in the main character that Mr. Miller somehow overlooked and thus makes the character more symbolic of the frustrated "little man". . . . The weakness of Mr. Miller's salesman, in this corner's opinion, is a petty and selfish disposition unredeemed by any outgoing love. Mr. March, by his personable nature, gives occasional fleeting glints of tenderness. Otherwise he is the shabby, cheap, dishonest, insufferable big-talker of the play. . . . Laslo Benedek's direction is commendable all the way . . . dismally depressing but it must be acclaimed a film that whips you about in a whirlpool somewhere close to the center of life.

Otis L. Guernsey, Jr. in the *New York Herald Tribune:*
March's Willy Loman is a breathtaking figure of pity as

With Kevin McCarthy and Patricia Walker

It's a Big Country

Metro-Goldwyn-Mayer / 1952

THE PLAYERS

Mr. March was *Papa Esposito* in this eight-episode film with a cast that included: Ethel Barrymore (*Mrs. Brian Riordan*); Keefe Brasselle (*Sergeant Klein*); Gary Cooper (*Texas*); Nancy Davis (*Miss Coleman*); Van Johnson (*Adam Burch*); Gene Kelly (*Icarus Xenophon*); Janet Leigh (*Rosa Szabo*); Marjorie Main (*Mrs. Wrenley*); George Murphy (*Callaghan*); William Powell (*Professor*); S. Z. Sakall (*Stefan Szabo*); Lewis Stone (*Sexton*); James Whitmore (*Stacey*); Keenan Wynn (*Michael Fisher*); Leon Ames (*secret service operative*); Angela Clarke (*Mama Esposito*); Sharon McManus (*Sam Szabo*); Elizabeth Risdon (*woman*); Bill Baldwin (*Austin*).

THE CREATORS

Clarence Brown, Don Hartman, John Sturges, Richard Thorpe, Charles Vidor, Don Weis, William A. Wellman (*directors*); Robert Sisk (*producer*); Helen Deutsch, Dorothy Kingsley, Isobel Lennart, William Ludwig, Allen Rivkin, Dore Schary, George Wells (*screenplays*); John Alton, Ray June, William Mellor, Joseph Ruttenberg (*photography*); Ben Lewis, Frederick Y. Smith (*film editing*); Johnny Green (*music supervisor*); Alberto Colombo, Adolph Deutsch, Lennie Hayton, Bronislau Kaper, Rudolph G. Kopp, David Raksin, David Rose, Charles Wolcott (*musical arrangements*); Douglas Shearer (*sound recording*); Malcolm Brown, William Ferrari, Cedric Gibbons, Eddie Imazu, Arthur Lonergan, Gabriel Scognamillo (*art direction*); based in part on stories by Edgar Brooke, Claudia Cranston, John McNulty, Ray Chordes, Joseph Petracca, Lucille Schlossberg.

Opened at the Trans-Lux 52nd Street Theatre, New York, January 8, 1952. Running time when released, 90 minutes.

THE PICTURE

Dore Schary, then head of Metro-Goldwyn-Mayer's production activities, put on the screen what was termed an "American Anthology" of eight unrelated episodes purporting to highlight various aspects of American life. It was far from a masterpiece, in fact so forgettable that once it had completed its run, little or nothing was heard of it again. A host of MGM stars got involved in this pedestrian attempt "to pay tribute to the wonder and excitement and drama and variety that is America," but all the king's horses and all the king's men and all the painstaking craftsmen, top directors, careful technicians, couldn't put this Humpty-Dumpty into any form that made sense or point. The consensus upon the picture's release was that all would have been better occupied with other projects.

March was one of those personalities who got mixed up in the business, and in an episode which was regarded as the weakest and most pointless of the eight, he essayed the role of an Italian-American, Papa Esposito, who bucks, for what seems endless length, at buying eyeglasses for his son Joseph, played by Bobby Hyatt. On hand as March's wife was Angela Clarke. Poorly written, inadequately, indeed obscurely motivated, the vignette is an outstanding example of a much-ado-about-nothing situation, and in what perhaps rates

With Bobby Hyatt and Angela Clarke

as the most forgettable of his screen appearances, March was no more than adequate; indeed, he must have been fully aware (too late) of what he had let himself in for, as his performance radiates (if that is the word) a half-hearted, half-baked quality that is distinctly not March.

The business takes twice as long as it should, with schoolteacher Nancy Davis trying to persuade March, who sports an Italian dialect, that it is not unmanly for his boy to wear the glasses that have been prescribed for him. Three of the eight segments are, indeed, not sketches but lectures (of a sort); Gary Cooper discusses Texas; William Powell analyzes the American mystique; a montage pays tribute to the accomplishments of American Negroes; the sketches include one of Ethel Barrymore as an Irish-American Bostonian complaining to the editor of the *Boston Post* that she has been omitted from the 1950 census; Keefe Brasselle as a wounded Korean vet who brings a letter to the mother of a soldier who has been killed in action (this sequence was regarded by many critics as the best); S. Z. Sakall and Gene Kelly as enemies of varying nationalities who are reconciled when Kelly wins the hand of Sakall's daughter; and Van Johnson, a substitute minister in a Washington church, gets to meet the President of the United States; he also learns he is not preaching just for the President.

THE REVIEWERS
Cue:
If this is the long-awaited Hollywood's short story film challenge to the three-and-four-part movie gems turned out in recent years by the British film-makers, our English cousins may relax. Presumably on the principle that bigger means better, more means merrier and eight episodes squeezed into a ninety-minute picture are finer entertainment than three (or four), *It's a Big Country* announces its eight stories (count 'em eight) and expects you to pop your eyes with excitement . . . the melting pot is melted into an MGM multiple-movie with mixed mediocre results—mostly soapy, sentimental, sugary and as elementary as a comic strip. All are animated by a

With Angela Clarke and Bobby Hyatt

spirit of sincerity. I wish they had been as well done as intended. The average is poor.

John Beaufort in the *Christian Science Monitor:*
One looks in vain for any subtlety in its message of hope and glory, any genuine depth of perception in its eight-sided view of life in the U.S.A. This is not to question the motives of Dore Schary and his MGM associates. Their hearts are undoubtedly in the right place. . . . But there are certain things missing . . . such as the spirit of humility and searching self-appraisal. One hesitates to think of the effect on overseas audiences of some of the film's sequences. . . . The individual sequences are developed economically and efficiently by their respective directors. In content and treatment there is a good deal to admire about the over-all purpose of the film. . . . Powerful reservations should perhaps be directed at the overblown commentary which ties the eight parts together and the booster-club heartiness with which it is delivered. Greater restraint might have helped [the film] come nearer to its purpose.

Man on a Tightrope

Twentieth Century-Fox / 1953

THE PLAYERS
Mr. March was *Karel Cernik* in a cast that included: Terry Moore *(Teresa Cernik)*; Cameron Mitchell *(Joe Vosdek)*; Gloria Grahame *(Zama Cernik)*; Adolph Menjou *(Fesker)*; Robert Beatty *(Barovic)*; Alex D'Arcy *(Rudolph)*; Richard Boone *(Krofta)*; Hansi *(Kalka the Dwarf)*; Pat Henning *(Konradin)*; Paul Hartman *(Jaromir)*; John Dehner *(the chief)*; Philip Kennelly *(the sergeant)*; Dorothea Wieck *(duchess)*; Edelweiss Malchin *(Vina Konradin)*; Margaret Slezak *(Mrs. Jaromir)*; William Castello *(the captain)*; and the Birnbach Circus.

THE CREATORS
Elia Kazan *(director)*; Robert E. Sherwood *(screenplay)*; Robert L. Jacks *(producer)*; based on a story by Neil Peterson; filmed entirely in Bavaria; Georg Kraus *(photography)*; Franz Waxman *(music)*; Earle Hagen *(orchestration)*; Hans Tost *(assistant director)*.

Opened at the Mayfair Theatre, New York, June 4, 1953. Running time when released, 105 minutes.

THE PICTURE
Man on a Tightrope was a thoroughly adult and extremely well made adventure drama that displayed March, then fifty-six, as the clown-acrobat-manager of a down-at-the-heels circus in Czechoslovakia, which he plots to maneuver out of the Communist zone into Western territory. Filmed on location in Bavaria, and with an actual circus troupe, the Birnbach Circus, lending authenticity to the background, the film profited from literate, apposite Robert Sherwood dialogue and the able direction of Elia Kazan, who guided the piece

With Terry Moore

along straightforward, non-polemical, actionful lines that made an anti-Communist statement by implication far more pointedly than grandiose speeches and impassioned stances ever could. In stressing entertainment, solid characterizations, colorful cinematics, Kazan and his able colleagues garnered a host of favorable reviews on the picture's release in 1953. Certainly it is one of March's better pictures of the fifties. March's own performance was skillful and often moving, and he was ably assisted by such sterling performers as Cameron Mitchell, Gloria Grahame, and Adolphe Menjou, who was particularly fine in his role of a Red investigator.

March's family, for generations, have been circus people. When the Communists take over Czechoslo-

Driving the car

turns like the proverbial worm and wins the respect of his young wife by masterminding an audacious escape plan. In full view of Red border police, he ostentatiously parades the entire circus in full regalia across a bridge, letting loose fierce dogs from cages to frighten the border guards, who think they are wolves. The elephants, too, come in for their share in diversionary tactics. Clowns and acrobats promote further confusion, and the troupe manages to force its way across the bridge into West Germany. But March is not there to rejoice with his followers, for he has been killed by Boone, who in turn is shot by the circus dwarf. March's young wife, determined to carry on, creates a defiantly colorful circus bombast from across the border.

With Adolphe Menjou

vakia, March is deprived of his ownership of the circus and merely allowed to operate it. His best workers are constantly drafted into the service of the state; his equipment distintegrates; and the state even attempts to tell him and his performers how they should entertain, suggesting political overtones and plants for his routine. In addition to the machinations of a rival circus owner whom March suspects is a Communist sympathizer, March must cope with the wayward romantic vagaries of his daughter, who is in love with the circus lion-tamer, a worthless adventurer; he also must weather the contemptuous indifference of his young second wife, who mistakes his quiet watch-and-wait philosophy toward the Reds as spinelessness.

March suspects his daughter's new suitor of being a spy for the Czech secret police, but he turns out to be an American GI on the loose behind the Iron Curtain. Richard Boone plays the circus aide in charge of equipment who turns out to be the true spy. Eventually March

THE REVIEWERS

Abel Green in *Variety*:

Director Elia Kazan has limned his characters with proper mood and shade . . . every detail of the freedom-hungry troupers in their camp is plausibly performed and presented. Even the side byplay of the Czech sentries and the Yank counterparts come across in the right key, never overdone, yet maintaining the proper pitch and excitement. All the components, from March, who is capital as the proud owner of a once-proud circus, through the rest of the cast . . . are big league.

Newsweek:

A highly atmospheric and timely melodrama, jammed with talent. . . . Fredric March once again a hero full of complicated agonies, and he has plenty of support from an elegant cast. . . . An absorbing picture.

Saturday Review:

Elia Kazan has staged the story frankly as an adventure film, a "chase" . . . as Cernik, Fredric March gives another of his beautifully turned performances, a man seemingly broken by events yet with the ultimate spiritual strength to defy authority. . . . The whole adds up to an unusually absorbing picture given added stature by its implications in our world today.

The New Yorker:

The methods employed to get out from under the comrades are so bizarre that they strain belief, but Mr. Kazan has arrayed his film with such ingenuity that before its winds up you are willing to put credence in almost anything. . . . The script is the work of Robert Sherwood, an old hand at these European affairs, and it is always adult.

Executive Suite

Metro-Goldwyn-Mayer / 1954

THE PLAYERS

Mr. March was *Loren Phineas Shaw* in a cast that included: Barbara Stanwyck *(Julia O. Tredway)*; William Holden *(McDonald Walling)*; June Allyson *(Mary Walling)*; Walter Pidgeon *(Frederick Alderson)*; Shelley Winters *(Eva Bardeman)*; Paul Douglas *(Josiah Dudley)*; Louis Calhern *(George Nyle Caswell)*; Dean Jagger *(Jesse Q. Grimm)*; Nina Foch *(Erica Martin)*; Tim Considine *(Mike Walling)*; William Phipps *(Bill Ludden)*; Lucile Knoch *(Mrs. George Nye Caswell)*; Edgar Stehli *(Julius Steibel)*; Mary Adams *(Sara Grimm)*; Virginia Brissac *(Edith Alperson)*; Harry Shannon *(Ed Benedeck)*.

THE CREATORS

Robert Wise *(director)*; John Houseman *(producer)*; Ernest Lehman *(screenplay)*; adapted from the novel by Cameron Hawley, Jud Kinberg *(associate producer)*; George Folsey *(photography)*; Cedric Gibbons and Edward Carfagno *(art directors)*; George Rhein *(assistant director)*; Douglas Shearer *(recording supervisor)*; Edwin B. Willis and Emil Kuri *(set decorators)*; Helen Rose *(gowns)*; Sydney Guilaroff *(hairstyles)*; William Tuttle *(makeup)*; Ralph E. Winters *(editor)*.

Opened at Radio City Music Hall, New York, May 6, 1954. Running time when released, 115 minutes.

THE PICTURE

March was never in better form than under Robert Wise's direction in the Metro-Goldwyn-Mayer film version of Cameron Hawley's *Executive Suite.* Ernest Lehman had given the screenplay his usual, meaning that Hawley's ideas were capsulized and intensified in admirably incisive vignettes, and moreover the production

values were lavish and there were stellar names galore, including William Holden, Barbara Stanwyck, Shelley Winters, Walter Pidgeon, and June Allyson.

This time March was involved in a highly unsympathetic role which gave him a chance to vary his portrayals (usually of an affirmative cast) with a "heavy" portrayal that was serpentine and devious—and as admiration-compelling as anything he had ever done when radiating his own special brand of sweetness and light. In this March was the controller of a large furniture company whose dynamic, forceful president has just dropped dead. March is hungry for the presidency himself, and sets out to win it by means fair or foul. His chief rival for the post, it develops, is a young vice-president (Holden) who specializes in design and wants the company to plump for quality and high standards as opposed to March's profits-any-way-you-can-get-them approach.

Meanwhile March is pressuring, and on occasion even blackmailing, right and left, all with the aim of enlisting his less decisive and less ambitious colleagues' support in his bid for the top spot. Among his foils are a vice-president who can't make decisions, a production man who is ready to quit anyway, a sales executive who is philandering with his secretary and is pressured accordingly by March, and a fancy moneyman who is a bit of a stock manipulator.

On and on the battle rages, with *the* board meeting coming up at which the new president will be chosen. William Holden continues to project his young-idealist plans. Then there is the secretary (Nina Foch) who is shattered by the late company president's death, and the ex-president's mistress (Stanwyck), who in the end

With Nina Foch

With Paul Douglas and Shelley Winters

casts the deciding vote to Holden. March garnered most of the good reviews, with some critics asserting that he had given the only solid performance in the ensemble, though in fairness it may be argued that his role was by far the most showy and complex of the lot. Whatever the pros and cons, it chalked up as March's best showing since *Death of a Salesman*, three years before.

THE REVIEWERS

Lawrence J. Quirk in *Current Screen*:
The versatility of Fredric March is on impressive display in this taut, well-made drama about corporate intrigue. In a far from sympathetic role, the usually sympathetic March gets across in spades all the crafty malice and manic ambition of a weasel-like company controller who stops at nothing to achieve the presidency after its occupant suddenly dies. The usually beneficent and positive-spirited March screen character, indeed, is not merely submerged; it is positively obliterated, in this brilliant study of a single-minded negativist—easily the best performance in a film graced by the likes of William Holden, Barbara Stanwyck, Walter Pidgeon, Paul Douglas, Shelley Winters, et al., all of whom must have found Mr. March a consummate scene-stealer—and not through shoddy tricks, either, but via the agency of his seasoned and formidable abilities.

Arthur Knight in *Saturday Review*:
A film with which both Houseman and Hollywood might well be pleased. Not a classic, not a milestone in movie-making, it does suggest a standard of product that could bring back to the box-office those vast audiences long alienated by trivia . . . where Mr. Hawley cluttered his story with irrelevant detail and personnel, the film has pruned scenes, combined characters and concentrated its attention on defining the motives of the six men struggling to assume leadership in their company. And where the author's technique occasionally failed him, the film sweeps along with incredible skill and certainty,

aided by inspired performances from Fredric March and Nina Foch, excellent ones from William Holden, Paul Douglas and Louis Calhern. True, there are moments when the script is just a bit too slick for its own good—too homey with June Allyson, too strident with Barbara Stanwyck, too pat with Holden. But underlying all is a ripe awareness of what makes the wheels go round, in business, in life and in the movies.

John McCarten in *The New Yorker*:
[This film] tries to interest us in the battle-for-succession that takes place when the masterful head man of a furniture company suddenly drops dead. The machinations of the firm's vice-presidents to assume control are related in some detail, but if by about the second reel you haven't put your money on the handsome, modest young executive who is outstandingly selfless in his devotion to shinier and sturdier veneer, then it's obvious that you couldn't spot Native Dancer in a paddock full of Clydesdales. . . . Of the actors engaged in this enterprise, only Fredric March, in the role of the bookkeeping genius, gives a performance of any substance. The others, including William Holden, Walter Pidgeon, Paul Douglas, Louis Calhern and Dean Jagger, are just shadows on the screen. Incidentally, the cast numbers among its ladies Barbara Stanwyck, June Allyson, Nina Foch and Shelley Winters. They seem to be out to prove that women connected with business don't have much fun.

With Nina Foch and Barbara Stanwyck

The Bridges at Toko-Ri

Paramount / 1955

THE PLAYERS

Mr. March was *Rear Admiral George Tarrant* in a cast that included: William Holden *(Lieutenant Harry Brubaker, USNR)*; Grace Kelly *(Nancy Brubaker)*; Mickey Rooney *(Mike Forney)*; Robert Strauss *(Beer Barrel)*; Charles McGraw *(Commander Wayne Lee)*; Keiko Awaji *(Kimiko)*; Earl Holliman *(Nestor Gamidge)*; Richard Shannon *(Lieutenant Olds)*; Willis B. Bouchey *(Captain Evans)*; Nadene Ashdown *(Kathy Brubaker)*; Cheryl Lynn Calloway *(Susie)*; James Jankins *(Assistant C.L.C. officer)*; Marshall V. Beebe *(pilot)*; Charles Tannen *(M.P. major)*; Teru Shimada *(Japanese father)*.

THE CREATORS

Mark Robson *(director)*; William Perlberg *(producer)*; a Perlberg-Seaton Production; Valentine Davies *(screenplay)*; adapted from the novel by James A. Michener; Loyal Griggs *(photography)*; Charles G. Clarke *(aerial photography)*; Lyn Murray *(music)*; Alma Macrorie *(editor)*; Wallace Kelley and Thomas Tutweiler *(second unit photography)*; Hal Pereira and Henry Bumstead *(art directors)*; Edith Head *(costumes)*; Wally Westmore *(makeup)*; Hugo Grenzbach and Gene Garvin *(sound)*; Commander M. U. Beebe, USN, *(technical advisor)*; color by Technicolor.

Opened at Radio City Music Hall, New York, January 20, 1955. Running time when released, 102 minutes.

THE PICTURE

March was reunited with William Holden in Paramount's *The Bridges at Toko-Ri*, this time playing an admiral who supervises aircraft carriers in the Korean conflict, waving his intrepid pilots off to battle and mourning the unwarranted loss of all too many of them. Holden is the derring-do pilot and Grace Kelly is wasted in an along-for-the-ride part as his worried wife, who pays him occasional visits in Tokyo. March and Kelly do a certain amount of philosophizing about the risks of war and the futility of bucking fate, but the planes and action steal the show, as well they should. Based on the novel by James A. Michener, with superb aerial photography by Charles G. Clarke supplementing Loyal Griggs' expert lensing, the film (one of a dying school by 1955) sported Edith Head costumes for Miss Kelly, Wally Westmore makeup, and let's not forget still a third photography set-up headed by Wallace Kelley and Thomas Tutweiler to catch the more flamboyant action (in the skies, not in the marriage bed, we hasten to add) and—well, just about everything—in fact, too much of everything.

Hailed with much chauvinistic hoopla in its own time, the film today seems flag-waving, posturing, falsely heroic—though the action sequences are excellent of their kind, and March gives the thing a solid and dignified look, especially when making such pronouncements as the one in which he speculates aloud on where such

With William Holden and Grace Kelly

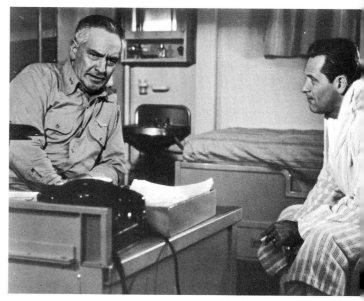

With William Holden

men as these come from—men who fly off a rolling deck, perform their difficult missions on an alien shore, then find once more their home ship that is a mere ocean speck, for a successful relanding.

The "Bridges" in question are strategic North Korean landmarks that must be destroyed to impede enemy operations, and Holden and Comrades destroy them, but at a cost—Holden's life and those of his men. Over-produced, overly busy with action that at times grows confusing, and under-generous in the footage allotted March, who deserved a far more fitting and less peripheral assignment, the picture was a feat of production skills and aerial photographic magic rather than a solid drama of human experience. Well-liked in 1955, *The Bridges at Toko-Ri* looks strident and dated in 1971—or perhaps in the intervening sixteen years audiences—and critics—have had enough of filmic glorification of wars.

THE REVIEWERS

Look:
This stirring film version of James Michener's novel of the Korean War is a story of heroism without heroics. It is focused upon one brave man, but it illuminates the gallantry of all the Navy's carrier-based jet pilots and their helicopter rescue teams. The action scenes were filmed in and around Tokyo and with a task force in the China Sea. The Technicolor cameras captured not only the breathtaking beauty of jets climbing into the sky but also, in chilly detail, the hazards of carrier operations.

Life:
A grimly realistic, exciting film . . . some of the most breathtakingly authentic flat-top footage to be seen in a long time.

Saturday Review:
There are heroics in this film but they are in what men do, not in what they say. Director Mark Robson filmed much of the footage aboard a Navy carrier in the Far East and his camera constantly documents the excitement of the business of taking off, flying, landing aboard a carrier . . . highly realistic battle scenes. . . . The fascination and danger of carrier flying are shown . . . beautifully.

John Beaufort in the *Christian Science Monitor:*
A thoughtful, beautifully photographed film which attempts the difficult task of appealing to popular taste, with a minimum of popular heroics. . . . In his screen adaptation Mr. Davies has done a skillful job of interweaving the flight episodes with those aboard the carrier in Japan. He moves the story forward persuasively, meanwhile keeping an even balance between military operations and personal drama.

With Grace Kelly

With Martha Scott and Richard Eyer

The Desperate Hours

Paramount / 1955

THE PLAYERS

Mr. March was *Dan Hilliard* in a cast that included: Humphrey Bogart *(Glenn Griffin)*; Martha Scott *(Eleanor Hilliard)*; Arthur Kennedy *(Jesse Bard)*; Dewey Martin *(Hal Griffin)*; Gig Young *(Chuck)*; Mary Murphy *(Cindy Hilliard)*; Richard Eyer *(Ralphie Hilliard)*; Robert Middleton *(Sam Kobish)*; Alan Reed *(detective)*; Bert Freed *(Winston)*; Ray Collins *(Masters)*; Whit Bissell *(Carson)*; Ray Teal *(Fredericks)*; Michael Moore *(detective)*; Don Haggerty *(detective)*; Ric Roman *(Sal)*; Pat Flaherty *(Dutch)*; Beverly Garland *(Miss Swift)*; Louis Lettieri *(Bucky Walling)*; Ann Doran *(Mrs. Walling)*; Walter Baldwin *(Patterson)*.

THE CREATORS

William Wyler *(producer and director)*; Robert Wyler *(associate producer)*; Joseph Hayes *(screenplay)* based on his novel and play. Lee Garmes *(photography)*; Gail Kubik *(music)*; Hal Pereira and Joseph MacMillan Johnson *(art directors)*; Sam Comer and Grace Gregory *(set decorations)*; Edith Head *(costumes)*; Robert Swink *(film editor)*; Wally Westmore *(makeup artist)*; John P. Fulton and Farciot Edouart *(special effects)*; Hugo Grenzbach and Winston Leverett *(sound recording)*.

With Richard Eyer, Martha Scott and Mary Murphy

213

Opened at the Criterion Theatre, New York, October 5, 1955. Running time when released, 112 minutes.

THE PICTURE

March, under the able direction of his *Best Years of Our Lives* guide and mentor, William Wyler, then co-starred for the first time with Humphrey Bogart, in the screen version of Joseph Hayes' play, *The Desperate Hours*, which had its Broadway run that same year, 1955. This was one of Bogart's final pictures before his death of cancer in 1957, and he played a considerably older (and considerably more tired) variation of the Duke Mantee characterization that had made him famous two decades before in the stage and screen versions of *The Petrified Forest*. Also on hand for a reunion with March was Martha Scott, who had played with him so affectingly in the warm and winning *One Foot in Heaven* fourteen years before. The criminal role was deliberately "aged" for Bogart's fifty-five years, the much younger Paul Newman having played it on the stage.

March was in fine fettle as the respectable citizen, husband, and father whose home, wife, and children are menaced by three escaped criminals who use their home as a hideout while awaiting get-away money. March gave an excellent portrayal of a decent, upper-middle-class citizen who encounters with raw courage and shrewd ingenuity the tough brutality of a criminal threesome.

Suspense mounts as the money fails to arrive, the wife grows more hysterical, and the little boy proves difficult to handle. March and his daughter are told to go daily into the outside world, performing their ordinary duties, so as to avoid community suspicion, with the wife and boy held as hostages to assure their silence. One of the criminals kills a suspicious tradesman, the girl's fiance becomes suspicious, and the police gradually draw a ring around the house. One criminal is killed when he leaves to strike out on his own, another in a gun battle with police outside the house—and Bogart gets his, of course, at the end, with a relieved March and his family once more restored to normal.

March was admirable in every one of his scenes, and

With Humphrey Bogart and Robert Middleton

projected tellingly such moods as calculated skill, determination, and fierce enterprise, as he at one point pleaded with police to adopt methods that would protect his family's lives, and later, outwitted and out-maneuvered the desperate Bogart.

THE REVIEWERS

Frank Leyendecker in *Boxoffice*:
It is Fredric March who gives the most memorable performance (equal to anything he has done on the screen) as the father, a fine, brave family man but one who is not ashamed to admit to his small son that he is afraid.

Hollis Alpert in the *Saturday Review*:
Wyler, a first-rate craftsman, has made a . . . polished production out of the situation. His cast leaves little to be desired . . . the performances are good, the direction solid, the settings reasonably believable. But again, we are shown human nature reacting to an extreme sort of

With Humphrey Bogart, Dewey Martin, Robert Middleton, Richard Eyer and Martha Scott

Fredric March, center

With Richard Eyer

situation. We aren't really told very much about the people who, of necessity, are types rather than characters.

John McClain in *The New Yorker:*
The cast of the picture is splendid. Fredric March has an impressive dignity as the citizen whose house has suddenly been taken over and Humphrey Bogart is frightening as the principal convict.

Life:
Made humanly convincing by the consummate skill of the film's entire cast and the . . . staging of its director, William Wyler. Humphrey Bogart is grimly perfect as the snarling ringleader. Fredric March is almost sure of an Academy nomination for his frightened but heroic father.

Time:
To melodrama fans, it may prove one of the most pleasurably prostrating evenings ever spent in a movie house. . . . Director Wyler has subordinated his actors with unusual severity to the pace of the plot, and most of them have taken to the rein like the thoroughbreds they are. . . . Fredric March, by the dignity of his performance, lends to the father's role a sense of legendary size that reminds a moviegoer—in a picture that might otherwise have had high-muzzle velocity but slight penetration—that he is witnessing not only an animated newspaper headline but also a plain parable about human rights and the majesty of the patriarchal principle, which, from the day of the cave to the advent of the split-level, has kept the wolf from the door.

With Robert Middleton

Alexander The Great

United Artists / 1956

THE PLAYERS

Mr. March was *Philip of Macedonia* in a cast that included: Richard Burton *(Alexander)*; Claire Bloom *(Barsine)*; Danielle Darrieux *(Olympias)*; Harry Andrews *(Darius)*; Stanley Baker *(Attalus)*; Niall MacGinnis *(Parmenio)*; Peter Cushing *(Memnon)*; Michael Hordern *(Demosthenes)*; Barry Jones *(Aristotle)*; Marisa de Leza *(Eurydice)*; Gustavo Rojo *(Cleitus)*; Ruben Rojo *(Philotas)*; William Squire *(Cachinos)*; Helmut Dantine *(Nectanebus)*; Friedric Ledebur *(Antipater)*; Peter Wynngarde *(Pausanius)*; Virgilio Texeira *(Ptolemy)*; Teresa Del Rio *(Roxane)*; Julio Pena *(Arsites)*; Jose Nieto *(Spithridates)*; Carlos Baena *(Nearchus)*; Larry Taylor *(Perdiccas)*; Jose Marco *(Harpacus)*; Ricardo Valle *(Hephaestion)*; Carmen Carulla *(Stateira)*; Jesus Luque *(Aristander)*; Ramsey Ames *(drunken woman)*; Mario de Barros *(messenger)*; Ellen Rossen *(Apites)*; Carlos Acevedo *(Orchas)*.

THE CREATORS

Robert Rossen *(writer, producer and director)*; Robert Krasker *(photographer)*; CinemaScope; color by Technicolor; Mario Nascimbene *(music)*; Ralph Kempler *(editor)*; Andre Andrejew *(set design)*; Gordon S. Griffith *(production executive)*; Cliff Richardson *(special effects)*; David Ffolkes *(costumes)*; Prince Peter of Greece *(technical advisor)*; shot in Spain and Italy.

Opened at the Capitol Theatre, New York, March 28, 1956. Running time when released, 143 minutes.

THE PICTURE

Robert Rossen next got March for a colorful role in costume, of the kind he had not done in years. This was his Philip of Macedonia in Rossen's lavishly produced *Alexander the Great*. Sumptuously mounted in CinemaScope and Technicolor, it starred Richard Burton as Alexander, with March getting co-star status as his tempestuous and quarrelsome warrior-king father Philip, who is eventually assassinated. Whereupon Alexander, now King of Macedonia, proceeds to conquer Greece, and then moves eastward as far as India, conquering and consolidating in his aim of uniting the known world under his sway.

Laid in the fourth century B.C., the piece is authentically set and costumed and the battle sequences were flashy and bloody in the usual style. Alexander, believing himself to be a god, as did his followers, went on from success to success, only to die of an allergy at thirty-two. There was some criticism of the long, talky, arid stretches, some of which featured much high-flown talk and abstract philosophizing. At times the spectacle was so overwhelming as to dwarf the characters, with Rossen obviously out to show DeMille how such things were done. March, in his scenes in the early part of the film, got across superbly the fierce passions and unpredictable whims of the highly masculine and brutally domineering Philip, and limned expertly the stark, tempestuous relationships of the bedevilled and bemused Macedonian ruler with his wife, played by Danielle Dar-

With Niall MacGinnis (third from left), Barry Jones and Richard Burton

With Niall MacGinnis and Richard Burton

rieux; with his followers and generals, and with his son, Alexander, portrayed by Burton with his usual flashing-eyed, stormy-browed intensity.

While Burton (being Alexander) got most of the footage, and handled the brunt of the action sequences (as well he should have at age thirty, March being then fifty-eight and past his prime for such physical exhibitionism) it was March's portrayal that came out best of the large cast's. Considering the nature of what he was given to do (and the relative brevity of it) March made the most of Philip of Macedonia with incisive deliveries of his speeches and a series of theatrically haunted and blazing expressions and stances. All in all he gave the role a bite and sharpness that recalled some of the other heroic roles of his more youthful period. If *Alexander the Great* does not deserve to rank with the better March films, it is primarily because March is not allowed to impress his personality on it beyond a certain point. The famous old cliche from *A Star Is Born* (when the producer assures the actor that the role is small but strong) could apply here: "They will be thinking of you all through the picture." And so they did. Had the film been made twenty-years before (and though there would have been no CinemaScope-color furbelows) March would have made a fascinating Alexander.

However, as Philip, he certainly has his moments. Philip's wife, Olympias, who once loved him greatly, later despises him for his constant infidelities and ever-lasting warmaking. Philip had had reason to believe that some other man sired Alexander, but treats the boy as his son, secures him an excellent classical education (Aristotle tutors Alexander and greatly influences him) and on occasion makes his regent in his absence.

Philip, however, alternates between promoting and distrusting his son. When Philip discards Olympias for a young wife, and has a son by her, the enraged Olympias, who wants to see Alexander king, engineers Philip's murder. Later, when he sets out on his world conquests,

Alexander cuts the famous Gordian knot; defeats Darius of Persia; copes with a mutiny in his ranks because he opens his soldiery to all nationalities, in line with his dream of a universal empire; and follows through on a dream Aristotle inspired in him, the spread of Greek culture and philosophy, which he believes to be the best in the world. Claire Bloom plays his great love, Barsine, giving what substance she can to an essentially sketchy and shadowy role. Death, of course, cuts short Alexander's dreams. As the above indicates, there was plenty of plot—indeed too much.

THE REVIEWERS
Variety:
Rossen is not always able to hold interest in his story

With Danielle Darrieux

and action, resulting in some long, dull stretches. Nor do the players have much chance to be more than puppets against the giant sweep of the spectacle. There are a number of single scenes that give the individual characters [some scope]; when they have them, artists such as Richard Burton and Fredric March give them a chance to grow.

Saturday Review:
Mr. Rossen has obviously striven to avoid most of the cliches of the spectacle form . . . the acting is several cuts above the level usually associated with this kind of movie. Fredric March as Philip of Macedonia is an heroic and stark figure. . . . Rossen would undoubtedly have had an easier time of it if he'd settled for something in the nature of a Greek horse opera. As it is, in spite of interesting open air sets, excellent costuming and some vivid CinemaScope photography, he has largely turned out a highly colorful pageant, with a good deal of the stiffness that the description implies. Alexander, as far as the movies go, is still a character in search of a plot.

John McCarten in *The New Yorker:*
While the picture has plenty of interesting pageantry, it doesn't offer quite enough drama to hold one's attention for its full length. . . . As Alexander, Richard Burton is a lot more satisfactory than the usual hero of costume epics and as Philip, Fredric March gives a credible portrayal of a mighty soldier slowly going to seed.

John Beaufort in *The Christian Science Monitor:*
Fredric March gives a robustly stimulating performance as that vigorous, shrewd and calculating warlord whose advice to his son was to trust nobody. . . . (The film) manages to suggest the complexities and contradictions, the contrasting barbarity and chivalry, the ruthless politics and the accompanying vision which characterized the behavior of Alexander, and to a lesser extent Philip.

With Richard Burton, Niall MacGinnis (second from right)

218

The Man in the Gray Flannel Suit

20th Century-Fox / 1956

THE PLAYERS

Mr. March was *Hopkins* in a cast that included: Gregory Peck *(Tom Rath)*; Jennifer Jones *(Betsy Rath)*; Marisa Pavan *(Maria)*; Ann Harding *(Mrs. Hopkins)*; Lee J. Cobb *(Judge Bernstein)*; Keenan Wynn *(Caesar Gardella)*; Gene Lockhart *(Hawthorne)*; Gigi Perreau *(Susan Hopkins)*; Portland Mason *(Janie)*; Arthur O'Connell *(Walker)*; Henry Daniell *(Bill Ogden)*; Connie Gilchrist *(Mrs. Manter)*; Joseph Sweeney *(Edward Schultz)*; Sandy Descher *(Barbara)*; Mickey Maga *(Pete)*; Kenneth Tobey *(Mahoney)*; Ruth Clifford *(Florence)*; Geraldine Wall *(Miriam)*; Alex Campbell *(Johnson)*; Jerry Hall *(Freddie)*; Jack Mather *(police sergeant)*; Frank Wilcox *(Dr. Pearce)*; Nan Martin *(Miss Lawrence)*; Tris Coffin *(Byron Holgate)*; William Philips *(Bugala)*; Leon Alton *(Cliff)*; Phyllis Graffeo *(Gina)*; Dorothy Adams *(Mrs. Hopkins' maid)*; Dorothy Phillips *(maid)*; Mary Benoit *(secretary)*; King Lockwood *(business executive)*; Lomax Study *(elevator operator)*; John Breen *(Walter)*; Renato Vanni *(Italian farm wife)*; Mario Siletti *(carriage driver)*; Lee Graham *(crew chief)*; Michael Jeffries *(Mr. Sims)*; Roy Glenn *(Master Sergeant Matthews)*.

THE CREATORS

Nunnally Johnson *(director)*; Nunnally Johnson *(screenplay)*; Darryl F. Zanuck *(producer)*; adapted from the novel by Sloan Wilson; CinemaScope; color by DeLuxe; Charles G. Clarke *(photography)*; Dorothy Spencer *(editor)*; Bernard Herrmann *(music)*; Alfred Bruzlin, Harry M. Leonard *(sound)*; Walter M. Scott, Stuart A. Reiss *(set decoration)*; Lyle R. Wheeler, Jack Martin Smith *(art directors)*; Hal Herman *(assistant director)*.

Opened at the Roxy Theatre, New York, April 12, 1956. Running time when released, 152 minutes.

THE PICTURE

Just as Richard Burton had been allowed to dominate *Alexander the Great* by sheer frequency of appearance, thus limiting March's over-all impact, so Gregory Peck was the leading character of *The Man in the Gray Flannel Suit* and the man on whom the lion's share of attention was focussed. Nonetheless, March, as in the earlier picture, made his relatively few scenes count heavily, and Peck was hard put to it to keep up with him in the scenes they played together.

This time March was a broadcasting tycoon who had sacrificed his family life to his chase for success, which in time had become an addiction. His disappointed and embittered ex-wife, Ann Harding, calls on him to help her with their spoiled, selfish daughter, Gigi Perreau,

With Ann Harding

who is getting out of hand. At the office, March gets to know Peck, who has been hired to write speeches for him, and finds himself admiring the younger man's independent spirit and forthright nature.

Peck is having problems with his wife, Jennifer Jones. Among other subplots worked into the picture, it develops that Peck had sired a child during his Army service in World War II (these flashback scenes are well presented) and Miss Jones, when she learns the news,

is unwarrantedly and indeed hysterically upset by the news, and takes some time to get back to a normal relationship with her husband.

Meanwhile at the office Peck must buck dour right-hand man Henry Daniell, who considers him too progressive and independent in his thinking to fit well into the corporate structure as he visualizes it. March, who takes a more mellow, tolerant view, has Peck up to his penthouse to discuss a speech he is about to make and once more finds himself admiring the young man's let-the-chips-fall-where-they-may views and opinions. March tells Peck a little of his own life, indicates that by sacrificing human ties for time-consuming, rat-race status-chasing, he has sacrificed human values and has only money to show for it.

With Gigi Perreau

Peck, who has been asked to take on greater responsibilities that would involve late hours and travel, elects for a low-pressure job and more time with his family; he has decided that ambition isn't worth the price.

This was one of March's most admirable roles; he was never more human, never more psychologically aware as he plumbed the depths of a man whose single-minded ambition had lost him all that was most precious in life, his family and human contact.

THE REVIEWERS
Fred Hift in *Variety:*
As the broadcasting tycoon, lonely in his power, Fredric March is excellent, and the scenes between him and Peck lift the picture high above the ordinary.... In adapting the screenplay from the book, Nunnally Johnson has caught the detail perfectly and the dialogue rings true. His direction is uneven, which accounts for

With Ann Harding

220

With Gregory Peck

against a recognizable and commonly shared contemporary background . . . a firm, fully packed drama with, it may be noted, some of the best acting we have had from the three principals mentioned.

John McCarten in *The New Yorker:*
[The film] has quite a few scenes that aren't at all badly constructed, and if it were an old-fashioned serial, I'm sure we might be able to tolerate it. In one massive dose, though, it's just too damned much and I think you'd be better off taking a tranquillizer pill than going through all this just for the sake of escaping the world and its woes.

the occasional lags. There are a great many imaginative touches in the picture.

Rod Nordell in the *Christian Science Monitor:*
Its [people] go farther than most movie characters in suggesting such things as integrity, loyalty and simple kindness. It is additionally refreshing to see a film plot proceed not through multiplied misunderstanding but through progressive understanding.

Cue:
Scenarist-director Nunnally Johnson, and a fine cast headed by Gregory Peck, Jennifer Jones and Fredric March, combine their distinguished talents to help make this an eminently satisfying, full-bodied, honest and mature drama of real people and real situations, set

With Frank Wilcox

With Henry Daniell, Gregory Peck and Arthur O'Connell

Middle of the Night

Columbia / 1959

With Kim Novak

THE PLAYERS

Mr. March was *Jerry Kingsley* in a cast that included: Kim Novak *(Betty Preisser)*; Lee Philips *(George Preisser)*; Glenda Farrell *(Betty's mother)*; Martin Balsam *(Jack)*; Albert Dekker *(Lockman)*; Lee Grant *(Marilyn)*; Edith Meiser *(Evelyn Kingsley)*; Joan Copeland *(Lillian)*; Betty Walker *(the widow)*; Rudy Bond *(Gould)*; Effie Afton *(Mrs. Carroll)*; Jan Norris *(Alice Mueller)*; Anna Berger *(Caroline)*; Audrey Peters *(Elizabeth)*; Lou Gilbert *(Sherman)*; Dora Weissman *(Lockman's wife)*; Lee Richardson *(Lockman's son)*; Alfred Leberfeld *(Ellman)*; Nelson Olmsted *(Erskine)*.

THE CREATORS

A Sudan Production. George Justin *(producer)*; Delbert Mann *(director)*; Paddy Chayefsky *(screenplay)*; from the play by Mr. Chayefsky as presented on Broadway by Joshua Logan; Joseph Brun *(photography)*; Frank L. Thompson *(costumes)*; Jean Louis *(Miss Novak's clothes)*; Edward S. Haworth *(art director)*; Jack Wright, Jr. *(set decorations)*; George Bassman *(music composer and conductor)*; Richard Gramaglia and Richard Vorisek *(sound)*; Irving Temaner *(production coordinator)*; Everett Chambers *(casting and dialogue supervision)*; Carl Lerner *(film editor)*; Charles H. Maguire *(assistant director)*; George Newman *(makeup)*; Marguerite James *(script supervisor)*; Lionel Kaplan *(technical advisor)*; Stephen Bono *(production manager)*; Flo Transfield *(wardrobe)*; filmed in New York.

Opened June 17, 1959 at the Odeon and Trans-Lux Theatres, New York. Running time when released, 118 minutes.

THE PICTURE

After a three-year absence from the screen March did Paddy Chayefsky's *Middle of the Night* for Columbia under Delbert Mann's direction. Originally the piece was a one-hour 1954 TV drama, also directed by Mann, starring Eva Marie Saint and E. G. Marshall. The long-running 1956 play version had starred Edward G. Robinson and Gena Rowlands. In the film the Gena Rowlands part was handed to Kim Novak, and her deficiencies as an actress were somewhat disguised by the fact that the character of the girl as visualized by Chayefsky was confused and not too bright to begin with.

March received his usual good reviews, though some critics insisted that he was hardly the type to portray a Jewish businessman convincingly. The story was one of those May-December affairs about a widower in his sixties who takes a fancy to his receptionist, a pretty young divorcee in her twenties. Circumstance and proximity draw the two together, the older man because he is lonely and rootless and does not want to settle for a staid second marriage with an older woman, and the girl because she was hurt in her marriage and tends to distrust younger men.

When the families of both parties discover what's brewing there are much dissension and countless protestations made about the essential unsuitability of the proposed union. The girl, in her confusion, is lured by her ex-husband into a night of love-making, which leads the older man to feel that she doesn't know her own mind. In his anguish, he breaks off with her. Later, having tried life apart and realizing that love is the only important thing, March and Novak elect for a happiness

based on their own instincts and not on the opinions of others.

Critics complained that the basic situation was unrealistic, and that such a marriage, especially in view of the girl's confusion and immaturity, would not last. Mann, however, gave the Chayefsky piece a realistic patina, and the excellent acting of March and some of his older colleagues, made it all seem reasonably credible. Once more Chayefsky's compassion for ordinary people caught in life's little culs-de-sac was manifest, and much in the picture was touching and true. It was the official 1959 United States entry at the Cannes Film Festival.

With Kim Novak

With Albert Dekker (second from right)

223

With Glenda Farrell. Kim Novak in rear

With Kim Novak

THE REVIEWERS

Bosley Crowther in *The New York Times*:
Mr. March is an excellent actor when it comes to showing joy and distress but he isn't successful at pretending to be a Jewish papa and business man. He goes with the flavor of his family, which is very colloquially played, about as poorly as spoonbread goes with lox.

***Time*:**
A cruelly beautiful and moving film. What most strikingly meets the eye is the profound and professional performance of Fredric March. Seldom have youth and crabbed age lived together in one face with so much suffering and meaning. Amazingly, actress Novak shows up not too badly, despite the distinguished company, and the credit for that seems to belong to director Mann.

With Edith Meiser

. . . Chayefsky, of course, is ultimately responsible for the passionate sympathy . . . of this film.

Paul V. Beckley in the *New York Herald Tribune*:
As penetrating as *Marty* and in some ways better. My zest for the personal trivia is more short-lived than Chayefsky's but who can deny his never-flagging insight into his characters or his truly remarkable ear for speech patterns. . . . Rich in good performances . . . from March one expects a good performance . . . This one is very solid. I doubt that any of his past performances, and there are fine ones to remember, is any more sharply realized than this one. . . . I never thought Miss Novak a great actress but she gives a reasonable facsimile here of a not too bright girl.

Hollis Alpert in the *Saturday Review*:
The story was more successful in its stage version. I suspect this was due to the playing of Edward G. Robinson and Gena Rowlands [and] Joshua Logan's direction. . . . The lines had humor and crackle, and the audience was able to put aside for a while its worry about what on earth would happen afterward. The movie, though, is a darker, gloomier affair. Fredric March, fine actor though he is, doesn't provide the appeal that Robinson brought to the role and Kim Novak, I'm afraid, isn't capable of sustaining any prolonged interest in the girl. Nor does Delbert Mann's direction spark the scenes between them to sustained life.

With Martin Balsam, Edith Meiser and Joan Copeland

Inherit the Wind

United Artists / 1960

THE PLAYERS

Mr. March was *Matthew Harrison Brady* in a cast that included: Spencer Tracy *(Henry Drummond);* Gene Kelly *(E. K. Hornbeck);* Florence Eldridge *(Mrs. Brady);* Dick York *(Bertram T. Cates);* Donna Anderson *(Rachel Brown);* Harry Morgan *(judge);* Elliott Reid *(Davenport);* Philip Coolidge *(mayor);* Claude Akins *(Reverend Brown);* Paul Hartman *(Meeker);* Jimmy Boyd *(Howard);* Noah Beery, Jr. *(Stebbins);* Gordon Polk *(Sillers);* Ray Teal *(Dunlap);* Norman Fell *(radio announcer);* Hope Summers *(Mrs. Krebs);* Renee Godfrey *(Mrs. Stebbins).*

THE CREATORS

Stanley Kramer *(producer and director);* Nathan Douglas and Harold Smith *(screenplay);* based on a play by Jerome Lawrence and Robert E. Lee; Ernest Laszlo *(photography);* Clem Beauchamp *(production manager);* Rudolph Sternad *(production design);* Ernest Gold *(music);* Frederic Knudtson *(editor);* Joe Lapis and Walter Elliott *(sound);* Bud Westmore *(makeup);* Larry Germaine *(hair styles);* Joe King *(wardrobe);* Anne P. Kramer *(assistant to the producer);* Ivan Volkman *(assistant director).*

Opened at the Astor and Trans-Lux 85th Street Theatres, New York, October 12, 1960. Running time when released, 127 minutes.

THE PICTURE

March got himself a colorful and challenging role in *Inherit the Wind,* one with many surface characterizational traits that suggested complex inner drives. The film (as was the play) was based on the 1925 Scopes "Monkey Trial" in Dayton, Tennessee. March's role of

385   *With Spencer Tracy and Harry Morgan*

Riding with Florence Eldridge

Matthew Harrison Brady was moulded on William Jennings Bryan, the fundamentalist who conducted the prosecution of the teacher who had violated the state's law against teaching evolutionary theories. Spencer Tracy co-starred as Henry Drummond, a character modeled on famed lawyer Clarence Darrow, who defends the teacher and pleads for reason, commonsense and freedom of individual thought.

Stanley Kramer produced and directed the film, which was based on the 1955 play starring Paul Muni and Ed Begley. March made himself up to closely resemble the legendary Bryan, complete with bald pate and flamboyant mannerisms. Florence Eldridge was on hand to play his wife. Tracy, as usual, underplayed, and elected, for reasons of contrast, to get his character across in a simple, direct manner, leaving the more colorful pyrotechnics (as was warranted) to March.

This was the first and only film Tracy and March appeared in together, and there was much excitement over the pairing of the two double-Oscar winners. They did not disappoint their admirers, playing their scenes together with an exciting complementary aplomb, each achieving his own well thought-out effects without infringing on the other's territory.

The chief characters are the fundamentalist Brady, a three-time Presidential candidate; E. K. Hornbeck (Gene Kelly), a cynical newspaperman who is out to drum up as much sensationalism as he can and gets his paper to

With Florence Eldridge and Donna Anderson

retain Drummond to defend the teacher. Though once friends, Brady and Drummond inject considerable bitterness into the trial. Brady professes to despise Drummond because he is a self-styled agnostic, but Drummond, slyly persistent, traps Brady in some pompous pseudo-religious bombast that undermines the prosecuting attorney's credibility, especially after Brady has used dubious fundamentalist witnesses and has refused to accept the scientific conclusions of Drummond's witnesses. Brady is made to look bad when he goes on the witness stand at Drummond's request and asseverates pompously that he considers his individual interpretation of the Bible to be the only correct one. Though the teacher is found guilty, the sympathetic judge imposes only a small fine. Brady is outraged by this and in a hysterical peroration tries to win the sympathy of the crowd, but

With Florence Eldridge

when it turns away from him, he has a fatal heart attack.

Drummond excoriates the cynical Hornbeck for his lack of compassion, and declares that Brady, for all his faults, had the right to his opinions and had the courage to express them. Brady's wife nails him down even more pointedly when she tells a doubting young girl that at least he stood for something, and how many people could say that?

THE REVIEWERS

Ivan Spear in *Boxoffice:*
Spencer Tracy as Darrow has the more sympathetic role but he is kept from stealing too many scenes by the consummate talents of Fredric March, who compensates with every trick in the histrionic bag, with subtle gestures and facial expressions, for what his part lacks in warmth.

Films in Review:
Fredric March actually looks like Bryan and enlivens his portrayal with little mannerisms which may not have been Bryan's but suggest aspects of his psychology. Florence Eldridge is very winning in a much smaller role. Spencer Tracy plays the Darrow character with his usual sincerity, which is not as uncouth and calculating as Darrow's essentially was.

Bosley Crowther in *The New York Times:*
One of the most intelligent, respectable and entertaining motion pictures of the year.... Mr. Kramer has wonderfully accomplished not only a graphic fleshing of his theme but he has got one of the most brilliant and engrossing displays of acting ever witnessed on the screen. Mr. March's extraordinary makeup and assumption of the mannerisms of Bryan is mainly a dividend for those who remember what Bryan looked like. The artistic virtue of it is that it gives a stunning comprehen-

sion of a proud, pompous, demagogic man, full of dogmatic assertion and theatrical flourishes who stands serenely encircled by ignorance until the locks of his mind are forced.... Mr. Tracy gives a fine, forceful simulation of a home-spun advocate of good sense ... since the clash of Mr. March and Mr. Tracy is not only the crux of the film but is also brilliantly, unsurpassably and fascinatingly played, it is the triumph of the picture.

Paul V. Beckley in the *New York Herald Tribune:*
Ingenious as it is, March's characterization puts too much stress on makeup and mannerisms. It is as though he was basically unsympathetic to the role, at least to the point of view it represents, and when making Bryan's better points had to smirk and overplay the man's vanity to keep from taking him too seriously.

With Spencer Tracy

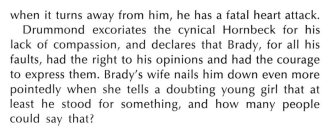

The Young Doctors

United Artists / 1961

THE PLAYERS
Mr. March was *Dr. Joseph Pearson* in a cast that included: Ben Gazzara *(Dr. David Coleman)*; Dick Clark *(Dr. Alexander)*; Ina Balin *(Cathy Hunt)*; Eddie Albert *(Dr. Charles Dornberger)*; Phyllis Love *(Elizabeth Alexander)*; Edward Andrews *(Bannister)*; Aline MacMahon *(Dr. Luxy Grainger)*; Arthur Hill *(Tomaselli)*; Rosemary Murphy *(Miss Groves)*; Barnard Hughes *(Dr. Kent O'Donnell)*; Joseph Bova *(Dr. Shawcross)*; George Segal *(Dr. Howard)*; Matt Crowley *(Dr. Rufus)*; Dick Button *(operating intern)*; William Hansen *(x-ray technician)*; Addison Powell *(board physician)*.

THE CREATORS
A Drexel-Miller-Turman Production. Stuart Miller and Lawrence Turman *(producers)*; Phil Karlson *(director)*; Joseph Hayes *(screenplay)*; based on the novel *The Final Diagnosis* by Arthur Hailey; Arthur J. Ornitz *(photography)*; Elmer Bernstein *(music)*; Jimmy Di Gangi and Angelo Laiacona *(art direction)*; Richard Sylbert *(production designer)*; Robert Swink *(editor)*; Ruth Morley *(costumes)*; filmed in New York City.

With Ina Balin and Ben Gazzara

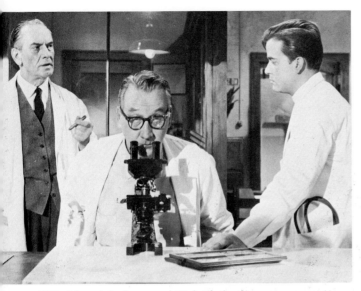

With Edward Andrews and Dick Clark

With Dick Clark

Opened at the Astor and Trans-Lux 85th Street Theatres, New York, August 23, 1961. Running time when released, 100 minutes.

THE PICTURE

In *The Young Doctors,* which was photographed in New York, March gave another excellent account of himself as an old-warhorse medico in a city hospital who is finally made to realize that he has run his course and must make way for a younger man. One critic stated that March's performance was so good that the picture was more rightfully concerned with old doctors than young ones. Be this as it may, the script by Joseph Hayes did get across the varying cross-currents of medical politics in a hospital setting, and also outlined the stresses and strains and varying crises that in time weed out the boys from the men. Based on a novel by Arthur Hailey, the story had originally debuted as a two-part CBS television drama presented in 1957. Titled *No Deadly Medicine* and directed by Sidney Lumet, it starred Lee J. Cobb in March's film role and William Shatner in the part Ben Gazzara later took over.

For the film version March took special instruction from a New York surgeon as to correct operating-room procedures; during the making of the picture four New York hospitals were made available to the producers for authentic locale work.

When Gazzara reports to the pathology section of the hospital, he is greeted coldly by the veteran chief pathologist, March, who is slipping with the years but won't admit it and considers the younger man a threat. When Gazzara demands a needed blood test for an expectant mother whose symptoms are suspicious, an irritated March countermands the order out of pique. When this results later in serious danger for the patient, March realizes that his time is indeed up and he offers his resignation. He leaves despite Gazzara's protests,

With Dick Clark, Ina Balin, Ben Gazzara and Eddie Albert

for the younger man has come to respect his colleague during their association.

In another instance a student nurse has a knee tumor; March diagnoses the condition as requiring amputation; Gazzara disagreed. This time it happens to be March who was right. March garnered some of the best reviews of his career for this film, in which his sound character insights were highy praised.

THE REVIEWERS

Joseph Morgenstern in the *New York Herald Tribune:* An often moving drama in which the people as well as the technical aspects have the stamp of truth upon them. . . . Fredric March gives a memorable performance as Dr. Pearson. The beauty of the part, which Mr. March makes poignantly clear, is that the old doctor not only learns but teaches. The dead teach the living, the young

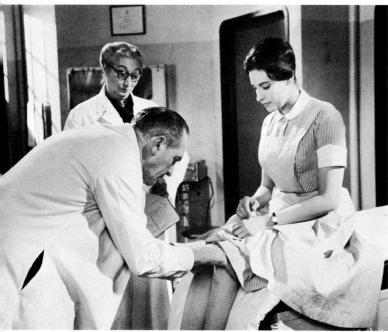

With Aline MacMahon and Ina Balin

teach the old, the old teach the young and the film teaches us without being pedantic about it.

Time:
A dissecting room meller that offers any moviegoer with the stomach for it a slice of hospital life.... As conceived, the story has dramatic force and psychological acuity. As realized, the film shows a distressing tendency to candy its corpses and the climax is a mere placebo. Hayes' screenwriting is often crude.... Phil Karlson ... clumsily misdirects his actors (but) he cannot rattle

With Arthur Hill and Ben Gazzara

actor March, who after a career of thirty-three years and sixty-five films stands almost without rival as a creative cinemactor.

Wilfred Mifflin in Films in Review:
Fredric March's performance is so artfully conceived and executed it proves anew he is today's most competent actor. In fact, his performance is so powerful you come away feeling "The Young Doctors" is about an old one.

Bosley Crowther in The New York Times:
A wistful realization was suddenly brought to mind as [the film] was unreeling. The realization was that the slightly senescent and headstrong pathologist who is a principal figure in this ... hospital film, could be the young Dr. Kildare of about twenty-five years ago. Yes, this aging and winning physician, played so finely by Fredric March that you have more regard and sympathy for him than for anyone else in the film, could be the middle-aged remainder of the alert and dedicated young medical intern whom Lew Ayres made a memorable example of medical devotion in the familiar old Metro series film.... Phil Karlson's sharp and taut direction is in the documentary-reenactment vein. So, all in all, this production is a fair memorial to Dr. Kildare.

Dr. Charles Begg, right, of the pathology department of New York's St. Luke's Hospital, demonstrates the proper way to dissect a human brain to an attentive Mr. March

The Condemned of Altona

Titanus-S.G.C.   20th Century-Fox / 1963

THE PLAYERS

Mr. March was *Gerlach* in a cast that included: Sophia Loren *(Johanna)*; Maximilian Schell *(Franz)*; Robert Wagner *(Werner)*; Francoise Prevost *(Leni)*; Alfredo Franchi *(grounds keeper)*; Lucia Pelella *(grounds keeper's wife)*; Roberto Massa *(driver)*; Carlo Antonini *(police official)*; Armando Sifo *(policeman)*; Antonia Cianci *(maid)*; Aldo Pecchioli *(cook)*.

THE CREATORS

Vittorio de Sica *(director)*; Carlo Ponti *(producer)*; Abby Mann and Cesare Zavattini *(screenplay)*; based on a play by Jean-Paul Sartre; a co-production of Titanus Films (Rome) and S.G.C. Films (Paris); Roberto Gerardi *(photography)*; *Music:* Symphony Number 11, Opus 203, by Dmitri Shostakovich, conducted by Franco Ferrara; Ezio Frigerio *(art director)*; Renato Guttuso *(drawings)*; Manuel Del Campo and Adriana Novelli *(editors)*; Ennio Sensi *(sound)*; Pier Luigi Pizzi *(wardrobe)*; Luciano Perugia *(production manager)*; Luisa Alessandri and Giuseppe Menegatti *(assistant directors)*; filmed in CinemaScope in Italy and Germany.

Opened at the Astor and 34th Street East Theatres, October 30, 1963. Running time when released, 114 minutes.

THE PICTURE

Neither cast nor creators emerged with any particular credit from *The Condemned of Altona*, which typical critcal reaction summed up—and correctly—as a muddled mess. Though March tried hard to lend conviction to his ineptly-directed and poorly written role of a Krupp-style German industrial leader with a skeleton in his family closet, the picture just didn't take—either with the reviewers or the public. It must be marked down as one of March's failures. Among the critical thumbdowns: "pretentious," "ponderous," "victim of its own ambitions," "interminable."

With Robert Wagner

Part of the problem lay with director Vittorio de Sica, who was not at home with German subject matter and did not comprehend the German mystique. Nor was the lustily Italianate Sophia Loren believable as a German *Frau*. Robert Wagner, as unmistakably American as Sophia was Italian, was even less credible as a scion of a corrupt German industrial clan.

The film was choppy, indifferently photographed, poorly edited, lacking in tension and pace, and all in all was a disaster for everyone concerned. March did manage to salvage a few good personal reviews from the debacle, though even he had by no means an unanimously favorable press, one critic for instance complaining that he "lacks Adenauer granite" (though how a corrupt industrialist should be granitic in an Adenauer style went unexplained by the critic).

The story dealt with the Gerlach family, obviously modeled on the Krupps, who head a vast German industrial complex. March, its head, learns he is dying of cancer and asks his younger son, Wagner, to return home. Wagner arrives with his wife, Miss Loren, and his father asks him to take over the business, but he refuses, as he disapproves of the entire operation and its indiscriminate toadying to whatever government happens to be in power.

Hidden in the attic of the family mansion is the older son, Maximilian Schell, who had once been cited at the Nuremberg trials for war crimes. He has deteriorated mentally over the years, and has been told Germany is poor when it is actually prosperous. Though he sees only his possessive sister, Miss Loren contrives to get in to him after learning of his existence, and at first is taken in by his persuasive charm. Later she learns that his earlier career was actually a nefarious one. Schell eventually leaves his attic and seeks out his father to kill him in order to exorcise both their tormenting guilts.

All this might have played plausibly and interestingly had director, photographer and screenwriters worked

With Robert Wagner

232

With Vittorio De Sica

together as a cohesive, disciplined unit, but the net result was confusion, discursiveness—and poor reviews galore.

THE REVIEWERS

Judith Crist in the *New York Herald Tribune:*
[The film] becomes a victim of its own ambitions. Its polemic assumes a vindictive monotony; its personalities divert rather than involve us in its thesis, and we are left with a domestic melodrama rather than a scathing insight into the evil of the day.... Fredric March, perfection as always, is the complete amoralist as the industrialist, but as the father he brings compassionate shadows to the black and white demands of the script. ... The film has an earnestness that is tiring, a gloom that is unrelieved. [It] pounds when it should prod, and its appeal is purely to the intellect rather than the heart and, above all, the conscience.

Time:
A ponderous, pretentious, interminable Germanic muddle of a movie, one of the year's nosier bombs ... on this Elbe of verbiage, Director de Sica sinks without a bubble. In scene after scene he simply aims his camera at a famous face and hopes for the best. He seldom gets it ... March, for want of anything better to play, plays March.

Stanley Kauffmann in *The New Republic:*
A pat anti-German tract. The dangers of rebuilt Germany are not slight but if anything is likely to make us recoil in the wrong direction, it is such material as Mr. Mann's hysterical superficialities ... the script is a reduction of Sartre's complexities of truth, responsibility and evil into simplifications of poster wickedness.... Fredric March lacks Adenauer granite as the father.

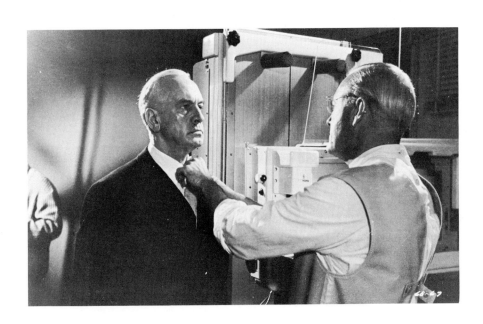

Seven Days In May

Seven Arts-Joel Productions   Paramount / 1964

THE PLAYERS
Mr. March was *President Jordan Lyman* in a cast that included: Burt Lancaster *(General James M. Scott)*; Kirk Douglas *(Colonel Martin "Jiggs" Casey)*; Ava Gardner *(Eleanor Holbrook)*; Edmond O'Brien *(Senator Raymond Clark)*; Martin Balsam *(Paul Girard)*; George Macready *(Christopher Todd)*; Whit Bissell *(Senator Prentice)*; John Houseman *(Admiral Barnswell)*; Hugh Marlowe *(Harold McPherson)*; Bart Burns *(Arthur Corwin)*; Richard Anderson *(Colonel Murdock)*; Jack Mullaney *(Lieutenant Howe)*; Andrew Duggan *(Colonel "Mutt" Henderson)*; John Larkin *(Colonel Broderick)*; Malcolm Atterbury *(White House physician)*; Helen Kleeb *(Esther Townsend)*; Colette Jackson *(bar girl)*.

THE CREATORS
John Frankenheimer *(director and co-producer)*; Edward Lewis *(producer)*; Rod Serling *(screenplay)*; based on a novel by Fletcher Knebel and Charles W. Bailey II; Ellsworth Fredricks *(photography)*; Cary Odell *(art direction)*; Edward Boyle *(set decorations)*; Jerry Goldsmith *(music)*; Ferris Webster *(editor)*; Joe Edmondson *(sound)*; Hal Polaire *(production manager and assistant director)*.

Opened at the Criterion and Sutton Theatres, New York, February 19, 1964. Running time when released, 120 minutes.

THE PICTURE
March gave one of the better performances of his recent period as The President of the United States in the John Frankenheimer-directed *Seven Days in May*. Rod Serling's screenplay captured all the excitement of the Fletcher Knebel-Charles W. Bailey II novel. March, in fact garnered the best personal reviews among a cast that boasted the likes of Burt Lancaster, Kirk Douglas and Edmund O'Brien, with his sincere, authoritative, dignified playing registering solidly.

When President Lyman arouses the disapproval of the military and some public resentment by signing a nuclear treaty with the Soviet Union, General James Scott, the Chairman of the Joint Chiefs of Staff, secretly plans a military coup. The plan is set for a certain date in May when the President will be relatively isolated during a military alert.

A friend tips off the chief executive to the conspiracy, and he sends one of his allies, a Senator, to investigate a certain top-secret base in Texas where the military have been allegedly hatching secret plans. The Senator is captured and held there, but later he breaks out. A Presidential aide flies to Gibraltar to get a statement from an admiral, one of the joint chiefs of staff who has indicated his disaffection with the coup. The admiral signs a statement that will nail the culprits, but the aide carrying it is killed in a plane crash returning to Washington. Then the admiral denies signing the statement.

The chief conspirator's mistress (briefly but fetchingly played by none other than Miss Ava Gardner) provides another of the President's allies with incriminating let-

ters. Later the President confronts Scott with the evidence of his guilt, but cannot bring himself to make public use of the letters. Scott feels that public opinion will support him, and that he and his aides will win the day. The President goes on TV to demand the resignations of the guilty members of the military. During the telecast the President is given the message that the Admiral's signed statement incriminating his coup-minded colleagues has been found in the wrecked plane. Scott and his cohorts are forced to resign and the coup is stymied before it gets off the ground.

Frankenheimer kept the suspense at a tense height; Serling, who had long since demonstrated a penchant for this type of story, delivered in fine style.

THE REVIEWERS
Time:
The movie is least successful when it tries to sound significant—as when March, stiffening up beside the flag, intones, "The enemy is an age. A nuclear age. And out

of this comes a sickness." Some of the dialogue in the final reels seems to have been cribbed from a prep school essay on "What Democracy Means to Me." But that seems fitting enough, too, for [the film] is the kind of fast-paced melodrama that is made to order for a rainy Saturday afternoon.

Judith Crist in the *New York Herald Tribune:*
The cast is excellent, with Fredric March's Presidential portrait marked by its sensibility, its mature dignity and its ease ... [the film is] in the best tradition of the suspense thriller—with the ultimate thrill our awareness of its actual potential.

Stanley Kauffmann in *The New Republic:*
The portentous smugness of the script is matched by the incessant trickiness of the direction. What passes for brilliance in Frankenheimer seems to me merely busy memory and egotism unhampered by taste or substance. ... Kirk Douglas, more restrained than usual, is the Marine colonel, Burt Lancaster more Lancastrian than usual. ... Fredric March is the President, easily the most skillful of the three.

Bosley Crowther in *The New York Times:*
Fredric March's performance is the finest ... a brave and forceful film.

With Edmond O'Brien

235

Hombre

20th Century-Fox / 1967

THE PLAYERS
Mr. March was *Alexander Favor* in a cast that included: Paul Newman *(John Russell)*; Richard Boone *(Cicero Grimes)*; Diane Cilento *(Jessie Brown)*; Cameron Mitchell *(Sheriff Frank Braden)*; Barbara Rush *(Audra Favor)*; Peter Lazer *(Billy Lee Blake)*; Margaret Blye *(Doris Blake)*; Martin Balsam *(Henry Mendez)*; Skip Ward *(Steve Early)*; Frank Silvera *(Mexican bandit)*; David Canary *(Lamar Dean)*; Val Avery *(Delgado)*; Larry Ward *(soldier)*; Linda Cordova *(Mrs. Delgado)*; Pete Hernandez *(Apache)*; Merrill C. Isbell *(Apache)*.

THE CREATORS
Martin Ritt and Irving Ravetch *(producers)*; Martin Ritt *(director)*; Ray Kellogg *(second unit director)*; Irving Ravetch and Harriet Frank, Jr. *(screenplay)*; based on the novel by Elmore Leonard; James Wong Howe *(photography)*; David Rose *(music composed and conducted)*; Frank Bracht *(editor)*; Jack Martin Smith and Robert E. Smith *(art direction)*; Jack R. Carter and David Dockendorf *(set decorations)*; Walter M. Scott and Raphael Bretton *(set decorations)*; Leo Shuken and Jack Hayes *(orchestration)*; Don Feld *(costumes)*; Ben Nye *(makeup)*; Margaret Donovan *(hair styles)*; Harry A. Caplan *(production manager)*; William McGarry *(assistant direc-*tor*)*; location scenes filmed in Arizona; DeLuxe Color; Panavision.

Opened at the Astor and 68th Street Playhouse, New York, March 21, 1967. Running time when released, 111 minutes.

THE PICTURE
After three years off the screen, March appeared with Paul Newman in 20th Century-Fox's *Hombre*. He had a strong part as Alexander Favor, an Indian agent who has been cheating the redmen by passing off dogmeat as beef and pocketing the profits. Favor and his wife, played by Barbara Rush, find themselves on an Arizona stagecoach (the story is laid in the 1880s), where there is discrimination against one John Russell (Newman) a white man who has been raised by Indians and has identified himself with his foster-folk to the point where he has taken on their manners and appearance. Favor's snobbish and stuffy bigotry forces "Hombre," as they call him, to ride outside with the driver and to be the sullen recipient of other minor humiliations.

But when gunmen, secretly in league with one of the passengers, Richard Boone, hold up the coach and

With Barbara Rush

make off with $12,000 of the money March had embezzled from the government via phony beef deals, it is Hombre who proves the most heroic and resourceful of the group. Hombre succeeds in killing two of the bandits and recovering the money, but the remaining outlaws, who are joined by Boone, have in turn taken March's wife as a hostage, and later offer to trade her for the money. Hombre doesn't wish to make the trade because, as he tells the group, March's wife made no protest during the years of her husband's chicaneries, though she knew of them.

The other members of the group under Hombre's protection are a boardinghouse keeper and a young married couple, along with the driver. Diane Cilento, the boardinghouse keeper, attempts to rescue the other woman by taking the money to the outlaws, but eventually Hombre goes in her place, a pitched battle takes place and though all the outlaws are killed, Hombre also dies while protecting his associates, who then realize belatedly that he has been the most courageous and worthy among them.

March's role, while it tended to be peripheral, did give him a few strong scenes in which he got across the essential cravenness of Favor, sketching in his character with sharp, sure strokes under Martin Ritt's able direction. March turned seventy the year the film was released, but his loyal admirers among the film audience found gratifying evidence here that he had not lost one iota of his skill and personality force.

THE REVIEWERS
Frederick H. Guidry in the *Christian Science Monitor*: An engrossing exploration of mankind's obligations and

With Diane Cilento, Margaret Blye, Peter Lazer and Martin Balsam

237

With Peter Lazer and Margaret Blye

frailties. Unfortunately, the film's emphasis turns negative, and the conclusion seems to be that sacrifice on behalf of another is useless. Nevertheless, the point is not lost that wisdom, courage and unselfish love are more attractive and inspiring than their baneful opposites (though *Hombre* apparently doubts that they are also more potent).... Fredric March, Diane Cilento and Martin Balsam are among the excellent actors portraying the waylaid passengers.

Murf. in *Variety*
Fredric March, essaying an Indian agent who has embezzled food appropriations for his charges ... scores in a strong, unsympathetic—but eventually pathetic—role.

Newsweek:
Like most good Westerns, *Hombre* really isn't about the West at all. *High Noon* was about responsibility, *Shane* about courage, and *Hombre* is about color, about the ambiguous role of the non-white American in a white society.... Two-faced Professor Favor, well-played by Fredric March, laments the evils done to the Indians but has swindled a fortune as their government agent. ... Director Martin Ritt builds his coachload of characters in pithy bursts of dialogue and gunplay.

With Barbara Rush and Martin Balsam

tick...tick...tick...

Metro-Goldwyn-Mayer / 1970

THE PLAYERS
Mr. March was *Mayor Parks* in a cast that included: Jim Brown *(Jimmy Price)*; George Kennedy *(John Little)*; Lynn Carlin *(Julia Little)*; Don Stroud *(Bengy Springer)*; Janet MacLachlan *(Mary Price)*; Richard Elkins *(Brad Wilkes)*; Clifton James *(D. J. Rankin)*; Bob Random *(John Braddock)*; Mills Watson *(Deputy Warren)*; Bernie Casey *(George Harley)*; Anthony James *(H. C. Tolbert)*; Dub Taylor *(Junior)*; Karl Swanson *(Braddock, Sr.)*.

THE CREATORS
Ralph Nelson *(director)*; Ralph Nelson and James Lee Barrett *(producers)*; James Lee Barrett *(screenplay)*; Loyal Griggs *(photography)*; Jerry Styner *(music)*; George W. Davis, Bill Glasgow *(art direction)*; Alex Beaton *(film editor)*; Robert R. Benton, Don Greenwood, Sr. *(set decoration)*; Franklin Milton *(sound)*; Mike Curb *(music supervision)*; Michael S. Glick *(assistant director)*; Panavision; MetroColor.

Opened at Radio City Music Hall, New York, February 12, 1970. Running time when released, 96 minutes.

THE PICTURE
After another three-year absence (March's following has found highly regrettable his recent three-year-interval pattern of screen appearances) March returned to film-making in Metro-Goldwyn-Mayer's *tick . . . tick . . . tick—* the three lower-case ticks of the title relating to the tense, increasingly explosive time interval before the whites of a Southern town erupt in rebellious rage against the installation of a black sheriff, ably played by Jim Brown.

The outgoing sheriff, George Kennedy, takes his demotion and retirement like a good sport, and, because he is an intrinsically fair man and knows the difficulties of the job, stands ready to help the duly constituted sheriff assert his authority if need be. Brown tries to handle matters in a civilized and firm manner, but the whites just won't let him, nor is his black deputy sheriff given any particular welcome either.

Though Brown arrests blacks and whites without discrimination whenever they trespass against law and order, the prejudice against him runs deep, and he even has trouble with his own people. March, as Mayor Parks, is determined to keep order, and being a shrewd psychologist who understands both the black and white approaches to issues, he warns whites that trouble-making will only bring Washington down on their ears. A series of nasty incidents occur, and when Brown jails a young white for killing a child with his car, and it turns out the boy's father is a bigwig from a nearby county, things get meaner.

With Jim Brown

Eventually, when an invasion of angry white folks from the next county, led by the jailed boy's father, and designed to free the prisoner despite his obvious guilt, threatens, the whites of the town are shamed by Kennedy into forestalling a gross miscarriage of justice and join their black sheriff in repelling the invaders.

Ralph Nelson got across a certain tautness and tension throughout the ominous proceedings, and fine perform-

ances from Brown and Kennedy. March gave a superior account of himself as the mayor who, for all his crustiness and minor eccentricities, has more basic common-sense than the other whites in town and deals with reality on its own terms. At seventy-two an alert, sharp March was plainly in top form, and his interpretation of Mayor Parks was filled with the creative insights and individual touches which have always distinguished his

With George Kennedy

240

With Jim Brown and George Kennedy

performances. The year the film was released, 1970, saw March celebrating his fiftieth year as an actor and his forty-first in films.

THE REVIEWERS
Lawrence J. Quirk in *Screen Slants:*
No matter that he is several years past the biblical three-score-and-ten; no matter that he looks grizzled and has every right to be weary (though he does not exercise that right); no matter that after fifty years as a professional actor, Mr. March could rest on his laurels and no one would blame him; a true star continues to shine undimmed, his lustre all the more radiant for all that has gone before. Mr. March adds needed substance and a welcome, leavening mellowness to the role of a Southern mayor who tries realistically to adjust to the reality

With George Kennedy

241

posed by a black Sheriff. Though plainly typical of his class and background, Mayor Parks, as delineated by Mr. March, comes through as human, likeable and down-to-earth; he is not, true, without his own brand of crusty rigidity, but for all that, he is aware, and in his way attuned to the realities of the human condition, and subtly, albeit rustically, sophisticated. . . . Mr. March's presence gives this picture a certain class; his lively performing is a joy to behold; he is an ornament to the proceedings, and his scenes contain a certain lift and elan that is not always discernible elsewhere in the film.

Murf. in *Variety:*
Ralph Nelson's apparent recipe for [this film] involves a racial reversing of *In the Heat of the Night* and a broad overlay of *Guess Who's Coming to Dinner.* Nelson, and Metro, should be so lucky. But they just might be, for the pic has a money look in it. Despite a hackneyed script, with huge plot-holes and turns marked as early as freeway off-ramps, plus a ten-tune song track that makes what story there is seem an interruption of a long-playing album, the comedy-drama about a Negro sheriff in Dixie works remarkably well as a general

audience film. . . . Within the rather severe limitations of credibility in the script, the performances range from excellent to poor. Brown, Kennedy, Lynn Carlin . . . Janet MacLachlan . . . Richard Elkins . . . are all on the plus side. March plays the Mayor as a Lillian Hellman caricature. Don Stroud again plays his usual role of a contemporary hippie-bum. . . . Nelson's direction and supervision of this mish-mash shows more of an eye on the [boxoffice] potential than the admiration of any film cult. Nothing wrong with that, of course, but it's a change from his recent previous pix.

Richard Schickel in *Life:*
The best thing about the film is the presence of Fredric March, too long away and certainly deserving of something more interesting to play than the crusty mayor of a dusty small town. The film is directed—cartooned would be a better word—by Ralph Nelson. As usual, his heart is in the right place but, again as usual, his directorial pulse is steady, predictable, without interesting leaps or murmurs. He simply lacks the ability of a Kershner or a Furie to fill out a film interestingly with details and divagations.

Notes on the MARCH Plays

Details are given only on the eighteen plays in which Mr. March opened on Broadway between 1920 and 1961. Among his other theatrical appearances were those outside New York in *Shavings* (1921); *The County Chairman* (1921); *Lei Aloha* (1921) (a Broadway show in which he appeared briefly at a later point in the run); *Zeno* (Chicago) (1923); *Tarnish* (on tour) (1923); *The Royal Family* (Los Angeles) (1928). He also toured in 1927-28 for the Theatre Guild doing such plays as *Arms and the Man, Mr. Pim Passes By, The Guardsman* and *The Silver Cord.*

MR. MARCH'S BROADWAY PLAYS FOLLOW
IN THE ORDER OF THEIR APPEARANCE

In his stock company days (1922)

Deburau / 1920

A tragicomedy in four acts adapted by Granville Barker from the French of Sacha Guitry. Produced by David Belasco at the Belasco Theatre, December 23, 1920.

THE PLAYERS
Lionel Atwill, Elsie Mackay, Bernard A. Reinold, Hubert Druce, Joseph Herbert, Rowland Buckstone, Margot Kelly, Pauline Merriam, Marie Bryar, Isabel Leighton, Edmund Gurney, Sidney Toler, Helen Reimer, Lydia Burnand, St. Clair Bayfield, Eden Gray, Rose Coghlan, John Roche, Sallie Bergman, Georgie Ryan, Morgan Farley, John L. Shine, Fred Bickel*, Robert Roland.

REVIEW
Heywood Broun in the *New York Herald Tribune:*
It is not a great play but it is a work of such distinction that some such statement must be made at the outset. Particularly the statement is necessary because there are moments when *Deburau* seems a great play, moments in which a thing now dead, which we call the grand manner, is animated so eloquently that it seems to be again the one true and perfect mood of The Theatre... though *Deburau* is a ghost, it is an apparition of sufficient stature to strike home to all beholders.

The Lawbreaker / 1922

A melodrama in four acts by Jules Eckert Goodman.

Produced by William A. Brady at the Booth Theatre, February 1, 1922.

THE PLAYERS
Frank Sheridan, Clifford Dempsey, John Cromwell, Frederick Bickel, William Courtenay, Morgan Wallace, Frank Sylvester, John Milton, Herbert Rathke, Blanche Yurka, Marguerite Maxwell.

REVIEWS
Alexander Woollcott in *The New York Times:*
Capital performances of general promise are thrown in for good measure by two young people, Frederick Bickel and Marguerite Maxwell. Mr. Brady has done quite well enough by the play.

Percy Hammond in the *New York Herald Tribune:*
A remarkably unaffected performance of the banker's weak and troubled son by Frederick Bickel.

The Melody Man / 1924

A comedy in three acts by Herbert Richard Lorenz. Staged by Lawrence Marston and Alexander Leftwich at the Ritz Theatre, New York, May 13, 1924.

THE PLAYERS
Eleanor Rome, Jerry Devine, Fred Starwer, Joe Lind-

*March was known as Fred Bickel in his initial stage appearances.

wurm, Dave Stryker, Al Schenck, Bill Tulker, Louise Kelley, Eva Pulk, Donald Gallaher, Sam White, Renee Noel, Betty Weston, Fredric March, Lew Fields, Jules Jordan, Joseph Torpey, Sara Chapelle, Jimmy Kapper.

REVIEW
John Corbin in *The New York Times:*
Neither the best nor the worst of its kind. The only question of importance with regard to it is just how easy it is to amuse those who are easily amused.

Puppets / 1925

A melodrama in three acts by Frances Lightner. Produced by Brock Pemberton at the Selwyn Theatre, New York, March 9, 1925.

THE PLAYERS
Ralph J. Locke, Fredric March, Michelette Buroni, Frank McDonald, Remo Bufano, Ascanio Spolidaro, Florence Koehler, Dwight Frye, C. Henry Gordon, Elizabeth Taylor, Miriam Hopkins, Stanley Grand, Charles D. Brown, Alexis M. Polianov.

REVIEW
Alan Dale in the *New York American:*
Perhaps the best work of the evening was contributed by Fredric March as one of the Italian lovers . . . but [the play] proved to be very small potatoes and if all the speaking parts could be cut out and the marionettes substituted, it would be rather nice.

Harvest / 1925

A play in three acts by Kate Horton. Produced by Messrs. Shubert in association with John Cromwell at the Belmont Theatre, New York, September 19, 1925.

THE PLAYERS
Louise Closser Hale, Elmer Cornell, Augustin Duncan, Ethel Taylor, Hilda Sprong, Wallace Erskine, Fredric March, Ronald Savery.

REVIEW
Burns Mantle in the *New York Daily News:*
For the better part of two hours, six or seven generally dull and uninteresting people sit around a Michigan farm house boring themselves and all within earshot. They talk much of their miseries, of the threatened failure of the corn crop, and particularly the complete failure of their lives. . . . Fredric March is not one of the rotten Marches known to Michael Arlen and The Green Hat. In fact [he] is rather a nice juvenile.

The Half-Caste / 1926

A play in three acts by Jack McClellan. Produced at the National Theatre, New York, March 29, 1926.

THE PLAYERS
John Gray, William Ingersoll, Isabel O'Madigan, Helenka Adamowska, Gertrude Moran, John O'Meara, Charles Lawrence, Fredric March, Veronica, Morris Armor, William Herring, Mabel Morgan, Bernice Hampshire, Leone Merriam, Virginia Bedford, Silvia Stoll, Henry Clark, David Munson, Charles Opunul, David Manaku, Gordon St. Cloud, James Kulalia, Frederick Perry, John O'Meara.

REVIEW
Percy Hammond in the *New York Herald Tribune:*
It was all a brazen and half-conscious caricature, depending on its sensational outbreaks to sell itself to the drama lovers. Fredric March, a good-looking and temperamental youngster, impersonated the unlucky debauchee as well as possible.

With Linda Watkins in The Devil in the Cheese, *1926*

The Devil in the Cheese / 1926

A fantastic comedy in three acts by Tom Cushing. Pro-

In The Royal Family, *1928*

New York, January 10, 1938. Staged by John Cromwell. Settings by Jo Mielziner.

THE PLAYERS
Fredric March, Florence Eldridge, Dame May Whitty, Brenda Forbes, Frieda Altman, Martin Wolfson, Marilyn Jolie, Harold Thomas, Walter Jones, Helena Glenn, Leslie Austin, John Pickard, Ethel Morrison, A. J. Herbert, Katherine Stewart, Montgomery Clift.

With Florence Eldridge in The American Way, *1939*

duced by Charles Hopkins at the Charles Hopkins Theatre, New York, December 29, 1926.

THE PLAYERS
Fredric March, Dwight Frye, Robert McWade, Catherine Calhoun Doucet, Linda Watkins, George Riddell, Bela Lugosi, Earl MacDonald, Frank Norman Hearn, Earl MacDonald, Hooper Bunch, Joseph Hazel.

REVIEW
Percy Hammond in the *New York Herald Tribune:*
Bright in its genial satire at times, it is at others a routine bib-and-tucker show, written for the nurseries . . . if you like cleanly dream plays sprinkled with picturesque melodrama, presenting sex as a lamb rather than a raging lion, you may enjoy yourself. . . . An unaffected actor named Fredric March plays the hero handsomely.

Yr. Obedient Husband / 1938

A comedy in three acts by Horace Jackson. Produced by Marwell Productions, Inc. at the Broadhurst Theatre,

REVIEW
Brooks Atkinson in *The New York Times:*
Mr. Jackson's eighteenth-century pastiche is written without much tingle in the lines or ideas and Mr. March plays it literally . . . he wears his costumes handsomely and plays with an attractive good will. But under the earnestness of his deportment in the drawing room there is little of the recognition of humor that underlies all good comic acting. To Mr. March, Mr. Steele is serious business.

247

The American Way / 1939

A spectacle play in two acts by George S. Kaufman and Moss Hart. Music by Oscar Levant. Produced by Sam H. Harris and Max Gordon at the Center Theatre, New York, January 21, 1939. Staged by George S. Kaufman. Lighting and technical direction by Hassard Short. Settings by Donald Oenslager. Costumes by Irene Sharaff.

THE PLAYERS
Fredric March, Florence Eldridge, James MacDonald, Eileen Burns, Jean Shelby, John Lorenz, Hugh Cameron, Le Roi Operti, Allen Kearns, Mary Brandon, Adrienne Marden, Alan Hewitt, David Wayne, Walter Kelly, Stephen Sands, Dora Sayers, Alex Courtney, Edward Elliott, Dicky Van Patten, Elinor Pittis, Claire Howard, Richard Lloyd, Walter Beck, Barbara Woodall, Gretchen Davidson, Witner Bissell, Jack Arnold, George Herndon, Ward Tallman.

REVIEWS
John Anderson in the *New York Journal-American*:
No audience that I can remember in my time on the stage aisle has been so shaken with emotion as we all were at the Center Theatre. . . . Here was no longer a theatre but a place of pilgrimage, no time to sit in judgment but to stand at attention. Salute!

Burns Mantle in the *New York Daily News*:
An expensive stage show, filled with crowds and hoopla, that rises now and then to moving heights by reason of its honest acting and playing. Especially fortunate is it in having enlisted the services of Fredric March, who has come back from Hollywood apparently, to recover such prestige as he sacrificed in playing *Yr. Obedient Husband* a year ago. . . . Well, Fredric may look in his mirror and indulge a smile of satisfaction this morning. He gave as finely sustained a characterization as the simple hero, as any actor has given in any drama this season. . . . Florence Eldridge gives fine support.

Hope for a Harvest / 1941

A drama in three acts by Sophie Treadwell. Produced by the Theatre Guild at the Guild Theatre, New York, November 26, 1941. Staged by Lester Vail. Supervised by Lawrence Langner and Theresa Helburn. Settings by Watson Barratt.

THE PLAYERS
Helen Carew, Judy Parrish, Fredric March, Florence Eldridge, John Marny, Arthur Franz, Shelley Hull, Edith King, Alan Reed, Doro Merande.

REVIEWS
Richard Watts, Jr. in the *New York Herald Tribune*:
Because [the play] has something of importance to say, and says it with sincerity, one has from the start a sympathetic concern with it and a far deeper respect for

With Florence Eldridge, Judy Parrish, Arthur Franz and Alan Reed in Hope for a Harvest, 1941

its heart and mind than for more expert dramas of lesser integrity. It really is striving to speak to the soul of America with gravity and idealistic fervor. The unfortunate thing is that in expressing the author's heartfelt interest in the future of the nation in a time of desperate crisis, the play goes in for some unpersuasive and undramatic theatrical matters which destroy the greater part of its effectiveness.

Burns Mantle in the *New York Daily News:*
Mr. March, with the fine sense of character that has brought him many successes . . . manages to make something more than a playwright's prig out of Cousin Elliott. Miss Eldridge's heart as well as her talent has gone into the playing of Carlotta.

The Skin of Our Teeth / 1942

A fantastic comedy in three acts by Thornton Wilder.

Produced by Michael Myerberg at the Plymouth Theatre, New York, November 18, 1942. Staged by Elia Kazan. Settings by Albert Johnson. Costumes by Mary Percy Schenck.

THE PLAYERS
Fredric March, Florence Eldridge, Tallulah Bankhead, E. G. Marshall, Reno Buffano, Andrew Ratousheff, Dicke Van Patten, Frances Heflin, Montgomery Clift, Arthur Griffin, Ralph Kellard, Joseph Smiley, Ralph Cullinan, Edith Faversham, Emily Lorraine, Eva Mudge Nelson, Stanley Prager, Harry Clark, Elizabeth Scott, Patricia Riordan, Florence Reed, Earl Sydnor, Carroll Clark, Stanley Weede, Seumas Flynn, Aubrey Fossett, Stanley Prager, Harry Clark, Stephan Cole, Morton Da Costa, Joseph Smiley, Ralph Kellard, Eula Belle Moore, Viola Dean.

REVIEWS
John Anderson in the *New York Journal-American:*
[What] Mr. Wilder is trying to say is by no means news but it is eternally pertinent since it is forever remembered, and always forgotten. It is the fact that humanity is as indestructible as its hopes, that from the glacial

With Florence Eldridge and Tallulah Bankhead in The Skin of Our Teeth, *1942*

age up to right now, from the invention of the wheel to the perfection of high-altitude bombing, man is forever improving himself, and eternally falling down in ruins, forever building and tearing down, but that somehow, through hell, high water and, as the playbill says, "double feature movies," he manages to survive.

Howard Barnes in the *New York Herald Tribune*: March plays the poor fool who goes on trying to make something of the wreckage of the world with immense power and Miss Eldridge is right behind him in giving a parallel human sympathy and warmth. . . . *The Skin of Our Teeth* is a bit crazy, but it is a vital and wonderful piece of theatre.

A Bell for Adano / 1944

A drama in three acts by Paul Osborn, based on a novel by John Hersey. Produced by Leland Hayward at the Cort Theatre, New York, December 16, 1944. Staged by H. C. Potter. Setting and costumes by Motley. Lighting supervised by William Richardson.

THE PLAYERS
Fredric March, Everett Sloane, Gilbert Mack, Tito Vuolo, Silvio Minciotti, Joe Verdi, Leon Rathiu, Miriam Goldine, Alma Ross, Florence Aquino, Harold J. Stone, Margo Bruce MacFarlane, Jack Arnold, Fred Barton, Harry Selby, Michael Vallon, Mario Badolati, Doreen McLean, Albert Raymo, Charles Mayer, J. Scott Smart, Rolfe Sedan, Clark Poth, Alexander Granach, Phil Arthur, Rex King.

With Margo in A Bell *for Adano, 1944*

With Florence Eldridge in Years Ago, *1946*

Burton Rascoe in the *New York World-Telegram*:
[We have the problem] of first learning for ourselves
what democracy, freedom and justice mean. They are
not merely principles but principles in action—in all
things big and little. Many Americans who think they
know what democracy is, don't.

Ward Morehouse in the *New York Sun*:
Mr. March brings humanness and warmth and force to
the role of the understanding, high-minded and sentimental soldier of Italian parentage who tells the GIs
why they're in Europe and what is expected of them. ...
A war play of great vitality.

Years Ago / 1946

A comedy in three acts by Ruth Gordon. Produced by
Max Gordon at the Mansfield Theatre, New York, De-
cember 3, 1946. Staged by Garson Kanin. Setting by
Donald Oenslager. Costumes by John Boyt.

THE CAST
Fredric March, Florence Eldridge, Patricia Kirkland, Bethel
Leslie, Jennifer Bunker, Richard Simon, Seth Arnold,
Fredric Persson, Judith Cargill; a cat.

REVIEW
Brooks Atkinson in *The New York Times*:
A pleasant, sentimental comedy, beautifully acted . . .
and since Fredric March is playing the part, Miss Gordon's father will now have to be added to the gallery
of stage worthies to be remembered and respected. For
Mr. March, acting in very high fettle indeed, has created
a vigorous, colorful character out of many simple details.
. . . In Mr. March's playing [the character] is a marvel-
ously entertaining person. For this is character acting of
great distinction by a master of the craft who has not
lost his respect for unrenowned people.

In Now I Lay Me Down to Sleep, *1950*

Now I Lay Me Down to Sleep / 1950

A comedy in three acts by Elaine Ryan. Based on the
novel by Ludwig Bemelmans. Produced by Nancy Stern
and George Nichols III at the Broadhurst Theatre, New
York, March 2, 1950. Staged by Hume Cronyn. Settings
by Wolfgang Roth. Costumes by John Derro.

THE PLAYERS
Fredric March, Florence Eldridge, Lili Valenty, Ray Poole,
Charles Chaplin, Jr., Henry Guertel, Charles Mayer,
Stefan Schnabel, Henry Lascoe, Norman Barrs, Richard

Abbott, Helen Seaman, Rick Jason, Rene Paul, Booth
Colman, Philip Gordon, Gregory Morton, Thomas E.
Noyes, Robert McCahon, Harold E. Gordon, Sally Anne
Parsons, Jacqueline Dalya, Hope Miller, Rene Paul, Helen
Scamon, Rudy Bond.

REVIEW
Howard Barnes in the *New York Herald Tribune*:
The acting supports a dozen or more scenes with great
effect. March swaggers delightfully as the general, wear-
ing fancy costumes with aplomb and working out his
love life with comical inflections. Miss Eldridge is not
far behind him. . . . [The play] has great wisdom as well
as humor—it is not all of a piece but it brightens the
season immensely.

An Enemy of the People / 1950

A play in three acts by Henrik Ibsen. Adapted by Arthur Miller. Produced by Lars Nordenson at the Broadhurst Theatre, December 28, 1950. Staged by Robert Lewis. Sets and costumes by Aline Bernstein. Production stage manager, Robert F. Simon.

THE PLAYERS
Fredric March, Florence Eldridge, Morris Carnovsky, Art Smith, Michael Strong, Martin Brooks, Ralph Robertson, Richard Trask, Ralph Dunn, Anna Minot, Fred Stewart, Lon Gilbert.

REVIEW
Richard Watts, Jr. in the *New York Post:*
Fredric March . . . gives a vigorous and earnest performance, being particularly effective in his scene of defiance to the mob. Florence Eldridge does well what little she has to do as the loyal wife. . . . Robert Lewis' direction is properly vital. It is interesting to note the timeliness of Ibsen but on the whole, I would rather see Mr. Miller writing his own plays.

The Autumn Garden / 1951

A comedy in three acts by Lillian Hellman. Produced by Kermit Bloomgarden at the Coronet Theatre, March 7,

1951. Staged by Harold Clurman. Settings by Howard Bay. Costumes by Anna Hill Johnstone. Production supervisor, Dee Hughes.

THE PLAYERS
Fredric March, Florence Eldridge, Fthel Griffies, Colin Keith-Johnston, Kent Smith, James Lipton, Margaret Barker, Joan Lorring, Maxwell Glanville, Carol Goodner, Jane Wyatt, Louise Holmes.

REVIEW
William Hawkins in the *New York World-Telegram & Sun:*
All the older characters have arrived at a point of payoff. There is not much chance left them beyond making the best bargain. This does not sound cheery but Miss Hellman has related most of her story with a great amount of wily humor. I cannot recall Fredric March, Florence Eldridge or Kent Smith in better form. March is the painter, vain and petty, noisy and shallow. It is a magnificent job of an actor exposing a character. Miss Eldridge plays the silly wife of the general with her inevitable taste. She acts this ridiculous woman with no thought of being comical or piteous. The result is an uncannily real person.

Long Day's Journey Into Night / 1956

A play in four acts by Eugene O'Neill. Produced by

Leigh Cornell, Theodore Mann and Jose Quintero at the Helen Hayes Theatre, New York, November 7, 1956. Staged by Jose Quintero. Setting by David Hays. Lighting by Tharon Musser; Costumes by Motley. Production Stage Manager, Elliott Martin. Stage manager, George Petrarca.

THE PLAYERS
Fredric March, Florence Eldridge, Jason Robards, Jr., Bradford Dillman, Katherine Ross.

REVIEW
Richard Watts, Jr., in the *New York Post:*
A magnificent and shattering play. . . . It seems to me that Fredric March gives the finest and most penetrating performance of his career as the father. Florence Eldridge is touching and real as the mother. . . . This is a play that gives the entire season stature.

Gideon / 1961

A play by Paddy Chayefsky. Produced by Fred Coe and Arthur Cantor at the Plymouth Theatre, New York, November 9, 1961. Staged by Tyrone Guthrie. Settings and lighting by David Hays. Costumes by Daningo Rodriguez. Production Stage Manager, Porter Van Zandt. Stage Manager, J. George Thorn.

With Florence Eldridge in Long Day's Journey Into Night, *1956*

253

With Douglas Campbell in Gideon, 1961

THE PLAYERS
Fredric March, Douglas Campbell, Martin Garner, Victor Kilian, Robert Weiss, Eric Berry, David Hooks, Alan Manson, Mark Lenard, George Segne, Alan Bergmann, Paul Marin, Edward K. Holmes, David Hooks, Lorraine Egypt.

REVIEW
Richard Watts, Jr., in the *New York Post:*
[The play] has distinction and a haunting fascination, and is beautifully acted by Fredric March and Douglas Campbell. . . . Mr. March is powerful and enormously impressive as The Lord. . . . Tyrone Guthrie's direction is characteristically brilliant. Despite the second-act decline, Mr. Chayefsky has written a powerful and provocative play.

Receiving the Tony Award for Long Day's Journey Into Night, *1957. Left to right, Judy Holliday, Rex Harrison, Margaret Leighton*